AGAINST ALL ODDS

THE IT STORY OF INDIA

'In the company of two excellent younger professionals—Dayasindhu and Krishnan Narayanan—Kris has ably demonstrated his avatar as a technology historian in addition to having been India's best software designer, a technology thought leader and an able corporate leader. He brings the same level of expertise, excellence and attention to detail in this book as he did in his earlier avatars. This book is the first written-down history of IT in India. It is a seminal contribution to advancement of the research of technology historians and the success of entrepreneurs. The three authors have herded between the covers of this book their narration of the good and the not-so-good aspects of policy, implementation and the use of computing and communications infrastructure right from the time of HEC-2M computer at ISI, Kolkata, to the ubiquitous and impactful presence of digitalization and 5G around us. What lends this book its authenticity are the myriad interviews with the various actors in this drama documented here— educationists, policy wonks, entrepreneurs, politicians, bureaucrats and industry leaders. The objective and the genteel personality of Kris and his co-authors shine throughout the pages of this important book. I would recommend it to every Indian interested in understanding the history of computing and software in India'—Narayana Murthy, founder, Infosys

'Kris, Dayasindhu and Krishnan have done a real service by writing this book. The rise of India as a power in the world of IT in the past few decades is a fascinating story. It has rarely been told with the depth and sweep that this book has. And that is very important because the story of IT is an integral part of the transformation of India in these decades, as also it is in this period that IT has become deeply embedded in almost all aspects of human life'—Azim Premji, founder, Wipro

'In this remarkable book, Kris Gopalakrishnan, N. Dayasindhu and Krishnan Narayanan have written the definitive account of the fascinating birth and rise of the Indian IT industry. As they have so evocatively described, it is a tale with many heroes, who all did their bit to collaborate and build a magnificent edifice that has done India proud on the global stage, created millions of jobs, laid the foundation for robust foreign exchange reserves and most importantly, gave our engineers and entrepreneurs the self-confidence to take on the world. This is a must-read to understand a great Indian success story!'—Nandan Nilekani, chairman and co-founder, Infosys, and founding chairman, UIDAI (Aadhaar)

'The historic, six-decade-long ascent of India's IT sector can now be better understood thanks to Kris Gopalakrishnan's research and compelling narrative. There is much to learn from the story of India's innovations and investments in hardware, software, services and the skills required to advance the world's digital imperative'—Satya Nadella, chairman and chief executive officer, Microsoft

'Indian IT is a wonderful example of *jhakaas*. This is a mindset of thinking outside the box and creating an entire world-class industry that is truly unique and awe-inspiring. Our IT industry has placed India on the global centre stage. Kris and his co-authors give us a captivating insider's view of Indian IT's revolution. This book captures the spirit of a confident India and is an inspiration for all of us'—Anand Mahindra, chairman, Mahindra Group

'A few decades ago, computers were only used as a tool to accumulate and process data. However, in the last thirty years, our computing abilities have evolved from organizing data to managing information to leveraging insights to augmenting intelligence. The Indian IT industry has come of age during this period. While we were handicapped initially, our entrepreneurs and professionals, with dreams to make India an IT force to reckon with, worked relentlessly to get the IT sector where it is today. This book is the story of how we took on this challenge and succeeded. Kris Gopalakrishnan, N. Dayasindhu and Krishnan Narayanan have written an inspiring book full of interesting anecdotes and insider nuggets of wisdom covering entrepreneurship, implementation excellence and scaling-up. This is the hallmark of Indian IT. I strongly recommend this book to anyone who is interested in knowing how Indian IT became world-class and world-scale' —S.D. Shibulal, co-founder, Infosys

'*Against All Odds: The IT Story of India* is a uniquely Indian story of capability and capacity-building, entrepreneurship, leadership, innovation and execution. Kris Gopalakrishnan, N. Dayasindhu and Krishnan Narayanan have written a compelling book that connects the remarkable milestones orchestrated by India's IT entrepreneurs in their journey towards global leadership. Indian IT is an exemplar of a revolution that created value and credibility as a front-running nation at a time when few countries understood the magnitude of the emerging digital opportunities. As a tech entrepreneur, I have admired the fighting spirit of IT entrepreneurs in their aspiration to build global leadership. Their efforts have delivered sustainable economic returns for India for generations to come'—Kiran Mazumdar-Shaw, executive chairperson, Biocon

'Five decades ago, when Indian IT was just an emerging topic in the IITs and IIMs, entrepreneurs in living rooms and college dorms were envisioning a future where Indian software would redefine the rules of global business. They dreamt of creating an industry from India that would one day lead the world. This book is about their dreams and hard work that resulted in the world-class Indian IT industry. Kris Gopalakrishnan, N. Dayasindhu and Krishnan Narayanan have captured the authentic insider stories of the rise of Indian IT through their meticulous research. This book is a must-read for all those interested in how a modern industry is architected on entrepreneurship, leadership and execution' —Ashank Desai, principal founder, Mastek

'*Against All Odds: The IT Story of India* provides a powerful account of the rapid ascent and continuing momentum of India's IT industry on the global stage and its impact in the broad spectrum of applications that benefit society. The book, which covers six decades of evolution through inputs and oral histories from the movers and shapers of India's IT story, is a particularly welcome and thoughtful document of archival significance as these technologies will increasingly define and influence every aspect of daily life in the twenty-first century. Kris Gopalakrishnan has been one of the pioneering leaders in the impressive accomplishments of India's IT industry and his perspectives, captured here in collaboration with N. Dayasindhu and Krishnan Narayanan, will be of considerable value not only to those interested in learning about historical information but also to successive generations of leaders shaping the future growth of the IT industry in India'— Subra Suresh, president and Distinguished University Professor, NTU Singapore, and former director, US National Science Foundation

'Few authors have a decades-long ringside view of the phenomena they write about. Here is a riveting history from such a trio of the emergence of the information technology industry in India. The helpful chronologies will orient any interested reader; the distillation of facts, and even revealing anecdotes, will enhance the understanding of even those familiar'—Tarun Khanna, Jorge Paulo Lemann Professor, Harvard Business School

AGAINST ALL ODDS

THE IT STORY OF INDIA

KRIS GOPALAKRISHNAN
N. DAYASINDHU
KRISHNAN NARAYANAN

INTRODUCTION BY GURCHARAN DAS

**PENGUIN
BUSINESS**

An imprint of Penguin Random House

PENGUIN BUSINESS

USA | Canada | UK | Ireland | Australia
New Zealand | India | South Africa | China | Singapore

Penguin Business is part of the Penguin Random House group of companies
whose addresses can be found at global.penguinrandomhouse.com

Published by Penguin Random House India Pvt. Ltd
4th Floor, Capital Tower 1, MG Road,
Gurugram 122 002, Haryana, India

Penguin
Random House
India

First published in Penguin Business by Penguin Random House India 2022
This edition published in Penguin Business by Penguin Random House India 2024

ISBN 9780670094158

Typeset in Janson Text LT Std by Manipal Technologies Limited, Manipal
Printed at Replika Press Pvt. Ltd, India

www.penguin.co.in

This is a legitimate digitally printed version of the book and therefore might not
have certain extra finishing on the cover.

Kris Gopalakrishnan
To my family, especially my wife, Sudha, and daughter, Meghana

N. Dayasindhu
To Akhila, Athmika, Kavitha, amma and appa

Krishnan Narayanan
To my amma, appa and Ramya

Contents

Introduction
by Gurcharan Das

INDIA'S CHEERIEST STORY

The quiet economic and social revolution unleashed by information technology (IT) is the cheeriest story of India's recent economic ascent, making one almost forget the nation's failure to create a broadscale industrial revolution. Conventional wisdom is that the software revolution took place from below, despite the state—a classic example of how 'India grows at night when the government sleeps'. Since software was invisible, landing on the customer's computer via the telephone, it escaped the clutches of the 'License Raj', dodging the Kafkaesque bureaucratic state that had killed the industrial revolution. This book challenges this hypothesis, revealing a remarkable, healthy collaboration between software companies via a unique trade association and a few rare government officials, who unobtrusively and unheroically, opened opportunities, cut red tape and helped shepherd the industry to glory. The IT industry's inability, however, to make a mark in hardware reinforces the 'conventional wisdom'.

The authors hang this sober, objective chronicle on the thread of personal experience of over fifty protagonists in the industry, whose stories are not only unique but also provide significant data of history. They have posted these 'video histories' on the web (https://itihaasa.com/History), creating a veritable museum of digital history. However, they have presented us with a fascinating puzzle. Like solid narrators of oral history, they have offered us dots of historical data, but have left it to the reader to connect the dots. My role in this division of labour is to help the reader make some of the connections via this introduction. This should not prevent independent-minded readers to challenge some of my dot-connecting to make up an entirely different story.

The chronicle begins with Prof. P.C. Mahalanobis, 'a physicist by training, a statistician by instinct and a planner by conviction' at the Indian Statistical Institute in Kolkata. He is credited with employing the first computer in India. Prime Minister Nehru had a scientific temper and he took a shine to the good professor, whose ideas about development resonated with his own. He did something extraordinary: he entrusted a statistician rather than a political or economic heavyweight to draft the country's Second Five Year Plan. Mahalanobis employed sophisticated models in 1955 with the HEC-2M computer to allocate investments in different sectors of the economy to optimize growth.

Thwarted by the License Raj

Although the authors shower legitimate praise on the professor for his pioneering role in computing, it should not blind us to the damage that his Soviet-style plan wrought on the nation. Since Nehru, Mahalanobis and the planners did not trust private entrepreneurs; they made the state the entrepreneur. Not surprisingly, they failed. India is still paying a heavy price for the decision to place the monopolistic public sector at the 'commanding heights of the economy', and then denying it an autonomy of working. The second mistake of the Second Plan was to close the economy—adopting an inward-looking, import-substituting road rather than an outward-looking, export-promoting one. As a result, the nation failed to capitalize on the great boom in world exports during the decades after the Second World War, and denied itself the prosperity that came to dozens of trading countries. Three, it over-regulated private enterprise with licensing and other controls, which not only diminished competition but throttled the entrepreneurial spirit of the Indian people. Four, it discouraged foreign capital and denied the nation benefits of new technologies that emerged after the War. One of these was electronic computing. In the end, India sacrificed two generations to the economic ideology of Nehru–Indira Gandhi and Mahalanobis' Plan.

The story moves into the 1960s, when the first Indian digital computer was born under the visionary leadership of Homi Bhabha and the tinkering talents of R. Narasimhan and P.V.S. Rao, created indigenously at the Tata Institute of Fundamental Research. Side by side in the 1960s, the Indian Institute of Technology (IIT) at Kanpur offered the first course in computer science. The authors describe vividly how an IBM computer arrived at IIT Kanpur in a bullock cart! Nehru didn't get his economic philosophy right but he deserves credit for founding the new institutes of technology across the country that nurtured the human capital and entrepreneurship for the IT revolution. This is a happier side of the story.

Blame Indira for Not Changing Course

The unhappier side is that the IT revolution had to wait till the late 1980s. It is difficult to blame Nehru's socialism for taking India's economy to a dead end. He was a product of his age, when the majority of intellectuals outside the US, was socialist. But one can blame Indira Gandhi for not changing course. By then, the world had witnessed the miracle wrought by the Asian Tigers—Japan, Korea and Taiwan. She not only ignored the East Asian marvel but turned in the opposite direction, towards the USSR, expanding the bureaucratic socialist state, creating a full-blown License Raj. By stubbornly persisting with the wrong model, she suppressed growth and jobs. Although she did it in the name of the poor, her policies in the end did very little for the poor. India's growth rate plunged to its lowest levels; other developing countries did far better. Most people are critical of her political failure—for declaring an Emergency in 1975, when India almost lost democracy—but they are unaware of the damage she wrought to the economy. When individuals blunder, it is a mistake and their families go down. When rulers fail, it is a national tragedy.

The IT story suffered during this dark period as did the entire Indian economy. Customs duties rose to 140 per cent. The income tax rate went up to 97.5 per cent, plus a wealth tax above it. With punishing taxes, there was little hope for accumulating capital for investment. Because of a closed economy with high tariffs, there was a persistent lack of foreign exchange to import goods. GDP growth plunged in this period to levels even lower than other developing countries. This book catalogues brave, pioneering efforts by entrepreneurs at HCL, Wipro, TCS, who tried to set up an IT business in the 1970s but they couldn't make much headway.

Because 'profit' was a dirty word, they were victims of continuing suspicion of business and the market. At this time, an air defence IT system was developed indigenously for the military. In another country it would have had a large impact on the hardware and systems engineering industries. It did not in the India of the License Raj, which 'once again lost an opportunity to build indigenous hardware capability', write the authors.

This book gives the example of an important report that would have allowed the private sector to make minicomputers in the early seventies. The computer market was changing from mainframes to minicomputers, requiring less capital to start up. Although presented to the Department of Electronics in 1973, the report languished for five years, seeing the light only in 1978, when it was too late— minicomputers would soon be made obsolete by the personal computer. Moreover, the policy itself was hugely flawed, limiting each company to making fifty minicomputers, so as to avoid anyone becoming dominant. No company could have survived with a sale of fifty machines per year. Not only were Indian companies depressed, but foreign companies were forced to divest their equity to 40 per cent. This led IBM, the market leader, to quit India. As the authors point out, IBM's departure had the unintended consequence in providing a fillip to Indian companies to enter the market of smaller computers. One company, HCL, launched a microcomputer, which came even before Apple's personal computer (PC).

Overall, it was a dismal scene in the IT industry as the country moved into the 1980s. Since hardware was a regulatory minefield, IT companies began to drift towards lightly regulated software. You were allowed to import a computer at a lower duty (35 per cent versus 150 per cent) against a commitment to export software. Narayana Murthy, one of the founders of Infosys, had made three trips to Delhi to get a licence to import a Data General MV/8000. The distinguished reformer, Montek Ahluwalia, has recounted this incident in his fine book, *Backstage*. By the time the licence was issued, the same computer was available with higher capacity at two-thirds the price. So, he had to make two more trips to Delhi to get the number changed on the licence. Finally, when the computer arrived, the customs official refused to clear it unless he was paid a bribe. The company refused to pay it. The official forced them to pay 150 per cent and the company went to court. It took nine years to recover the extra duty paid.

Enter a White Knight, Rajiv Gandhi

Indira Gandhi died in 1984, and her son Rajiv Gandhi became prime minister. With his coming, the country experienced the first winds of liberalization. Rajiv Gandhi was a pilot, who instinctively understood the significance of the computer. He was advised by able technocrats like N. Seshagiri, the founding director of the National Informatics Centre and the architect behind the computerization success at the IX Asiad Games held in New Delhi in 1982. Shocked at the controls on the private sector, Rajiv Gandhi announced a number of policy changes. The first in November 1984 simplified computer manufacture. Within a year, the number of computers doubled in the country; prices dropped to half. In 1986, there was further liberalization, allowing duty-free import of computers against exports. People in the government laughed at Rajiv Gandhi's 'childish obsession with high-tech toys' but he was undeterred. As a symbolic message, he had a personal computer sent to every district office in the country. His untimely death prevented him from seeing the IT revolution, which came about in the following decade. Fortunately, following the pioneering lead of IIT Kanpur, students at all IITs had embraced computer education. They were ready to meet an explosive demand for human capital that came in the following decade.

The King's Horse Did, Indeed, Fly

The story is apocryphal. Akbar, the Mughal emperor, sentenced Birbal, his witty minister, to death. But then he changed his mind, agreeing to hold off for a year because Birbal promised to make the king's horse fly. When asked by friends, Birbal explained that one of three things could happen in a year—the king could die, or Birbal could die, or the horse could fly. N. Vittal, secretary of the department of electronics, narrated this story to a vast audience of NASSCOM, the IT industry's excellent organization. Led by the charismatic Dewang Mehta, NASSCOM had been pestering him to remove obstacles in the way of the industry, principally the one that would give seamless access to customers' computers abroad. 'I shall do all that you want, but you must return the favour like Birbal. Guarantee me, your export revenues will quadruple in five years.' The industry captains didn't know what to say but the reckless Mehta embraced the outlandish target. Exports, in fact, soared from $164 million in 1991 to $1 billion in five years. The king's horse did, indeed, fly.

Even a Garage Becomes a Technology Park

True to his promise, Vittal worked hard to cut red tape, introducing the revolutionary Software Technology Parks of India (STPI) in 1991, wherein even a garage qualified as an STPI, as long as it was enabled by the STPI Earth Station, giving the user access to global delivery of software. The industry returned the compliment, making offshore delivery real via a robust global delivery model. Vittal was aided by a changing national mood as a result of the historic economic liberalization of 1991. This, in turn, was helped by the fall of communism and the Soviet Union at the end of the 1980s. The articulate Indian Left, as well as the powerful left wing of the ruling Congress Party, became defensive. The nation's mindset had begun to change, questioning for the first time socialist principles that had dominated policymaking for forty years. Private enterprise began to become more respectable.

But the Telecom Revolution Had to Wait Another Decade

The nation still needed a telecom revolution if global delivery of software was to be seamless. The government telecom monopoly for overseas telephony, Videsh Sanchar Nigam Ltd (VSNL), was Vittal's bête noire. It put one obstacle after another in the way of the software industry, almost scuttling the STPI's Earth Station. Eventually, Vittal managed to get his way when he threatened to set up another government company, Satcomm, in competition with VSNL. Rajiv Gandhi had recognized this problem earlier, in the eighties. Telephones were a prized possession then, with long waiting lists, and you had to know someone to get a phone. There were only one million telephones in India in 1980; only 10 million in 1990 for a billion people. Gandhi brought in Sam Pitroda, a US-based entrepreneur to help. But Pitroda failed to create a telecom revolution, and the nation had to wait another decade before the Vajpayee government finally broke the monopoly of state-owned companies, unleashing ferocious competition in the marketplace.

Technological change also contributed with the coming of the mobile phone, which went on to become ubiquitous as the majority of Indians leapfrogged the landline stage. Quickly, users rose to a billion.

To his credit, Sam Pitroda did create the 'STD booth revolution' giving urban India universal access to long distance calling through retailers in the bazaars of country. But he didn't achieve his dream of village connectivity through his invention of a simple, digital, village-size exchange. Montek Ahluwalia blamed Pitroda's woes on the public sector. When Pitroda was heading C-Dot, a public sector entity, on which depended the rural revolution, Montek suggested he set up a private company to achieve the same goal. Pitroda, however, was wedded to the Congress Party's mantra of public sector supremacy. It is ironical that, at the same time, a Chinese engineer in the People's Liberation Army, Ren Zhengfei, got the same idea and created a similar, small digital exchange. But he set up a company. That Chinese company is known today as Huawei.

Y2K—Problem or Opportunity?

There are many reasons for the software industry's success. I have alluded to some, but one that I have not, so far, is to have been in the right place at the right time. The industry came into its own just as the global economy was changing from an industrial to a knowledge economy. Indian software rose on the coat-tails of this transformation. But it is true also in a more specific sense. The year 2000 mattered. People believed that 2000 would result in large-scale blackouts in cities, airplanes might crash, and other doomsday scenarios. The reason was the 'Y2K problem' or a flaw in computer coding: 2000 was written as '00' in computer systems; if computers misread it as '0000' or '1900', it might be catastrophic. The authors of this book describe vividly how this problem kept people awake in the late 1990s, resulting in a mad scramble to fix computer systems at a cost estimated between 300 to 600 billion US dollars. For India's software industry, it turned into an opportunity. More than revenue, it opened doors for Indian IT suppliers into the Fortune 500 companies to showcase their skills. The world, in the end, did not end in 2000 and earnings from Y2K in 1999 were higher than total industry earnings in 1998, thanks to this tailwind.

Jack Welch Joins the Party

Another factor in the industry's success is the power of reputation. Indian software companies were rapidly acquiring a formidable reputation for quality work at an affordable cost. Multinational companies didn't want to be left behind. They began to come to India in droves, where they set up 'capability centres' in the Deccan cities of Bengaluru, Hyderabad and Pune. These were sometimes called 'back offices'; at other times, they were 'R&D centres'; still other companies outsourced their business processes to Indian 'call centres'. One of the early converts was the legendary General Electric, under the entrepreneurial Jack Welch. This book narrates his visit to India, where he witnessed such a centre processing mortgage and car loan applications at Six Sigma quality. He would tell his audiences that, in America, he ran around fast-food restaurants, failing to persuade anyone willing to work in a back office. 'In India, there are qualified graduates, ambitious, energized and loving the same work.' On his return to America, he told his top global team, 'Anyone who hasn't been to India is an idiot!'

By 2019, 1250 international companies had created 1750 capability centres, handling remote, sophisticated problems, in all fields of business. Their rapid growth was only possible because India was adding a million engineering students a year. IBM was back, this time with over a hundred thousand Indian employees. R&D services in India began as extensions of headquarter departments, hiring Indian PhDs in many domains. Gradually they became independent as they began inventing new products. Cisco India, for example, developed the Advanced Services Router (ASR) 901; Veritas engineers in Pune developed the cluster server and a data replication server for financial services. As these matured, some of their talent departed, as individuals caught the entrepreneurial bug. Some of these start-ups went on to become unicorns.

Heavens, a Scandal!

A scandal in 2008–09 sheds light on a key reason behind IT's success story. It concerns Satyam, one of the largest, most respected IT companies. It had satisfied customers, proud employees and a board with impeccable credentials, enjoying shareholders' trust. Audited by one of the big four firms, it had twice won an award for corporate governance. Yet, its founder, B. Ramalingam Raju, executed one of the greatest frauds in Indian corporate history—a deceit that had gone on for seven years. The public lost Rs 20,000 crore in the value of its shares and 53,000 employees faced an uncertain future. There was huge public outcry, and calls for regulatory reform. Concerned about reputation, the industry worried about its customers abroad. The Left parties, on whose support the government depended in Parliament, termed it a failure of capitalism, and called for nationalizing the company.

Fortunately, the industry's stellar organization, NASSCOM, jumped in to reassure the world that this was an isolated case of individual fraud, not broadscale misgovernance of the system. One individual at the helm of one company had misused its funds, managing to deceive employees, auditors and the board. And confessed theatrically that he 'was riding a tiger, not knowing how to get off without being eaten'. Now the law would take its course. In the next seventy-two hours, all major customers received a reassuring phone call to this effect. In India, leaders of NASSCOM convinced the government not to wring their hands about regulatory reform but to energize enforcement agencies, get at the root of this ingenious crime and quickly punish the guilty. They led by example, using the scandal as a wake-up call to ensure that each of their employees was honest, establishing policies of zero tolerance for dishonesty in their own companies.

NASSCOM worked incessantly with the government to save Satyam, an outstanding company with outstanding employees. In a fit of maturity, the government agreed not to nationalize it but put it up for sale. Another feather in NASSCOM's cap, meanwhile, was its ability to enforce an agreement among members that no company would poach the employees of Satyam during the transitional period. All Satyam customers abroad, and employees, suppliers and banks in India, received this reassuring message. Eventually, Tech Mahindra bought it in a fair, transparent manner, and a prized jewel of the industry was saved.

The Government Joins the Act

The Indian government eventually woke up to the power of the computer. Dr N. Seshagiri founded a number of e-governance organizations and connected all government offices countrywide through satellite. He set in motion powerful e-governance initiatives that have transformed citizens' interface with the state. Aadhaar, devised by Nandan Nilekani, one of Infosys' founders, has been adopted by 1.2 billion users to become the world's largest biometric identity system. It brought significant savings to the government's welfare programmes, reducing waste and corruption in public food distribution, the rural job guarantee programme and many others. It was not an easy journey, as Aadhaar was accused of creating a surveillance infrastructure, infringing the privacy of citizens. It successfully defended these challenges, securing a legal stamp of approval in 2018 from the Supreme Court.

Under Prime Minister Narendra Modi, digital technologies got a tremendous fillip. The Jan Dhan Yojana, combined with Aadhaar and mobile technology, heralded financial inclusion in the country. Technology helped dramatically reduce a bank's cost of onboarding a new customer from Rs 1500 to Rs 10 and brought banking to the masses via the mobile phone. Initiatives like Digital India, Make in India and Startup India put the spotlight on technology-enabled entrepreneurship and paved the way for India to become the third-largest start-up ecosystem in the world.

So, Why Did the Horse Fly?

When Vittal narrated Birbal's tale to the IT industry, he was inspiring them to raise their sights. But never in his wildest dreams, did he imagine what the industry achieved. Revenues rose from less than $200 million in 1991 to $5 billion in a decade, climbing further to $50 billion in the next decade, and again growing to $200 billion in the following one. Birbal's horse, did indeed, fly! Why did it do so? I have tried to answer this question in this introduction and shall summarize the factors behind the IT revolution here.

As one reader of this history of the IT industry, I have tried to connect the dots of the puzzle. Conventional wisdom is a good starting point. Yes, there is truth in the belief that because software was invisible, it managed to escape the clutches of the 'licence, permit, inspector raj' that still dogs the rest of India's industry. Despite the 1991 reforms, and a big rise in the nation's economic growth rate, India has failed to create an export-led manufacturing revolution that would have created masses of jobs, transforming the nation into a middle-class society much like East Asia.

This failure also explains why India didn't create a hardware revolution in the IT sector. To come up with this answer, I merely had to connect the dot relating to the government's outrageous five-year delay in opening the manufacture of minicomputers to the private sector in the late seventies, to a dot that showed the approval came when the minicomputer was about to be made obsolete by the personal computer; then to another one limiting each company to fifty machines a year, making the business unviable; finally to Murthy's nine-year saga about importing a computer.

On the other hand, it wasn't only 'benign neglect' by the state that explains software's success. This book has sensibly highlighted two unique factors. One, the role played by the extraordinary trade association, NASSCOM, which depended on a healthy collaboration between the software companies, driven by the talented, passionate Dewang Mehta. Second, a group of government officials, but above all, N. Vittal. He quickly grasped the amazing possibilities before the industry; then, patiently he removed the main obstacles laid by the Indian bureaucratic state. If one has to name a single act that made it all possible, it was Vittal's Software Technology Parks of India, a deliberate misnomer, I suspect, to lull the Indian bureaucracy into the complacent belief that that all was tickety-boo (btw, a phrase picked up by the British in India from the Hindi, '*Sab theek hai babu*') inside the leafy parks that were not parks.

I also believe that the storied success of the sector was built on the foundations of 'middle-class values' of the founders of IT companies. Most of them were first-time entrepreneurs, not stepping into a family business. Most of them came with advanced degrees in engineering or management. And most of them had an early exposure to the Western world because of their teachers and computers. The book is replete with tales of grit, such as TCS acquiring an IBM mainframe computer whose value was higher than all other assets of TCS at the time. Or of Infosys' founders living under extremely meagre circumstances, while working fervently on projects in client locations. Its generous ESOP programme or 'when in doubt, disclose' sentiment at Infosys reflected a spirit of egalitarianism, merit and corporate governance. The IT sector has proved that a world-class industry can be created in India.

Other factors contributed to the software revolution. The government's modest liberalization in the 1980s turned the tide, transforming the industry's mood. The timing of the take-off in the nineties was also right. The momentum in software exports came just as the global economy was changing from an industrial to a knowledge economy. The Y2K problem turned out to be an opportunity, which opened doors of Fortune 500 companies to Indian companies to showcase their skills. 1250 multinational companies jumping on the bandwagon, creating 1750 capability centres in India to remotely handle sophisticated problems in the form of back offices, R&D centres and call centres, was important.

Finally, the government's e-governance initiatives have played an important part in the software revolution. Not only have they touched every Indian's life, but they are also helping to make Indians comfortable with digitization.

Ab Initio: The Indian IT Industry Discovers a New Normal

30 January 2020 seemed like any regular day in India; the national newspapers carried stories on rising vegetable prices in New Delhi, the worsening traffic congestion in Bengaluru (Bangalore), and the surprising growth of fountain-pen sales in Kolkata (Calcutta).[1, 2] It was very much a typical day—but only until 1.33 p.m.

That was the time when the Union ministry of health and family welfare put out a press release announcing the first positive case of the novel coronavirus in India. The patient was a young woman studying medicine at a university in Wuhan, China, who had recently returned to her hometown in Thrissur, Kerala.[3] It would be only many days later, on 11 February 2020, that the World Health Organization (WHO) named the new disease Covid-19.[4]

The Indian IT industry, given its significant presence worldwide, had got early-warning signals of the global outbreak.

The IT companies went into a state of alert but, like several entities worldwide, they initially believed that the problem would be largely localized to China. Antoine Imbert, chief operating officer of Capgemini in India, said, 'We don't see a big impact at this stage across global operations but we are analysing our business continuity plans to see if more employees need to work from home.'[5] Pravin Rao, vice-chairperson of NASSCOM, the Indian IT industry association, and COO of Infosys, said, 'The IT sector may see some indirect impact in the medium to long-term as some of the clients have exposure to manufacturing in China.'[6] NASSCOM felt comfortable enough to conduct its Technology and Leadership Forum conference in Mumbai in mid-February 2020.

But things began to unfold dramatically from there on, and by March 2020 the pandemic spread across Asia, and from there to Europe, the UK and the US. By end May 2020, Covid-19 had affected more than 200 countries, with confirmed cases at nearly 6 million. India witnessed its first surge incident in early March in Jaipur, and on 24 March 2020 announced a nationwide lockdown for twenty-one days.[7] Phrases like 'lockdown', 'social distancing' and 'flattening the curve' began to enter the common vocabulary of the people. Worldwide, the pandemic dramatically impacted the functioning of governments and businesses, not to mention the lives of people.

The Indian IT industry responded swiftly to the evolving crisis. At Infosys, the Business Continuity Management core response team, chaired by Pravin Rao, met in March 2020 to take stock of the situation. Rao said, 'In the four decades of our operations, we've had occasion to fine-tune our plans for employee safety and business continuity over several crisis situations, and that has taught us invaluable lessons. It is this handbook, shaped from our collective and shared experience, that is helping us navigate towards stability in the face of the unprecedented disruption triggered by Covid-19 globally.'[8]

Within a week, 93 per cent of the Infosys global workforce began working from home. Infosys rapidly mobilized laptops and desktops, ensuring access to secure virtual work environments wherever necessary. It shipped 35,000 such 'assets' to employee residences. The company expanded its own virtual private network bandwidth by ten times and ensured a fourfold increase in backend capacity to support the increase in concurrently connected remote users. Infosys set up a twenty-four-hour help desk to support employees in emergency and unfamiliar situations.[9]

TCS moved with similar alacrity and established a Covid-19 Emergency Response Apex committee in March 2020 itself. This committee would drive a holistic action plan and coordinate TCS's global efforts to cope with the pandemic. Rajesh Gopinathan, CEO and MD of TCS, said, 'Our priority has been to safeguard the health and well-being of our associates while continuing to support mission-critical IT backbones globally. Early on we took proactive measures like travel restrictions, cancellation of events and large internal meetings, safe working environments and processes, which helped minimize the impact [of the pandemic].'[10]

TCS seamlessly switched from a highly centralized model—consisting of work spaces set in large delivery campuses and capable of accommodating thousands of employees—to a work-from-home model called Secure Borderless Workspaces. Gopinathan provided a context to this: 'Our current operating model is currently a twenty-year-old legacy. In some ways, this crisis actually leapfrogs us into a new model.'[11] TCS managed to make the dramatic transition as rapidly as it did because it leveraged its prior investments and learnings around open agile workspaces and standard service delivery environments, digitized governance processes and extensive use of collaborative and cloud-based technologies. By end March 2020, 90 per cent of TCS employees were working remotely and securely from their homes.

The rest of the Indian IT industry, too, soon made this transition to remote working. NASSCOM worked with the government to get the IT–BPM (Business Process Management) industry acknowledged as an essential service, which allowed a small percentage of employees performing mission-critical functions for their global clients to work out of their offices even during the lockdown. Debjani Ghosh, president of NASSCOM, described the partnership, 'The responsiveness of DoT (Department of Telecommunications) in relaxing Other Service Providers' terms and conditions to enable work-from-home (which allowed equipment to be shifted from Special Economic Zones or SEZs to a home), the quick action by the Directorate General of Export Promotion to ease the customs-related process, and the support of MeitY (Ministry of Electronics and Information Technology), the commerce ministry, and some of the key state governments relevant for our sector, have been particularly helpful.'[12]

The Indian IT industry embraced the new normal of remote work as well as a hybrid model (a combination of working from home and working from office) with aplomb, successfully managing client projects. Mars Incorporated, the US-based multinational manufacturer of confectionery, food, and pet care products and services, was an example of a client that worked extensively with partners in Indian IT. As global chief digital officer at Mars and former president and head of Americas for Infosys, Sandeep Dadlani is no stranger to the Indian IT industry. He was pleasantly surprised by the transition. 'I thought we would do 20 per cent less work due to unavailability of people during the crisis. But the Global Delivery Model has been more resilient than I expected. The mindfulness and focus shown by the IT teams have been exemplary. The service providers were able to bring in automation of business processes on their own, resulting in increased productivity. During this time, we had one of the smoothest financial closings in our company's history,'[13] he said.

The pandemic also triggered global enterprises to accelerate their digital strategy formulation and implementation. N. Chandrasekaran, chairperson of both Tata Sons and TCS, described the pace of acceleration, 'In many sectors, digital channels have gone from being secondary, nice-to-have options to become the primary channels, and in some instances, the only channels. Schools, colleges and even courts have shifted to an online-only mode. Farmers' cooperatives are taking online orders and directly delivering fresh produce to city-dwellers. This is the transformation that we had spoken of five years ago when we said that Default is Digital, but even I am still amazed by the scale and speed of the change.'[14]

At Infosys, Nandan Nilekani, chairperson, and Salil Parekh, CEO and MD, echoed similar sentiments in the context of their global clients seeking resilience in their businesses. 'In many ways the recent crisis has accelerated our clients' move along the direction of digital. We pivoted our attention to the new needs of our clients—cloud, workplace transformation, cost efficiency and automation,'[15] said a statement in the Infosys annual report for FY 2019–20.

Not only did the global clients move to new digital technologies but they also moved more of their traditional IT work offshore to

India. Consequently, the top Indian IT firms hired 44 per cent more employees in the pandemic-hit financial year FY 2020–21 than in the previous year. NASSCOM expected the Indian IT industry to grow by 2.3 per cent in FY 2020–21. Its CEO survey done in January–February 2021 revealed an optimistic picture—71 per cent of CEOs expected global tech spending to be significantly higher than in 2020, and 67 per cent expected the Indian tech industry to grow significantly.

It was not by chance that the Indian IT industry successfully navigated the turbulent waters of the pandemic. Ravi Kumar, president of Infosys, explained how the industry had built its digital capabilities over the decades and had become ready to catch a break when the opportunity arose. 'Think of the first wave of global technology development that gained momentum in the nineties as IT service providers the world over tackled the Y2K problem that threatened to bring us all to a grinding halt. Then, around 2007, a few years following the dotcom bubble burst, the (Indian IT) model proved its mettle again. The ride to recovery, backed by expanding telecom infrastructure and massive uptake for smartphones, came with the development of full-stack digital services that leveraged cloud and big data. Now, the post-coronavirus economy will usher in the next wave backed by always-available telecom infrastructure and accelerated adoption of 5G. In this there's great opportunity for us to absorb the shock of the recent crisis by accelerating our all-round digitization—localizing more atoms by globalizing more bits.'[16]

It was not just the IT industry whose appetite for technology soared during the pandemic. Other industries, governments and start-ups too embraced digital technologies in a significant way as part of their pandemic response.

Government, Industry and Start-ups Embrace Digitization during the Pandemic

On 2 April 2020, the government of India developed a contact-tracing app to track people who had contracted Covid-19 and others with whom they might have come into contact. The mobile app Aarogya Setu—which in Sanskrit means 'bridge to health'—made use of cutting-edge Bluetooth technology, algorithms and artificial intelligence to monitor Covid-19 cases and manage the pandemic.[17] Overseen by the MeitY, the app was developed by National Informatics Centre (NIC) in collaboration with volunteers from industry and academia, in an inspiring spirit of public–private partnership.

Aarogya Setu became one of the most downloaded apps in the world. On 15 April 2020, Amitabh Kant, CEO of NITI Aayog, the policy think-tank of the Indian government, tweeted: 'Telephone took seventy-five years to reach 50 million users, radio thirty-eight years, television thirteen years, Internet four years, Facebook nineteen months, Pokemon Go nineteen days. #AarogyaSetu, India's app to fight Covid-19, has reached 50 million users in just thirteen days—the fastest ever globally for an app. Salute the spirit of India!'[18] A year later, Aarogya Setu had over 176 million users.[19]

At the same time, several voices of concern were raised—about the app's security vulnerability, about whether it invaded the privacy of individuals, about its efficacy vis-à-vis those of competing technologies like Decentralized Privacy-Preserving Proximity Tracing (DP3T),[20] and the extent and purposes for which the data collected would be used. The sub-text pointed to the potential imbalance between compassionate healthcare provision and over-reaching surveillance by the government.

On the medical frontline, Aarogya Setu proved useful in the country's Covid-19 management efforts. By August 2020, more than 6.6 million contacts were traced using Aarogya Setu, of which 27 per cent tested positive (whereas the second national Covid-19 serosurvey estimated the prevalence of antibodies in only 7 per cent of the population[21]), thus proving that the technology was highly effective. More than 30,000 disease hotspots, with pin-code level accuracy, were identified and shared with state governments in whose jurisdictions they fell.[22] Since its release, the app has seen constant innovation, resulting in introduction of features like e-pass and QR code scanning—used, for instance, by security personnel to allow people into airports or lockdown zones—and an open application programming interface (API) service, which is a connection between computer programs to enable organizations to obtain information on the health status of their employees in real time.

In January 2021, the Indian government pushed its digital boundaries further when it developed a technology platform—Co-WIN—to support India's Covid-19 vaccination drive, the largest such programme in the world. Citizens could register on Co-WIN by simply providing their mobile phone number and an identification number, such as that of their Aadhaar (India's unique identity platform), and schedule their vaccination slots at the nearest vaccination centres. Commenting on this digital backbone, Nandan Nilekani said, 'We are the only country in the world where everybody gets a digital vaccination certificate immediately. And this can be printed, it can be on the person's smartphone, it can be kept in the Digital Locker, (and) is encrypted, digitally signed and it is QR coded so that we can authenticate that certificate anywhere—offline or online.'[23] Although the vaccination programme faced logistical and availability challenges, especially in its third phase when it was opened up to Indians over eighteen years of age, the programme's digital platform functioned well from an e-governance perspective. A country like India also needs to take along citizens who do not have access to technology and digital apps or portals. Citizens could register on the spot at the primary healthcare centre. Their information was captured in the Co-WIN back-end, and available online when they revisited the centre for their second shot of the vaccine.

Several Indian states too made innovative use of technology and collaborated with start-ups as part of their Covid strategy. For instance, the governments of Kerala, Telangana and Gujarat leveraged Geographic Information System (GIS) based apps to monitor movement of home-quarantined patients; the government of Jharkhand used robots, called Co-Bots, to handle automated delivery of food and medicines to patients; and the government of Maharashtra launched 'Swadhyay', an online remedial learning programme for school students. Seen from the lens of technology adoption, these Indian governments demonstrated a sense of digital enterprise in their pandemic response.

The Indian industry and start-ups too picked up the gauntlet thrown by the pandemic with determination and digital preparedness. A Confederation of Indian Industry study found that Indian industries were keen to adopt technologies that helped their Covid response when it came to their factory/office. These technologies facilitated teleworking, remote working and online collaboration; they augmented cybersecurity and brought in resilience to the organization, achieved automation of business processes and assisted in online learning in organizations.[24] The healthcare sector, expectedly, witnessed a flurry of activity. Shobana

Kamineni, vice-chairperson at Apollo Hospitals, declared that 'home care with digital' would be the next biggest revolution in healthcare. She said, 'In the post Covid-19 context, Apollo got more than 5000 of our doctors online. Accelerating the use of online tele-consultation, merging of biology and technology, data science and AI in personalized healthcare will be the new changes.'[25]

Several innovators, including deep-tech start-ups from academic incubators in the IT, healthcare and allied fields, rose to the challenge. IIT Madras incubated Modulus Housing, which developed a quickly installable portable hospital unit. PathShodh Healthcare, an IISc start-up, developed a unique electrochemical test for Covid-19. CoronaSafe Network, a tech-volunteer group, developed open-source software for pandemic management war rooms. Nocca Robotics, an IIT Kanpur-incubated company working on autonomous waterless solar panel-cleaning robots, quickly pivoted. In just ninety days the company developed Noccarc V310, a fully-functioning ICU ventilator costing less than similar global models. Commenting on how a good quality indigenous medical product was created, K. Radhakrishnan, former chairman of ISRO and chairman of the board of governors at IIT Kanpur, placed this effort in perspective: 'The ventilator project is not only a case study for entrepreneurs or the start-up ecosystem of India, but also for our premier educational institutions and the critical role they will have to play in the *aatmanirbhar* (self-reliant) movement whilst strengthening our economy.'[26]

The financial payments sector drove the use of contactless digital technologies. The distinctive QR codes that enabled digital payments became highly visible in the *kirana* store (the neighbourhood grocer's), found in every nook and corner of India.

Payment start-ups and apps like Google Pay, Paytm and PhonePe got a tremendous fillip to their growth. Data from the Reserve Bank of India showed that India, in mid-2020, made around 100 million digital transactions a day, clocking a volume of Rs 5 trillion (approximately US$67 billion), which represented a fivefold jump from 2016. Much of this digital transformation was powered by the United Payment Interface (UPI), a real-time payment system developed by National Payments Corporation of India.[27] Sameer Nigam, founder and CEO of PhonePe, said, 'The first two lockdowns led to an artificial, but sustained boost as far as all digital bill payments and recharges were concerned. UPI payments are now growing because of massive network effect at the societal level. Ten to fifteen million new customers are coming on board the platform every month.'[28]

A market study in 2019–20 had found that the education sector in India too was poised for digital disruption. The study predicted that by 2022, online K–12 education offerings (across grades 1 to 12) would increase sixfold and the post-K–12 market would grow nearly fourfold.[29] The Covid-19 pandemic only seemed to turbo-charge this transformation. With schools and colleges shut during the pandemic, education shifted online across the world, and in India too. Start-ups like Byju's, Unacademy and UpGrad experienced a sharp growth in the number of users on their platforms. Venture capital firms seized the opportunity and, according to Venture Intelligence, pumped in US$1.7 billion into India's ed-tech sector in the first nine months of 2020, registering a fourfold jump from the whole of 2019.[30]

Ronnie Screwvala, co-founder and chairman of UpGrad, a start-up focused on the post-K–12 market, believes that the shift to online learning holds significant potential for societal change:

'Whether we like it or not in India, the socio-economic reasons force people to take up a job very early in their lives and therefore skip education more as a necessity rather than as a choice. And that's what I think online will substitute for, where you can continue to work and learn and get a degree.'[31]

The last two years since the advent of Covid-19 have been remarkable—they have been truly a test of the survival instincts and fighting spirit of humanity and businesses facing the onslaught of the pandemic. The adage—'There are decades when nothing happens, and then there are weeks when decades happen'— captured well the state of digital transformation sweeping across the various fields of human activity worldwide, and in India too. And the Indian IT and technology sectors seemed to have done particularly well, leaving many amazed at how quickly they adapted to the situation.

We were not surprised, though. This was not the first time that such a turn of events, calling for dramatic transformation and agility in response, was taking place in Indian IT. We had come to expect how adroitly the Indian IT industry would manage this crisis, how sharply the government would implement mission-mode IT projects, and how smartly a new wave of digital start-ups would rise to the occasion. The watchword was resilience. For us, history was simply repeating itself.

Important Universal Lessons from the History of Indian IT

In our exercise to understand the history of Indian IT over the last six decades, we spent considerable time with over fifty stalwarts who have built and shaped the IT sector in the country. They shared their experiences, their trials and triumphs with us . . . and there emerged a tale of persistence and resilience, of luck and of being at the right place at the right time, of foresight, of planning and being ready when luck knocked on their doors, of a spirit of adventure and, above all, of an abiding sense of faith in technology and the belief that it would do good for the country. Their accounts presented some important universal lessons for business and life, and also offered a historical explanation for how well Indian IT reacted to the crisis of the Covid-19 pandemic.

The first lesson of their lives was the value of having faith in computing. For some time since the arrival of the first computer in 1955 (it was being used primarily for statistical and scientific purposes), we witnessed a rather sedate growth in computing in the country. In 1978, only 1000 computers existed in all of India![32] So, what motivated academic institutions like IIT Kanpur and its band of enthusiastic professors like V. Rajaraman to start teaching computer programming in India in the 1960s? Prof. H.N. Mahabala spoke for all the early pioneers of Indian IT when he described how he decided to choose computer science: 'Here was a "stupid" machine which, at every step, had to be told what to do. And one day, that it would exhibit what you might call rudimentary intelligence was something hard to believe. I can't say if I knew that it would happen, but I had a gut feeling that it might. It was a great challenge, and so I chose to be in computer science. And time has proven that my faith in computing was correct.'[33] What propelled young students like N.R. Narayana Murthy to sign up for computer courses in that era? In later years, many colleges, besides the IITs and IISc, offered programmes in computer science and IT, and those who graduated from these programmes became the bedrock of the Indian IT industry. Now, in 2022, when the world has not yet recovered from the pandemic, is it surprising that the voices in Indian IT are optimistic about the digital future of Indian business and society?

The second lesson is about achieving resilience and scalability by using world-class systems. India's focus in the 1970s and early 1980s was self-sufficiency and indigenous manufacture, and the ensuing policies made it very difficult to import computers into the country. Consequently, the IT industry was dominated by firms manufacturing and selling hardware. From the mid- to late-1980s, the policy changes made it easier for Indians to import computers, and the government provided incentives for software through the Software Technology Parks of India (STPI) scheme. Many hardware-focused emerging firms like Wipro and HCL transformed into software-services exporters. Pivoting at Indian 'start-ups' was indeed not a new phenomenon.

Indian IT companies found that exporting software services in the 1980s was a challenge. It was not easy to convince global clients about the merits of Indian IT, especially those who had never been to India or were even aware where the country was located on the world map. Scalability and being process-driven thus became the mantras for the entire Indian IT industry, and from this emerged the Global Delivery Model. The industry also embraced the software quality movement with great gusto and adopted the Software Engineering Institute Capability Maturity Model (SEI CMM) standards. Kris Gopalakrishnan spoke for the industry when he said, 'We invested in all aspects of the business—world-class campus that looked more like a university than an office, world-class quality system, world-class education and training, world-class financial management processes, administrative processes, and I think all of these allowed us to create that foundation of a scalable organization.'[34] The industry got a lucky break with the Y2K (year 2000) opportunity. Although the task this entailed was essentially remediation of a software bug, the Indian IT companies adopted a factory-like approach and did such a good job in solving this problem that global CIOs retained them to maintain their IT systems. Was it any surprise then that they managed a process-driven, smooth transition to nearly complete remote working during the pandemic?

It was not all smooth sailing for the Indian IT industry in the 2000s, when it had to weather the storms of the dotcom bust of the early 2000s and the global financial crisis in the latter years of the decade. But Indian IT companies seemed to be able to convert every moment of crisis to one of new opportunities and continued to achieve growth. Inherent to their spirit of resilience was also the camaraderie among the fiercely competing Indian IT companies. Kiran Karnik, former president of NASSCOM, described this camaraderie as a 'coalition of competitors': 'This capability of coming together in the Indian IT industry is something that very few other industries have. It is based on the principle "let's grow the pie, and within that we will compete". The best example was in the Satyam case. People understood right away that if Satyam went under, the whole industry would take a hit. NASSCOM helped the industry work together on several other issues such as human resources, visa or taxation.'[35] Such a spirit of cooperative competition and resilience will stand the world in good stead as it navigates a new normal.

The third lesson is the importance of entrepreneurship, and how vital it is to infuse new ideas and innovations into the ecosystem. The current groundswell of start-ups in India has followed multiple waves of IT entrepreneurship in the country. Commenting on this evolution, Kris Gopalakrishnan reminisced: 'The first wave happened in the late 1970s and early 1980s after IBM left India. There was a need to maintain these computers (the IBM mainframes). And it was also an opportunity for minicomputers to be introduced to India. So, the big companies you know now, such as HCL and Wipro, were established in that period. TCS came in earlier and Infosys later. And by mostly first-generation entrepreneurs, and that's why we consider that as a first wave of entrepreneurship. The second wave of entrepreneurship happened in the late 1990s—thanks to the Internet, new skills and capabilities were required, new opportunities were created, and so new companies also emerged. Mindtree is an example from this period. The late 2000s saw the emergence of IT start-ups beyond pure-play IT companies with application of IT in retail, logistics, food delivery and healthcare.'[36] This sense of entrepreneurship led to an expansion of services offered by the Indian IT services companies (such as expansion of the GDM model beyond application development to other services like ERP implementation, software testing and IT infrastructure management) as well as the explosion of IT-enabled start-ups. Was it then any surprise to find so many digital start-ups in the Indian ecosystem smartly responding to the Covid situation? We can indeed expect another wave of new start-ups in the post-pandemic world.

The fourth lesson is about leadership. The founders and the management teams at Indian IT companies were typically college educated and often with advanced engineering or management degrees. They established a new model for businesses in India, one that was professionally run and meritocracy-based, which was systems- and data-driven, and followed world-class quality and corporate governance standards. They changed the world's perception of India as a land of snake charmers to one of technology-savvy professionals. A research study on leadership lessons from India found that the source of the competitive advantage Indian companies had lay in their investment in people.[37] Indian IT companies took this to a different level—with their focus on training and skilling of employees, stock options that made many of them millionaires, and campuses that often housed saunas and gymnasiums for all. This was a point that Narayana Murthy evocatively reinforced when he said: 'We believe that our asset is primarily our people. Our asset walks out mentally and physically tired every evening. It is our responsibility to make sure that asset comes back enthusiastic in the morning.'[38] This lesson in compassionate capitalism, where corporations have to account for the costs they impose on their employees and vendors, environment and society, becomes particularly relevant in the context of conducting business during the pandemic. Does not the remarkable system for learning that the Indian IT companies developed for their employees offer a model for other businesses as they look at reskilling their employees in an increasingly digital world?

We believe that all these leadership lessons from the history of Indian IT are relevant for today's professionals and policymakers.

Why the Book, What It Contains and What Is Different about It

Firstly, this is personal. Chronicling the history of Indian IT has been a labour of love. We have been part of the Indian IT industry ourselves over the last three decades and more. We have been software programmer, architect, consultant, researcher, educator and salesperson at different times; we have been in leadership roles at Infosys, consulted clients worldwide and managed global IT transformation programmes. Kris Gopalakrishnan, of course, has been a pioneer entrepreneur in the industry. This project is one way in which we can pay back the industry from which we have benefited immensely.

So, we jumped at the opportunity to capture the stories of Indian IT, an industry that has played a seminal role in shaping modern industrial India. Firstly, we recorded its history in the voices of over fifty of its extraordinary protagonists. We spent a year interviewing them, following a two-step process for most of the interviews— the first consisting of a semi-structured, conversational, in-depth research interview, and the second a structured video interview. We then made available these oral histories through a mobile app and then on the web (https://itihaasa.com/History). Trust the geeks in us to go the digital way, and we were thrilled to create a first-of-its-kind 'digital museum' on Indian IT.[39] And now we are writing this book, which weaves the leaders' individual narratives into one cohesive story.

Secondly, we believe that business history is a powerful tool. History can be used to inspire collective effort and to devise smart strategies for the future.[40] As Prof. Geoffrey Jones, faculty chair of the Business History Initiative at Harvard Business School says, 'History provides rich and nuanced evidence on many key debates in the world today, including the evolution of leadership, the sources of innovation and entrepreneurship, the drivers and consequences of globalization, the role of business in political systems, and the responsibilities of business to creating a more sustainable world.' Global businesses can learn from the history of Indian IT.

Thirdly, this book is a response to what we heard from many young IT professionals who visited our website on the history of Indian IT. We realized that many of them had limited knowledge of the rich professional heritage that they were part of, and they wanted to learn more. But they sought this information in the form of stories written in a conversational style. They desired to learn about the origins of their companies, about their interesting early projects and the stories of their founders, who were programmers or hardware engineers first and CEOs only later.

So, here's our book—an engaging analysis of the evolution of Indian IT based on the oral narratives of the key actors who shaped it over the decades. For, who better to tell us stories about the industry than the people who created them. This book is replete with interesting recollections shared by the key actors in the Indian IT industry.

You, the reader, will get an anecdote-rich history of Indian IT over the decades from this book. For instance, if you take the topic of 'brushes' with first computers, you will learn about the journey from England of the HEC-2M, India's first computer; the arrival of the IBM 1620, the first computer at IIT Kanpur, by air and then by bullock cart; and the creation of TIFRAC, India's first indigenously built computer. The book will also connect the past with the present. There are several business lessons that one can learn from different points in the evolution of the IT industry. Many Indian start-up unicorns today, who find scaling up profitably a challenge, may learn from the ability of the Indian software services companies to scale up rapidly and with high profit margins. Another challenge that start-ups face is successful pivoting from their existing business model to something new when the situation calls for it. The best examples of successful pivots were when HCL and Wipro shifted from a domestic hardware focus to a software-services export focus. There are also stories about existential and crisis situations that Indian IT companies found themselves in and how they changed them to opportunities—TCS purchasing an IBM mainframe which cost more than the company's gross worth in the 1980s, or Infosys choosing not to renew a contract with GE, one of its largest customers in the mid-1990s. Looking back, these were audacious decisions at critical points in the evolution of these companies.

The IT industry has placed India in the global spotlight within a short span of six decades. Indeed, we have come a long way, but how did it all start? You have already read about the remarkable response of the Indian IT industry to the Covid-19 pandemic, and how even the government agencies and Indian start-ups responded bravely and admirably to the crisis through their digital efforts. In many ways, it is the events over the last six decades and more that have made Indian IT ready for such a stern examination. We believe that history is repeating itself. And the current situation provides us a good opportunity to travel back in time to the start of computing in India.

The Chapters in This Book and What They Contain

Chapter 2: Emergence of IT in India and Capability-Building

The focus of this chapter is to understand how modern IT came to India in the 1950s; and how Indian policymakers and thinkers, such as P.C. Mahalanobis and Homi Bhabha, envisioned the evolution of computing in the country. The word 'computation' made its first appearance only in the second Five-Year Plan,[41] and the word 'computer' made its grand entrance only in India's third

Five-Year Plan. We present the stories of HEC-2M at ISI Kolkata, the first computer in India, and its use in India's Five-Year Plans; TIFRAC, the first digital computer for scientific applications to be built in India at the Tata Institute of Fundamental Research; and the first-ever computer programming course in India at IIT Kanpur. Computers made very slow progress in India and were predominantly used for scientific and educational purposes.

We also cover the earliest contexts for the use of computers by industry in India, especially by the jute mills and the MNCs. IBM became the dominant technology provider in the country. And you will discover how India built capability in computers and computer programming based on refurbished technology offered by the IT multinationals to their Indian clients. In 1969, Tata Sons created Tata Consultancy Services (TCS) and appointed F.C. Kohli, who had deep connections with American institutions such as Massachusetts Institute of Technology (MIT) and Institute of Electrical and Electronics Engineers (IEEE), as its general manager. This era also witnessed the creation of Computer Society of India, a forum that would go on to successfully bring together computing researchers and industry professionals. One anecdote that you will relish is what happened when Narayana Murthy saw a computer for the very first time.

Chapter 3: Emphasis on Self-Reliance and the Domestic Hardware Industry

We look at how the IT industry managed to survive under the constraining computer policies of the 1970s. The 1974 Computer Imports for Software Export policy allowed Indian companies to import computers against their undertaking to use these computers to export software. In fact, it was this scheme that helped TCS import a Burroughs mainframe computer, which eventually opened the doors for software exports.

IBM was asked to leave India during this period. One unlikely aspect of the nascent Indian IT industry which emerged in this crucible of trying conditions was the germination of entrepreneurship. The minicomputers policy was announced in 1978, and soon 'start-ups' like DCM, ORG and HCL (founded by Shiv Nadar and team) and Wipro Information Technology (founded by Azim Premji and team) started to make microprocessors-based minicomputers. How these companies originated and grew in their early days is a fascinating story of grit and determination.

Computer education, which had a defining influence on the careers of India's IT entrepreneurs, flourished in various institutions. A BTech programme in computer science introduced at IIT Kanpur became a runaway success; India's, and probably Asia's, biggest computer of its time arrived at the IIT Madras computer centre; there is the story of IIM Ahmedabad and its sophisticated computing facility; and the government's recommendations led to the creation of a new master's programme in India called Master of Computer Application (MCA). One interesting anecdote is about how Prof. Kamala Krithivasan's work on theoretical computer science was inspired by the intricate *kolam* patterns of south India.

Several government initiatives—like the National Informatics Centre, the National Centre for Software Development and Computing Techniques, and the Education and Research Network (ERNET) project—were established. You will read about India's first email, which was sent during this decade.

Chapter 4: Growth of Software Services and Mission-Mode Government IT Projects

In the 1980s, the Indian IT industry welcomed new start-ups like Infosys (founded by Narayana Murthy and team), NIIT (founded by Rajendra Pawar and team) and Mastek (founded by Ashank Desai and team). Other start-ups too emerged, focused on different domains in the IT sector—FutureSoft in niche telecom software, IIS Infotech in offshore-based software services, and Tally in software products for the enterprise. The industry also saw the first trickle of IT MNCs, like Texas Instruments (TI), setting up their software subsidiaries in India. New industry associations like MAIT (Manufacturers Association Information Technology) and NASSCOM (National Association of Software and Services Companies) were formed in this decade, lending voice to the hardware and software companies.

The government played a big role in this era—the New Computer Policy announced in 1984 recognized 'software' as an industry and played an important role in spurring the growth of export-oriented software services. It also initiated some of the most impactful IT projects to touch the lives of ordinary citizens—the Railways Passenger Reservation System (PRS) and the banking mechanization project, where computers were euphemistically referred to as 'advanced ledger posting machines'. The government also established the Centre for Development of Advanced Computing (CDAC), approved creation of the National Supercomputer Education and Research Centre (SERC) in IISc, and kick-started the Knowledge Based Computer System (KBCS) initiative.

You will no doubt be chuffed to bits when you read about the doyens of the Indian IT industry cutting vegetables and washing dishes! And you will be amazed to learn how general elections in India, robots in a factory in Japan, and a three-hour delay at the reservation counter for a CEO of an Indian IT company led to the success of the iconic PRS project.

Chapter 5: The Rapid Growth of Indian IT Services

In this chapter, we focus on how the Indian IT industry morphed into a predominantly software services industry and had a period of spectacular growth. This was an era characterized by a concomitance between conducive policy, enabling technologies and business model innovations. The Indian software industry grew and, as the 1992 World Bank report predicted, reached US$1 billion by the mid-1990s.

The Department of Electronics (DoE), under the leadership of N. Vittal, introduced the Software Technology Parks of India (STPI) programme. The soft-touch STPI scheme was revolutionary and almost freed the software services export industry from regulation in return for its ability to bring dollars into India. The negotiations between a fledgling NASSCOM and DoE offer a fascinating case study of how India's potential was unshackled when policy and industry talked to each other.

The software services industry invented the Global Delivery Model (GDM), which included offshore delivery of services. The value chain in software services—recruitment, training, delivery operations, quality and finance—evolved into fine-tuned capabilities that provided the momentum for the rapid growth of software services, predominantly from India. The Y2K (year 2000) opportunity materialized, and the Indian IT industry lapped it up.

In this decade, MNCs like IBM came back to India, often in joint venture with Indian partners. Large-scale offshore development centres (ODCs) emerged, pioneered by the efforts of companies like GE and Nortel. There was a second wave of IT entrepreneurship in the 1990s when companies like Cognizant, Mindtree and Microland were established.

You will find in this chapter the fascinating stories of two 'firsts' for India in the 1990s—the launch of India's indigenous supercomputer, the PARAM; and the average Indian citizen's first brush with the Internet as VSNL, the national telecom carrier, made it available for public access.

Chapter 6: Indian IT Comes of Age

The 2000s saw a golden period of expansion and rapid scaling of the Indian IT industry. The IT industry brought GDM into adjacent services like infrastructure management services, testing services, systems integration and business process outsourcing/management (BPO/BPM), and expanded its service offerings. In this decade, the IT industry also grew geographically—beyond the US and the UK and into continental Europe, Latin America, Australia and other regions. Indian IT also achieved global leadership in the product category of core banking. This decade also saw a rapid increase in the number of subsidiaries of MNCs and their global capability centres in India focused on engineering, IT and BPM.

The Indian IT industry also witnessed some dark moments in this decade. We explore the challenges of the 2008 global financial crisis and its subsequent impact on the IT industry. There was a breakdown in corporate governance in one company in the IT industry, leading to the Satyam scandal. But the way the IT industry and NASSCOM closed ranks and worked with the government to resolve this crisis is a one-of-a-kind case study in the world.

We will also deep-dive into the new wave of IT start-ups and companies that pushed the boundaries of the industry; some of them were Genpact (in BPO), Ittiam Systems (in video technologies) and Pico Peta Simputer (in hardware devices). This period also saw the advent of new IT-enabled start-ups—B2C or consumer-facing start-ups—like Flipkart, Ola and Paytm; and B2B product and SaaS companies like InMobi, Druva and Zoho. In this era, India became host to the third largest start-up ecosystem in the world.

The various governments in India, both at the Centre and in the states, created forward-looking IT policies. They were themselves at the forefront of adopting IT through impactful e-governance initiatives and transformative mission-mode projects like the Aadhaar, the world's largest biometric identity system for people, and Unified Payments Interface (UPI), a real-time payment technology.

You will love the anecdotes about frugal innovations that powered Indian BPO. And your heart will race as you read about the events of the first seventy-two hours after the Satyam scandal broke out.

Chapter 7: Quō Vādis: Where Are We Heading?

In this concluding section, we gaze into the future of Indian IT. What are the emerging technologies and emergent business opportunities that are shaping IT today and will in the near future? We will look at how a mix of technologies, like Artificial Intelligence (AI), Machine Learning (ML), Internet of Things (IoT), robotics and genomics are helping reimagine businesses and unlocking human productivity. Indian IT has the opportunity to create emerging technologies, such as 5G radio interface technology, and to become an integrator of these global technologies. It also has the obligation to harness these technologies to meet the needs and aspirations of all sections of its own society.

We will see how Indian IT services companies and the global capability centres of MNCs in India are becoming the preferred partners in digital transformation and engines of innovation and digital capabilities. We will also examine the rise of deep-tech start-ups from India. They will put us on a path where we will be able to solve some of India's difficult problems using technology. Deep-tech start-ups are also important for boosting human productivity in a resource-constrained economy like India's. We will look at some systemic models—like academic incubators, research parks and deep-tech alliances—that are in play in India, supporting these start-ups. We will then explore some IT-led government mission-mode programmes, including the National Digital Health Mission and the National Programme on Technology Enhanced Learning.

The engine of success for the IT industry, IT deep-tech start-ups and government is the capability of the Indian IT professional, which is increasingly being powered by digital learning and skilling platforms. We will then examine the emerging trends in science research in India. AI/ML is among the most foundational of technologies in which India must acquire national capability. We look at some key strategies to achieve research excellence in this space. We also explore what India is doing in brain sciences, one of the most promising interdisciplinary domains of the future.

All the IT elements in the country that we have discussed so far—industry, start-ups, government and research—will be driven by data and algorithms. We will look at why regulations are becoming important as technologies become more pervasive in our lives. We will delve into some groundbreaking regulations around data that India is proposing. And we will explore why AI systems need to be governed better.

To us, this book is more than just a homage to the past or a nostalgia-tinged walk down memory lane. It is a narrative of triumph, and a missive of optimism for the future. Happy reading!

2

Emergence of IT in India and Capability-Building

The Information Technology (IT) industry has become the poster child of modern industrial India. As of 2021, IT contributed to 8 per cent of India's GDP, around 52 per cent of total Indian services exports, was the largest private employer in India employing around 4.5 million IT professionals, and housed 1000-plus IT and R&D services subsidiaries of MNCs.[1] Indeed, we have come a long way. But when and where did it all start in India?

In fact, several questions spring to mind. When did the first modern computer come to India? When was programming first taught in India and how did education in computer science evolve in the country? How did India embark on its journey to manufacture computers and software? Who were the earliest IT entrepreneurs? What were the policies that shaped the industry? How did the industry grow?

Delving into the Minds of India's Policymakers and Understanding the Scientific Temper of Modern India Through Its Five-Year Plans

Modern India's 'tryst with destiny' began in 1947, and soon the Five-Year Plan became the principal planning mechanism. The Plans provide a unique snapshot of the thinking that shaped India's development. Let us analyse the first three Five-Year Plans, especially from a technology perspective.

	First Five-Year Plan (1951–56)	Second Five-Year Plan (1956–61)	Third Five-Year Plan (1961–66)
Number of times the words 'technology', 'technological', 'technologically' or 'technologist' appear	28	61	142
Number of chapters containing the word 'technology' or related words	8 of 39	17 of 30	24 of 35
Number of times the words 'computer' or 'computation' appear	0	1	2

Table 1: A word-analysis of the first three Five-Year Plans for use of the words 'technology', 'computers' and their derivatives.

We can see a steep increase in the occurrence of the word 'technology' and its derivatives with each successive Plan. The word 'computation' made its first appearance only in the second Five-Year Plan, and the word 'computer' made its grand entrance only in India's third Five-Year Plan.

In the first Five-Year Plan,[2] the planners held a dichotomous view on the influence of technology in society. While they recognized the importance of technology, they were also wary that technology might unleash excessive unemployment.

In 1954, Prime Minister Nehru entrusted P.C. Mahalanobis, founder of the Indian Statistical Institute (ISI), with the responsibility of preparing the draft for the second Five-Year Plan.[3] Mahalanobis leveraged sophisticated statistical models to determine optimal allocation of investments to different sectors in order to maximize economic growth in the long run. This emphasis on statistics meant an emphasis on large-scale data collection, and this necessitated significant computational capabilities. The word 'computation' thus made its first appearance in the second Five-Year Plan when it talked about ISI's 'electronic computation laboratory'. We will soon see the story of India's first computer coming to ISI.

The second Plan emphasized ideas like government control of industry (industrialization through public companies) and fiscal prudence, which influenced the nation's policies on technology development and procurement of computers. These policies are discussed in greater detail in the subsequent chapters. In the second Plan, the foundation was laid for establishing an Indian Institute of Technology (IIT) each in Mumbai, Kanpur and Chennai. These institutions went on to play an important role in developing computer education in the country and in nurturing the Indian IT sector.

It was in the third Five-Year Plan that the word 'computer' appeared for the first time.[4] The influence of Homi Bhabha, founder of the Tata Institute of Fundamental Research (TIFR), in shaping the computer-related technology capability of the nation was evident in the third Plan, which said, 'It is proposed to install one of the latest types of fast transistorized digital computers in the institute (TIFR). It is also planned to design and build a computer with a higher speed and more powerful computational facilities than any commercially available today.'

The third Plan also placed great emphasis on scientific personnel. A national register for scientific and technical personnel was maintained by the Council of Scientific and Industrial Research for providing temporary placements for highly qualified scientists, especially those returning to India from foreign countries. We will see how similar networks enabled Bhabha to get enterprising candidates to join TIFR and the Atomic Energy Establishment (AEE).

Computing at the Indian Statistical Institute in the 1950s and 1960s and the Story of Jute Crop Surveys, Five-Year Plans and the Advent of India's First Computer

The story of computers in the country's east is deeply intertwined with the story of Prashantha Chandra Mahalanobis, who has been described as 'a physicist by training, a statistician by instinct and a planner by conviction'.[5]

In 1913, just as Mahalanobis was to set sail to India from England, Prof. Macaulay, his tutor at King's College, drew his attention to some bound volumes of *Biometrika*, a journal of statistics.[6] Mahalanobis devoured the entire set of journals during his journey and discovered statistics as a new area of interest in his life. But, due to the First World War, Mahalanobis remained in India. He joined Presidency College in Kolkata as a professor of physics. But his interest in statistics grew stronger, and he soon discovered interesting areas for application of statistics, such as meteorology and anthropology. In the 1920s, he ran a workshop called 'statistical laboratory' from his university room and conceived the idea of a statistical institute in the country. The Indian Statistical Institute was thus founded in 1931 and soon developed a new statistical technique for estimating acreage and yield of crops in a large region by random sampling. This was applied to estimate the jute crop in the province of Bengal in 1937.

In 1950, Mahalanobis helped establish the National Sample Survey (NSS) for collection of socio-economic data such as consumer expenditure, public opinion, forecasts of acreage and yield of crops. These surveys provided the copious amount of demographic and economic data required for running the Mahalanobis model of the second Five-Year Plan.

Mahalanobis reasoned that the only way to keep up with so much data was by means of a computer. He said, 'We must proceed with electronic computers with all possible speed. Otherwise, we will never be able to cope with the tremendous volume of primary information which is accumulating . . . I know that real planning would require the use of such computers.'[7]

Early Computers at ISI

The story of 'computers' at ISI actually began in the 1930s when the jute crop surveys were undertaken. These were unusual computers— unusual from the point of view of the conventional understanding of what a computer is. They were actually humans. Mahalanobis designated a few statistical staff members as computers, who calculated and tabulated the large-scale sample surveys conducted at the institute.[8]

Pickering's Computers or Harvard Computers[9]

Since we are on the subject of humans being classified as 'computers', let's take a small detour and meet the other human computers—Pickering's Computers or Harvard Computers from the United States of America.

Edward Charles Pickering was director of the Harvard College Observatory in 1877 and started amassing what would eventually become the world's largest collection of photographic plates of stars. He hired a number of women, who were skilled workers, to process astronomical data.

As Dava Sobel explains in her book *The Glass Universe: How the Ladies of the Harvard Observatory Took the Measure of the Stars*, 'Much of the women's work entailed computing the actual positions and brightness of individual stars by applying mathematical formulae to the nightly notations made by the male observers. With the glass plates, they could discover new stars. While some of the photographs portrayed the stars as dots to be counted and catalogued according to sky coordinates, other images displayed the stars' light as tiny strips, or spectra, bearing distinct patterns.'

These women went on to produce a stellar classification system and methods to assess the relative size of stars and distance markers in space.

Mahalanobis also realized the importance of scientific instruments to aid the statistical efforts of the institute. In 1953, the first general report on the NSS, conducted under Mahalanobis's leadership, noted: 'Since much of the work of tabulation and analysis of the primary data was to be done by tabulating machines,[10] training was also given to a large number of punchers and verifiers in the Institute . . . Arrangements were made to hire the latest types of tabulating machines from the International Business Machine Corporation (IBM) of New York; and by the latter part of 1951, the Institute had two new models of IBM tabulators, a new multiplier (an electronic calculator) and several sorters (for sorting punched cards), reproducers (for copying information from one deck of cards to another), etc., in addition to some of the machines of the British Tabulating Machine Co. which the institute had been using for some time. An Electronic Statistical Machine (a high-power combined sorter-tabulator) was also rented from the IBM.'[11]

That same year, the Electronic Computer Division at ISI built, with salvaged materials from the disposal depots of Kolkata's Chandni Chowk market, India's first electrical analogue computing machine that could solve simple linear equations. Around the same time, V. Rajaraman, a student at the Indian Institute of Science, was working on a differential analyser.

According to the ISI annual report for 1952–53,[12] these machines were used for a variety of surveys, such as the National Sample Surveys, model sampling experiments in connection with crop surveys (jute, cinchona, etc.) and population surveys (of Mysore, refugees in West Bengal, etc.).

The HEC-2M Comes to ISI

As we saw earlier, Mahalanobis soon realized the importance of getting a digital computer with enhanced capabilities to process data that India was collecting as part of its planning process. In 1954, he convinced the Soviet Ambassador Menshikov to help India acquire a digital computer. Eight months later, the USSR and the United Nations agreed to fund India's purchase of a Hollerith Electronic Digital Computer-2M (HEC-2M) from the British Tabulating Machine Company for a princely amount of Rs 2 lakh.

Describing the events surrounding this digital computer, Rajaraman said: 'In 1955, ISI got a digital computer imported from England, made by the British Tabulating Machine (BTM) Company. Two of their professors, Amresh Roy and Monimohan Mookerji, went to England and worked with Prof. Booth, who was building that machine at Birkbeck College London. BTM was not willing to instal and maintain the machine in India, because only one machine was coming to the country. The ISI professors came back to India after their training, and sometime in the middle of 1955 when the machine arrived, they installed it and made it work. The machine had all of a 1024-word memory. It was a drum memory. (It did not have a printer or a tape and used punched cards.) The arithmetic was elementary and there was no language; they had to use machine language. They solved some interesting problems for ISI. That's probably the first machine that came to India.'[13]

Indeed, the HEC-2M was the first digital computer not only in India but also possibly in mainland Asia.

Andrew Booth, Computer Pioneer and Inventor of the HEC-2M Computer[14, 15]

Andrew Donald Booth was a distinguished pioneer in the development of computers in the UK. Booth received a PhD from University of Birmingham during the Second World War on crystallography of explosive materials.

In 1945, Booth was building one of the first computers in the UK. He recognized the need for a compact data storage device and developed the world's first rotating storage device in the form of a drum. Later, researchers adapted his technology to create the now familiar computer disk.

In 1947, Booth built the prototype Simple Electronic Computer, followed by his All-Purpose Electronic Computer (APEC) in 1951, which was among the first generation of electronic computers. In fact, the first version of APEC was built in Booth's family home barn. Booth sold his computing technology to the British Tabulating Machine Company (BTM).

Raymond 'Dickie' Bird and his colleagues from BTM replicated Booth's machine, and their product was called the Hollerith Electronic Computer, HEC-1. By the late 1950s, it became the UK's bestselling range of computers. BTM delivered seven or eight systems of its second-generation machines, the HEC-2M, worldwide. One of them came to the Indian Statistical Institute.

In 1958, with a grant from the United Nations Technical Assistance Administration (UNTAA), ISI got its second digital computer, the URAL. Unlike the HEC-2M, the URAL came with a complete set of detailed manuals and eight Russian engineers to help with the installation and training of personnel. The URAL was a 32-bit-word-sized 2Kb-memory machine with a horizontal magnetic tape, punched celluloid tape and a printer. Soon the computer division had around thirty people working full time to crunch NSS data and create optimal economic plans for the Planning Division.

A circuit from the Ural computer in ISI. Courtesy: Subroto Bagchi and itihaasa Research and Digital

In 1961, ISI, in collaboration with Jadavpur University, decided to design and build two solid-state electronic digital computers. The machines were planned to be character-based, having a syllable structure, unlike the word structure of the HEC-2M and the URAL, and was expected to be adaptable to automatic programming using a universal programming language such as 'ALGOL'.[16] The computer was commissioned in 1965–66 and was christened as ISIJU-I (ISI Jadavpur University - I). However, the project was not highly successful—it was not able to get the card reader and line printer free of charge from the United Nations, and the input-output equipment that was designed consequently did not function satisfactorily. The computer's projected data link could not be operated continuously due to serious fluctuation in the voltage of electric current at the institute.

Soon, ISI procured an IBM 1401, and the computation services at ISI consisted mostly of programming on this computer. The research and training school at ISI imparted training in efficient programming and the operation of tabulating and computing on machines. Their three-month evening course on 'Punched Card Systems' in Kolkata became popular. ISI was a strong contender in the race to become the first National Computational Centre in India. But it lost that race to TIFR.

By the 1960s, the east had ceded its leading position to the west of India. Institutions like TIFR and AEE, and people like Homi Bhabha, took centre stage. We now head to Mumbai to witness what happened there in the 1950s and 1960s.

Homi Bhabha and TIFR: Genesis of an Indian Computer and Laying the Foundation for a National Policy on Computers

While Mahalanobis was pioneering the use of computers in Kolkata, another Indian stalwart, Homi Jehangir Bhabha, was independently doing so in Mumbai. In the same way that the disruption of the First World War made Mahalanobis return to Kolkata permanently, Bhabha's return to India in 1939 for a duration longer than he anticipated was thanks to the disruption caused by the Second World War.

Bhabha's achievements as a young student in Cambridge in the 1920s and 1930s gives us a glimpse into his genius. He was awarded the Salomons Studentship in Engineering and obtained a first class in his Mechanical Sciences Tripos exam. Bhabha then switched to study mathematics. He obtained a first class in the Mathematical Tripos exam and was awarded the Rouse Ball travelling studentship in mathematics. This helped Bhabha work with stalwart physicists like Wolfgang Pauli, Enrico Fermi and Paul Dirac. It was when Bhabha was in India for his annual vacation in 1939 that the Second World War broke out and he had to postpone his trip back to Cambridge. To India's luck, Bhabha accepted the post of reader in physics at IISc, and continued to work on nuclear physics and particle physics. C.V. Raman, then director of the institute, described Bhabha as 'a great lover of music, a gifted artist, a brilliant engineer and an outstanding scientist . . . He is the modern equivalent of Leonardo da Vinci.'[17] Not surprisingly, Bhabha was nominated for the Nobel Prize in Physics many times in the 1950s.

While in India, Bhabha developed a rapport with the leaders of the Indian National Congress, including another University of Cambridge alumnus, Jawaharlal Nehru. This camaraderie would go on to influence a significant part of India's science and technology policy during the 1940s, 1950s and 1960s. Bhabha convinced Nehru on the importance of an Indian nuclear programme even before India became independent. He also made a successful appeal to the Tata Trusts for funding in 1945, to establish the Tata Institute of Fundamental Research (TIFR), an institution focused on cutting-edge basic science research, including nuclear and atomic physics. In 1948, immediately after Independence, the government of India set up the Atomic Energy Commission (AEC), chaired by Bhabha. The AEC set up a specialized applied research and engineering facility, the Atomic Energy Establishment (AEE), in 1954.

Bhabha was not only an exceptional physicist but also a keen student of emerging modern technologies. He obtained a copy of the famed John von Neumann report published in 1945 during one of his visits to the US in the early 1950s. Formally titled 'First Draft of a Report on the EDVAC', it had the first description of the logical design or architecture of a stored program computer. The Electronic Discrete Variable Automatic Computer, EDVAC, was built at University of Pennsylvania's Moore School of Electrical Engineering in 1949 and was a successor to the Electronic Numerical Integrator and Computer (ENIAC), which was the first general-purpose programmable electronic computer. Bhabha immediately understood the importance of the pivotal role digital computers would play in all domains of science and technology, and felt that India, and especially TIFR, should possess a digital computer.

TIFR's TIFRAC: India's First Indigenous Digital Computer

Bhabha was always on the lookout for exceptional Indian scientists for TIFR. He found help from the officers at the Tata Trusts who managed the J.N. Tata Endowment for Higher Education, which funded meritorious Indians studying in the US and England. They would send freshly minted PhD scholars visiting their Mumbai office to meet Bhabha. One such scholar was R. Narasimhan, who returned to India in 1954 after completing his master's in electrical engineering from California Institute of Technology and a PhD in mathematics from Indiana University. Bhabha recruited him as a research fellow at TIFR. Apart from having stellar qualifications, Narasimhan was thoroughly familiar with the concepts enunciated in the von Neumann report, which Bhabha hugely appreciated. Not surprisingly, Narasimhan's first seminar at TIFR was on the designing of an electronic computer. In the words of M.G.K. Menon, a noted Indian physicist, a director of TIFR and the first chairman of the Department of Electronics, government of India, 'Prof. R. Narasimhan was quite a unique personality. He was certainly one of the pioneers, a doyen and indeed a father figure in Indian computer science research.'[18]

Narasimhan and other young scientists in the TIFR team, which included P.V.S. Rao, who joined TIFR immediately after his master's in physics from Banaras Hindu University, decided to build a 'pilot' digital computer first. It was their maiden attempt at building such a complex machine from scratch. The team had, apart from the von Neumann report, some sketchy technical information on the University of Illinois' ILLIAC (Illinois Automatic Computer). The pilot computer was successfully completed in 1956. And a more powerful and larger computer was completed in 1959. This

The TIFRAC computer at TIFR. Courtesy: TIFR archives

computer was tested only in early 1960, since the air conditioning system for housing the computer was delayed. It was in 1962 that this computer was formally inaugurated by Prime Minister Jawaharlal Nehru, who christened it TIFRAC—TIFR Automatic Calculator.

Fabrication of the TIFRAC was entirely an internal operation. Narasimhan reminisced, 'We couldn't have gotten any help from outside, because there wasn't any organization outside which was doing this kind of work. Basically, we depended on our own workshop. So, the fact that we were able to put together a machine like this says something about the capability of the workshop. The main systems, that is CPU plus memory, were built as plug-in units. They were all built locally and maintenance was so much simpler. If you trace the fault to a particular plug-in unit, you pull it out, put a new one in and the computation keeps on going while you can service the plug-in unit. Tricks like that were tried out and we were able to design them to implementation stage and it was implemented using the workshop capabilities.'[19]

The TIFR archives give us a fascinating insight into Bhabha's vision and Narasimhan's planning in 1959, when the TIFRAC was just getting ready. In a note titled 'Electronic Computers', Bhabha highlighted the importance of computers and described his discussions with scientists in the US and England to assist TIFR in building or acquiring a computer. He discussed the possibility of computer scientists from the University of Cambridge spending time at TIFR, and the strengths of the Manchester University computer group. In the US, the University of Illinois Urbana-Champaign suggested that it would be possible for one or two TIFR computer scientists to visit their computer centre that built and operated the ILLIAC. Bhabha's discussions with the head of research at IBM are also interesting. It appears that IBM was interested in selling a powerful computer to TIFR. It also appears that Bhabha, faced with a 'make vs buy' decision, decided to make TIFR's first digital computer in-house.

Narasimhan's 1959 note, 'A Proposal for the Establishment of a Computer Group in TIFR', dwelt on the importance of TIFR having a separate 'computer group' with its own mission. The twin objectives of this group were identified as (1) maintaining and operating the digital computer (the TIFRAC) and helping users in programming, and (2) basic and applied research in digital computer theory and operations.

Coming back to the TIFRAC, one of the fascinating aspects about it was that its performance compared favourably with—or was perhaps even better than—IBM's best-selling scientific computer at that time, the IBM 701. Based on our research of publicly available information about these computers, this is how the TIFRAC compared with the IBM 701.

	TIFRAC	**IBM 701**
Focus	Scientific calculations	Scientific calculations 'Defence Calculator', first commercial scientific computer
Launch	1959	1952
Memory	2048 words of 40 bits, 3D ferrite core	2048 words of 36 bits, tubes, later ferrite core
Cycle time	15 microseconds (µs) Addition: 45 µs Multiplication: 500 µs	12 µs Addition: 60 µs Multiplication: 456 µs

Table 2: Comparison of the TIFRAC and the IBM 701

Notes: 1) The larger the number of bits that a computer has, the better. 2) The 3D ferrite core for TIFRAC's memory was a state-of-the-art technology imported from the UK. 3) Times are in micro (µ) seconds or one-thousandth of a second. The lesser the time it took to do computations, like addition and multiplication, the better the computer.

The faster 'addition' on the TIFRAC was possible because of an innovative method developed by TIFR researchers, P.V.S. Rao and

B.K. Basu. According to Rao, 'These (features of TIFRAC) were trendsetters in that time. One that I can think of was the adder. This was something that I was personally associated with. We cut down the time taken to do an 'addition' by a factor of 70 per cent . . . overall speed of the computer could be increased by that much . . . because (functions like) multiplication, division and subtraction were implemented in terms of addition.'[20]

Another very innovative feature of the TIFRAC was its cathode ray tube (CRT) display. It was perhaps a world first that the TIFRAC could display both text and graphics on its CRT display. This was in an era when computer output was mainly through electromechanical teletype writers (similar to typewriters) that were not capable of displaying graphical output.

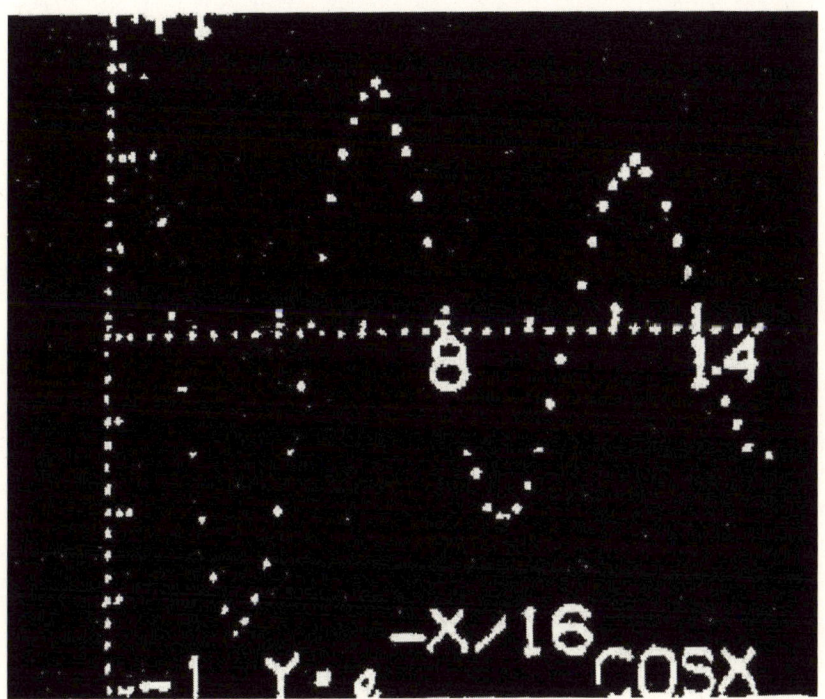

CRT Display of the TIFRAC. Courtesy: P.V.S. Rao

Take a moment and reflect on the achievement of the TIFRAC team in building world-class computer hardware in India in the late 1950s, especially in the context of today, in the second decade of the twenty-first century, when we still have debates on Indian skills in computer hardware and product engineering.

The TIFRAC was used extensively by scientists in India—to train the cadre of young scientists being drafted into India's atomic energy programme on computers. It was also used to perform data analysis of the air shower experiments of the cosmic ray physics group at TIFR and the crystallography group in the physics department of the University of Madras. This was also the start of the symbiotic relationship between India's atomic energy programme and Indian endeavours in computer hardware.

Young scientists recruited into India's nascent space programme were also given an opportunity to work on the TIFRAC. According to one of them, 'Immediately after the interview, my selection as a rocket engineer for the space programme was communicated to me by Prof. M.G.K. Menon. Before going to NASA's Wallops Rocket Station, Goddard Space Flight Centre, Maryland, US, I was posted to the Atomic Energy Establishment at Trombay. The first assignment given to me was to work with the TIFRAC computer team. TIFRAC at that time was under development and certain capabilities were in operation.'[21]

That young scientist was none other than Abdul Kalam, who went on to become the President of India.

The TIFRAC played an important role in introducing strategic Indian public-sector organizations to computers. Within a couple of years of its unveiling, researchers and professionals from many Indian organizations were using it. The demand for the computer was so high that TIFR was operating it in two shifts. The TIFRAC was operational till about 1965. TIFR was supposed to shift it to IISc and instal it there. It is not clear why this did not happen—or, more importantly, it is not clear at all why India's first indigenous digital computer was not preserved.

This was also the time when TIFR was seriously thinking of developing an even more powerful computer.

CDC 3600, a Modern State-of-the-Art Computer Comes to TIFR, Which Becomes India's National Computation Centre

Computer hardware in the 1960s was rapidly evolving, but the harsh truth about this evolution was the ever-increasing performance-to-cost ratio. While the TIFRAC was a world-class computer to start with, it could not keep pace with computers worldwide. Another shift that was taking place in the US, the country at the forefront of computer technology, was that computers were being built increasingly by commercial organizations. They were no longer experimental machines built in universities. Companies there, like IBM, had the research capability, funds, and the benefit of a favourable ecosystem to build more powerful computers. India did not have any of these companies or the ecosystem the US companies operated in. This meant that Indian computer hardware efforts had to take a back seat, post the TIFRAC. Thankfully, Indian researchers and policymakers in the 1960s realized that computers were essential in scientific, and increasingly, business contexts. Even if India could not manufacture its own computer hardware, they decided that India could import state-of-the-art computer hardware. This foresight, and the way India, especially TIFR, went about choosing a cutting-edge computer, strengthened the foundation of information technology in India.

Bhabha formed a committee, comprising members of the TIFRAC team and headed by Narasimhan, to evaluate computers in the US for TIFR. Once the TIFRAC was completed, Narasimhan had moved to the University of Illinois Urbana-Champaign as a visiting scientist at its digital computer laboratory. P.V.S. Rao was also there as part of the design team of the ILLIAC II computer. The committee members visited IBM, Burroughs, Control Data Corporation (CDC) and other computer manufacturers in the US to evaluate their latest computers, even those that were still prototypes, and to interact with their design teams. The committee chose a computer that was in the final stages of development—the CDC 3600—with a 160-A computer as a satellite. This was bought with the assistance of a United States Agency for International Development (USAID) loan.

The document 'Extract from Report of the Narasimhan Computer Committee Choice Between CDC 3600 and IBM 7090 Systems' provides insights into the analysis that went into the choice of the CDC 3600 computer.[22] The CDC 3600 won hands down in terms of its best-in-class design and provision for enhancement of future performance. However, since the IBM 7090 was an existing computer, it had better programming facilities and was cheaper. How did the committee break this tie? Keeping in mind a realistic delivery time for these machines, they decided to evaluate the 3600 and 7090 based on the conditions likely in two years' time. They also noted that Argonne National Laboratory and laboratories in Oak Ridge and Livermore in the US were likely to opt for the CDC 3600. These were labs in the US that were doing work in atomic and nuclear physics, similar to TIFR and the Atomic Energy Establishment. Nowadays it has become standard practice to consider technology obsolescence before buying computing hardware. That the Narasimhan Committee was doing much the same, at a time when there were only a few large computer installations in the world and probably none in India, is a hallmark of the foresight of our computer pioneers.

P.V.S. Rao was given charge of installing the CDC 3600 at TIFR, a task that was challenging since there was no prior infrastructure or experience in India of setting up a high-speed state-of-the-art computer. TIFR had to design and fabricate false floors in their own workshop. An amusing fact was that to effectively sound-proof the rooms that would house the CDC 3600, TIFR asked for and received from CDC high-fidelity recordings of various parts of the computer at work. The infrastructure was ready before the CDC 3600 landed in Mumbai in 1964. However, there were last-minute hiccups. The TIFR team realized that they had forgotten to procure card punch machines. (Programs had to be punched into these cards, which would then transfer the programs to the computer.) Using its old boys' network, TIFR procured one from the Geophysical Research Institute, Mumbai. And another came from IIT Kanpur by train, accompanied by a young faculty member, V. Rajaraman, who went on to become an important player in the history of Indian IT. And soon, the computer was installed.

Opportunity Missed: Core-memory Manufacturing[23]

The TIFRAC and the CDC 3600 used ferrite core memory. Though the ferrite cores for the TIFRAC were imported from the UK, the memory system was built in-house by the TIFR team. As P.V.S. Rao wrote, 'The team actually strung the memory matrix together, designed the special Plexiglass frames, and threaded the hair-thin enamelled wires through sub-millimetre magnetic ring cores—80,000 of them. Each core carried 4 wires! It was a combination of careful design, engineering skill, and dexterity of this team that accomplished this challenging task.'

Incidentally, J. Schemy, manager of the far east operations of CDC, made a proposal in 1965 for setting up a core stringing operation in India. It proposed a 50:50 venture with an Indian

Core memory of TIFRAC. Courtesy: TIFR archives, from the report 'The National Computation Centre'

partner, with CDC absorbing all the production of core memory from this factory. The proposal also mentioned that the foreign exchange earnings from this operation could be used to import CDC computers for sale in India.

It appeared that this proposal went into cold storage. Bhabha was also considering an Indian semiconductor manufacturing facility, which again did not take off at the time. Indians even today bemoan the fact that while we are globally renowned for software and allied services, we have not made any meaningful contribution in hardware manufacturing. Did we miss an opportunity in the 1960s? Imagine what would have happened if India had then become a hub for computer memory production and had kept pace with technological changes over the years. One of the reasons for India not catching this wave could be the untimely and tragic death of Bhabha in an air crash in 1966. India lost a technocrat leader who could persuade the government to make big technology bets in multiple domains.

After the installation of the CDC 3600 computer, TIFR became India's National Computation Centre. Going by TIFR reports, the CDC 3600 operated on a 24/7 basis, and the up-time of this computer system was over 98 per cent in the years from 1965 to 1970. During the first year, users were provided free access to the CDC 3600 computer. The only demand on the users was that they wrote and debugged their own programs. To help users, the TIFR staff programmers conducted many short courses on programming.

The CDC 3600 spawned Indian research and consultancy in computer applications. Some of the interesting software research projects included a time-sharing operating system, computer animation for generating dynamic visual displays, a flexible speech synthesis based on a phonetic alphabet, optimized bus scheduling for Brihanmumbai Electricity Supply and Transport (BEST), an optimal electricity distribution system for Mumbai, and simulation and optimization of multistage satellite launch vehicles. In terms of basic research in computer science, there were projects on the formal theory of computation, modelling language and numerical analysis. There was applied hardware research too. For instance, a visual display console with a light pen useful for computer-aided design was designed to be used with the CDC 3600.

The CDC 3600 was used not only by TIFR scientists but by over 100 institutions across India. This was truly a national computing facility in India. For F.C. Kohli, the legendary head of Tata Consultancy Services for about three decades, the CDC 3600 in TIFR was among his first encounters with a state-of-the-art computer. It left a deep impact on him in terms of what a computer could do. Recollecting his experiences from the mid-1960s, when he was at Tata Electric, he said, 'Then came the installation of the CDC 3600 at TIFR. And we discussed with them (TIFR). They said we will allow you about 20 per cent or 30 per cent of the time for Tata Electric Company. Of course, we didn't need that much time. But we did train up people in programming at Tata Electric Company.'[24]

Genesis of an Indian Policy on Computers: Bhabha Committee, Sarabhai Committee and Creation of the Department of Electronics

A successful TIFRAC project, the installation and running of the CDC 3600 as the National Computation Centre, and an active research programme in computer science and applications made TIFR the pre-eminent Indian organization with expertise in computers. This, along with the fact that the core instrumentation team for atomic energy-related projects came from TIFR, made it only natural that India's electronics policy, including policy on computers, was driven by Bhabha and his team at TIFR.

An acute shortage of critical electronic components for equipment like radar used by our defence forces in the India–China war of 1962 made electronics a strategic focus area for the government of India. A committee was formed in 1963 with Bhabha as its head. A.S. Rao, who was leading the electronics group in the AEE, was a member of this committee. The committee's agenda was to study the requirement for electronics equipment in India, including computers, and identify how these could be obtained for the short term—whether they should be bought or made. The long-term agenda of the committee was to recommend how India could become self-reliant in electronics equipment.

Though the final report of the committee was reviewed by Bhabha, it was formally presented to the government of India only after his death. Vikram Sarabhai, a noted physicist, considered the father of India's space programme and the pivot in establishing the Indian Institute of Management in Ahmedabad, was a committee member and was given the responsibility of nurturing electronics in India, post-Bhabha. The Bhabha Committee report, as it came to be known, was India's first plan to nurture use and production of electronics, including computers. Like many other strategic national programmes of the day, a big focus was on achieving self-reliance. Let us look at its recommendations related to computers.

The Bhabha Committee projected that there would be a requirement of about ten large computers, a few hundred medium-sized computers and a few thousand small computers in India over the next ten years. The committee noted that while the large computers might need to be imported, the medium and small computers could be manufactured in India based on the engineering expertise in TIFR and AEE. The government of India accepted the recommendations of the report and set up another committee in 1966 under the leadership of Vikram Sarabhai to implement these recommendations.

The Sarabhai committee spent four years on assessing the current state of electronics, including computers, from the usage and production perspectives. It became clear that India was lagging behind the world leaders in both use and production of electronics. India had a stated policy of self-reliance, thanks to the wars India had fought in the 1960s and the global context defined by the Cold War. Another important consideration in this era was conservation of foreign exchange. This was a time when India was embarking on large physical infrastructure projects and, more importantly, importing food. This presented a dilemma for the Sarabhai committee since the status quo and lack of policy was putting India further behind in the rapidly evolving domain of computers and related technologies.

The biggest policy recommendation that came from the Sarabhai Committee was creation of the Department of Electronics (DoE) in the government of India in 1970, and a policymaking apex body, the Electronics Commission (EC), in 1971. The TIFR connection to India's electronics and computer industry continued, with its director, M.G.K. Menon, being selected as the Secretary of DoE and chairman of the EC. In 1970, as a culmination of the work of the Sarabhai Committee, a National Conference on Electronics was conducted.

The proceedings of the National Conference on Electronics provided interesting insights into the shaping of policy on computer hardware and software.[25] Narasimhan's pragmatic note, 'Meaningful

National Goals in Computer Development, Production and Use', remarked that there were only about 111 computers in operation in India in 1968. Given this actual number, it appeared that India was lagging behind with respect to the Bhabha Committee's goal of having a few thousand computers by the mid-1970s. Again, self-reliance seemed central, and the aim was to indigenously manufacture everything else other than large computer systems.

Narasimhan made a key observation on the growing importance of software: 'A computer system is only as versatile as the software that is made available with it. Sophistication in software has grown so enormously in the last decade that, in the computer systems of the [19]70s, the hardware to software cost is likely to be in the ratio 30:70. Currently, it is roughly 50:50. A decade ago, it was 70:30. An important feature of software development is that it can be farmed out to several organizations.'[26]

He also foresaw the importance of data links when he wrote, 'In the next ten years, there is bound to be growing demand in the country for reliable, fast and cheap communication links for transfer of data between computers . . . This aspect should be kept in mind while planning for the upgrading of the communication technology during the decade of the [19]70s.'[27]

Narasimhan projected the size of the workforce that would be required for different domains of computer hardware and software in India at 2000 system programmers and analysts, 1000 maintenance engineers, and 1500 to 3000 application programmers. He also made an important recommendation—creation of Regional Computer Centres in multiple locations in India. He felt that very large computer installations should be treated like national facilities. And that was the only way to get India to leverage computers on a large scale and in quick time.

V. Rajaraman's note in that conference, titled 'Strategies in Education and Training for Computer Development in India', advised that regional computer centres be linked to centres of education and research in the emerging domain of computer science. 'Creating a core of computer professionals in both hardware design and in software design should be done by initiating computer science programmes at the master's and doctoral levels to cater to both streams.'[28] Simultaneously, Rajaraman also identified important domains for computer applications, such as management decision making, engineering design, real-time control and communications, and modelling of physical and behavioural systems. Rajaraman's recommendation under 'Strategy for Indigenous Design and Development' ended with an innocuous but prescient line— 'Foreign exchange can also be earned by software export.'[29] This was probably the first time that software export was mentioned as a strategy for India.

Attempts to Produce Indigenous Hardware: Birth of ECIL

The influence of TIFR and AEE (which was renamed Bhabha Atomic Research Centre, BARC, after Bhabha's demise) on computer and electronics-related activities in India also led to the formation of Electronics Corporation of India Limited. ECIL, a spin-off from BARC's electronics division, was started in Hyderabad in 1967 as a public-sector company for the development of indigenous hardware and for design and development of electronics equipment in India.

The first computer that ECIL manufactured had its origins in TIFR's On Line Data Processor project (OLDAP), which also had participation from the electronics group in BARC. According to P.V.S. Rao, one of the design objectives of OLDAP was to maximize use of Indian components to build an indigenous computer. This was interesting, since in the mid-1960s the only electronics components to be manufactured in India were transistors for making miniaturized radios, and none for digital electronics. So the OLDAP team had to work with diodes and transistors that were used for radio receivers, which were too slow for a computer. The OLDAP with modifications would become the TDC 12, India's first indigenous, commercially manufactured computer. (TDC 12 stood for Trombay Digital Computer 12—Trombay was the locality where BARC was headquartered; the computer had 12-bits word-length).

In 1969, while in the midst of the OLDAP project, the computer development team at BARC was shifted to ECIL as its computer division, to design a production version of the TDC 12 that could be manufactured in ECIL's new factory. Later that year, the TDC 12 was launched. The machine was primarily aimed at Indian universities and research organizations. While the TDC 12 was a vacuum tube machine, its next version based on transistors, the TDC 312, was launched in 1974. Between 1971 and 1978, there were twenty-one installations of the TDC 12, which had a standard price of Rs 6 lakh, and thirty-two installations of the TDC 312, whose standard price was about Rs 10 lakh.[30]

The software development for compilers and interpreters for the TDC 312 was carried out by teams in TIFR, IIT Kanpur, IIM Ahmedabad and ECIL. N.R. Narayana Murthy, who was leading the computer centre at IIM Ahmedabad at the time, played a vital part in this exercise. Murthy reminisces about this project, 'We had to work from 10 p.m. to somewhere around 3 a.m. to 4 a.m. in

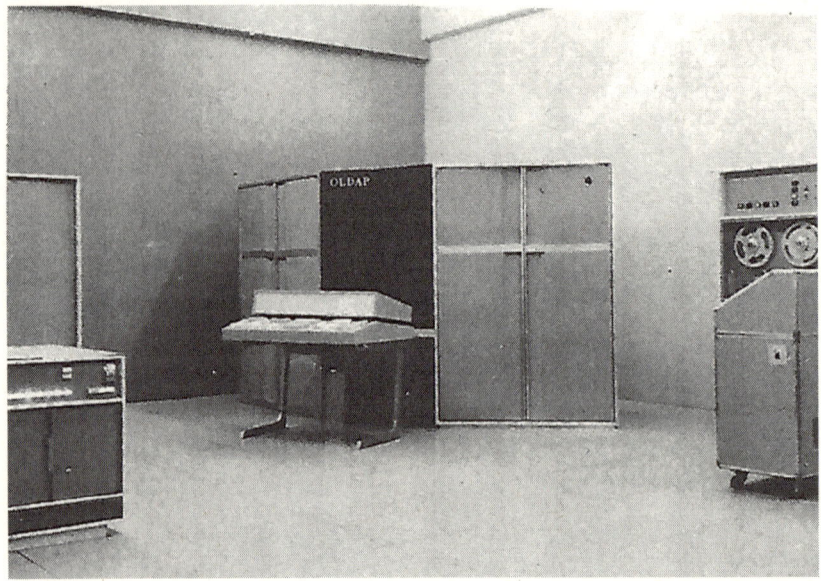

The OLDAP, precursor to ECIL's TDC 12, the first indigenous, commercially manufactured computer in India. Courtesy: TIFR archives; from the report 'The National Computation Centre'

writing a simulator first for the ECIL machine and then a BASIC interpreter on that . . . T.P. Rama Rao, who later on became a faculty member there (IIM Ahmedabad), and myself, we worked very hard . . . If I'm not wrong, TIFR and IIM Ahmedabad were the only two institutions that completed what they were supposed to do on time. TIFR was developing an assembler for the ECIL machine, while we were developing a BASIC interpreter.'[31]

MNC Computer Companies Service the Indian Market: IBM Operations in India

IBM's installation of a 1401 computer in petrochemical company ESSO Standard Eastern Ltd in Mumbai in 1961 was probably the first instance of a multinational selling computers in India. IBM started manufacturing key-punches in India from 1959 and began refurbishing 1401s in India from 1962 to service the local market.[32] IBM requested the government of India to grant it a licence to manufacture mechanical key-punch machines, which would be 80 per cent indigenous, for export. With the foreign exchange earned from exporting key punches, IBM wanted permission to import used 1401 computers, which it planned to refurbish and sell in India. This was a classic arrangement, typical during the foreign-exchange-constrained years of the 1960s in India.

The IBM 1401 was used in India in the 1960s in an unlikely business context—in jute mills. The business environment, in general, and the payroll function, in particular, were heavily regulated in India. And for the owners of these jute mills, time-bound payroll was like the proverbial sword of Damocles. Subroto Bagchi, who started his career as a management trainee in the textiles division of Indian conglomerate DCM and was later part of Wipro's leadership team before he co-founded Mindtree, reminisces about the IBM and jute-mill era, 'This calculation of payroll had to be done dynamically based on workers' allocation, (and the categories of) temporary and permanent workers. It was a nightmare. If the establishment failed to disburse wages on time, then you not only had a trade union problem but you could also be shut down. So, the jute mill owners were the first bunch of people who were open to the idea of computerization.'[33]

IBM India sold the jute mill owners a payroll processing service. Yes, it was service! The jute mill owners, who could not afford the 1401, leased computer time from IBM to process their payroll. IBM sometimes provided for cards and card punch machines on the premises of the jute mills. All the relevant daily payroll details of an employee would be punched in a card and used as his record. The cards would be collected weekly by IBM and processed for payroll at its service bureau, which had the 1401 computer. This was a precursor to outsourcing and computing as a service. Once IBM was entrenched in a company as the payroll service provider, it would cross-sell inventory control and financial accounting services too.

By 1965, about thirty IBM 1401s were installed in India.[34] The machines became popular not only for their functionality but also for the excellent service that IBM provided. Commenting on the operations of IBM, S. Srinivasan, a graduate of the first batch of the BTech course from IIT Madras, and who worked in IBM India in the mid-1960s, says, 'We were supporting a few punched card installations that gradually gave way to computers. At that time, it was an expensive proposition to go for a computer. For example, the largest configuration was 16 Kb of memory and four disk drives of 2 Mb each. And into this system you had to push the entire production planning, inventory control and operations of companies like TISCO, TELCO, Indian Telephone Industries. That was a challenge. So, customers did require a lot of support, and even though it was expensive, IBM excelled in support. That was the first thing you learnt, that you needed to handhold your customers . . . For example, if there was a hardware problem, the moment the problem was located, IBM had a norm that if it was not solved within four hours by the local engineer, the regional engineer would get an air ticket, to fly in and support!'[35]

Indigenous Software Services: Genesis of TCS

The 1960s also witnessed the setting up of the first Indian corporate computer services group in Mumbai. Lalit Kanodia, a graduate of the first batch of the BTech course from IIT Bombay, pursuing a PhD from Sloan School of Management in MIT in the mid-1960s, was a young man well conversant with the latest trends in computers. He spent a few months in India in 1965 when he consulted for Tata Sons, the holding company of India's largest conglomerate, the Tata group. One of Kanodia's recommendations to Tata Sons was to set up an in-house data processing centre for the Tata companies. Accordingly, the group started the Tata Computer Centre in 1967. Kanodia joined them.

Kanodia recounts those days: 'A lot of time was spent on going to the Tata companies. I went to TELCO, TISCO, and that time CEAT was a Tata company. We did a lot of lectures. I remember once J.R.D. Tata attended for a whole day. We had to explain to him what a computer was! It was fun. And we took on small little projects from Tata companies—we computerized the Taj (Hotels) processes at that time. We took over the share department, and we computerized the share accounting of all Tata companies. We also computerized fixed deposit accounting which was very popular in those days.'[36]

The Tata Computer Centre was hived off as a separate division of Tata Sons and was named Tata Consultancy Services (TCS) in 1968. The focus was not only computerization of Tata group companies but also of non-Tata group companies. F.C. Kohli, an alumnus of MIT and a deputy general manager in Tata Electric Company, joined TCS in 1969 as its general manager. Kohli's visionary leadership is described later.

A TCS brochure from this era proudly proclaimed its computer expertise: 'And what is more we have a computer to assist us—one of the most powerful 1401 configurations in the country.' There were about twenty PhDs working at TCS in the late 1960s, when its total employee strength was less than 100. Another aspect of the

THE SERVICES :

The T.C.S.'s capabilities cover six major areas of management consultancy :

☐ Operations Research
☐ Industrial Engineering
☐ Management Information Systems
☐ Computer Systems
☐ Software Development
☐ General Management.

A typical project would require skills in more than one of the above areas.

In addition to the above services, the T.C.S. offers to the engineer, scientist and mathematician a technical advisory and programming service as well as computational facilities.

Since we are equipped with an E.D.P. section, (both computer and unit record) we can follow-up systems and programming work with an offer of data processing facilities to the client. This is an efficient service at a competitive price.

Within the next two years the T.C.S. hopes to acquire a third generation, time-shared, multiprogramming computer which will

☐ provide for maximum utilisation of expensive hardware
☐ cut down software, development and programming costs
☐ provide instantaneous access to on-line data banks.

THE CLIENTS :

The Tata Consultancy Services, though recently formed, have successfully completed projects for a number of major companies. In addition there are some fifteen projects on the anvil.

Our clients include a textile company, an oil mill, a printing press, a hotel, an electrical utility company, a radio manufacturer, a machine tool firm, a marketing organisation and a switchgear manufacturer. They have consulted us in such diverse fields as management accounting, organisation, credit control, sales forecasting, financial accounting, inventory control, production planning and scheduling, mathematical models for decision making, work study, critical path methods, statistical analyses and quality control.

Against this background of varied experience, T.C.S. offers a mature and comprehensive service to the prospective client.

3

A page from a 1968 TCS brochure. Courtesy: Lalit Kanodia

brochure that is hard to miss is the significant share of women IT consultants in the company. Nergish C. Ghadialy was a systems programmer and developed programs for share accounting; Zarine P. Khergamwala did systems and programming work related to sales invoicing and statistics; Vimal D. Kshemkalyani developed packaged programs for share accounting; Usha M. Rao worked on programming for utility billing and payroll processing; Vera Umrigar worked on sales accounting applications. This tradition of gender diversity at the workplace endures even today in the industry. The Indian IT industry has among the highest share of women among all industries in the country.

The Minsk II Computer in IIT Bombay

While Mumbai was becoming the 'hotbed' of computers, an IIT was established in the city in 1961 with assistance from the erstwhile USSR. Naturally, the first computer in IIT Bombay was Russian, the Minsk II, which was installed in 1967. Deepak Phatak, who joined IIT Bombay as a master's student in electrical engineering in 1969 and completed his PhD and became a faculty there, says, 'The Minsk II computer had a paper tape input. It would take hours to transcribe your program into paper tape. And then you submitted that paper tape. And then the output itself would be a paper tape, which you fed to a teleprinter and got your printouts . . . It was a very large computer. But, in today's terms, it was as powerful as one hundredth of a PC.'[37] That was the rather innocuous start of IIT Bombay's journey to become one of India's powerhouses in computer science education and research in later years.

What was happening in the north of India around this time? We head to Kanpur, an oasis of computing in the hinterland of India.

Computing at IIT Kanpur—the Story of How MIT, an IBM 1620, a Bullock Cart and Enthusiastic Faculty Played Their Part in Its Journey

As we saw earlier, the government of India had signed an agreement for establishing an IIT in Kanpur in 1959. Based on a request from India, the US government provided funding for the institute, amounting to US$13.5 million from the US-owned PL 480[38] wheat loan funds.[39] The US Agency for International Development (AID) and the Education Development Center (EDC) collaborated to create the Kanpur Indo-American Program (KIAP), with Massachusetts Institute of Technology (MIT) as the primary university partner, along with eight other universities. A contract was signed in February 1962, and the KIAP Consortium remained in place for over a decade.

A unique educational design was forged at IIT Kanpur. Firstly, a big computer became central to the education system. As P.K. Kelkar, the first director of IIT Kanpur, wrote, 'I once again became convinced that the computer represents the future far more significantly than any other device I have known.'[40] Secondly, an emphasis on experimental laboratory work played a key role in the development of computer skills at the institute. All IIT Kanpur students learnt how to program. The computer facility, which went on to include an IBM 1620, 7044, 1401 and 1800, was in use twenty-four hours of the day. It became an essential component in the work of the faculty and students.

Kelkar was convinced that a large percentage of the faculty had to be found from among Indians studying and working abroad. H.N. Mahabala was one such faculty who relocated from Toronto, Canada, and joined IIT Kanpur's electrical engineering department in June 1965. He says, 'A close friend of mine, Dr Vishwanathan, and I joined as faculty at IIT Kanpur. We didn't know where Kanpur was and it was even spelt differently then—Cawnpore. In fact, the first day we drove to the institute from Kanpur city, we wondered whether we had made the right decision. But when we landed at the institute, we were amazed to see nearly 50 PhDs from top universities around the world had joined as faculty there!'[41]

Mahabala went on to have a lasting impact on computer education at IIT Kanpur, and later at IIT Madras too.

The IBM 1620 in IIT Kanpur

An IBM 1620 computer arrived in IIT Kanpur in August 1963. Talking about the machine, V. Rajaraman says, 'The machine was state-of-the-art, at that time. It was a very popular machine with the universities. It was a reasonable-cost machine and was probably of the order of (Rs) 25 lakh or so at that time.'[42] The IIT Kanpur computer centre had a central processor with 40,000-digit core storage (IBM 1620), three 7330 magnetic tape units, a 1622 card input-output unit, twenty key-punch machines, and an IBM 407 accounting machine that was used as a printer.[43]

Narrating the story of how the IBM 1620 arrived in Kanpur, Rajaraman says, 'The machine arrived by plane at Chakeri airport at Kanpur, and from there they took it (to the institute) by bullock carts with inflated tyres. They were worried about bringing it by truck the vibration of the truck on the bad roads of Kanpur might essentially ruin a lot of the electronic circuits. When the machine was brought, we found that the door (of the IIT Kanpur computer centre) was too small to take in the machine. One of the walls was broken and the computer was installed.'[44]

Prof. Harry Huskey, who, along with his American colleagues, Prof. Forman Acton and Prof. Irving Rabinowitz, oversaw the installation of the computer, adds some more colour to the arrival of the IBM 1620 in India: 'The logistics of shipping the computer from the US to India was not easy. So, when the computer came up,

The IBM 1620 arrives at IIT Kanpur. Courtesy: V. Rajaraman; from the report by Normal C. Dahl, 'Revolution on the Ganges: A Report on the Indian Institute of Technology, Kanpur', *Tech Engineering News*, April 1967

they set it out by a chartered DC-8. One problem with DC-8s was that you couldn't land them at the commercial airport in Kanpur. So, they flew it down to the military airport there. So, we had to load the stuff and bring it through the town.

'And in India, they had road blocks every once in a while, where they collected customs taxes to pay for roads and so on. So, the question was how do we get AID to pay this customs fee. And we decided, we'll breeze through like we owned the place. And it worked, and we got the computer out to the institute. But the trouble was the computer room still wasn't finished. This was monsoon season and there was about an inch of water on the floor in the room where the computer was to go!

'Also, India power is 50 cycles and a slightly different voltage. And the computer was 60 cycles. So, we had to convert from 60 to 50 cycles and adjust the voltage a little bit. There were a lot of telegrams sent back and forth between IBM and Kanpur. But anyway, we got the power on, and in about three weeks we had the machine up and running.'[45]

Take a moment to imagine this unlikely scenario—a state-of-the-art digital computer being hauled on bullock carts in 1963 through the dusty, potholed roads of an Indian city, surviving the scrutiny of zealous customs officials, and the computer centre having to contend with the Indian monsoons and getting ready to instal the computer in typical Indian style!

The IBM 7044, PDP-1 and Other Computers in IIT Kanpur

It was decided that an IBM 7044 computer would follow the IBM 1620 to Kanpur. Commenting on the technical negotiations with IBM, Gio Wiederhold, who was a KIAP professor, says, 'IBM was not anxious to provide its most up-to-date equipment. Fortunately, I had worked at IBM in the US and knew about their latest machines. I insisted on, and got, the latest high-density tape drives which used error-correcting codes. The older models only had error-checking and in effect had a much worse failure rate in dusty surroundings.'[46]

In 1968, IIT Kanpur had two batch-processing second-generation computers—an IBM 7044/1401 and an IBM 1620. The IBM 1620 was used primarily to teach programming to all students, and the IBM 7044/1401 was used by research students and faculty, besides by a large number of guest users from several neighbouring universities and research laboratories.[47]

Around this time, John McCarthy, a faculty at Stanford University and the person who coined the term 'artificial intelligence', visited the computer centre at IIT Kanpur and offered to donate the time-sharing machine installed at the Stanford Artificial Intelligence Laboratory. Thus the PDP-1 came to IIT Kanpur in 1969, and became the first time-shared computer to be installed in India. One of the first computer games, Spacewar!, was developed on the PDP-1 at MIT. The IIT Kanpur students would play the game and many of them got addicted to it. Some things were not very different from today!

Computer Science Education at IIT Kanpur

The First Computer Science Course at IIT Kanpur

Courses in computer programming were initiated in 1963 soon after installation of the IBM 1620, and continued at the rate of two or three per year. Rajaraman says, 'The machine came to IIT Kanpur in August and sometime in October or so, the KIAP professors decided to teach students how to use the computer. They started intensive courses of ten days' duration, which had components of FORTRAN programming. The IBM 1620 was one of the first machines which came to India that had a high-level language programming.

'The ten-day course had three aspects: 1) how to program using FORTRAN, 2) numerical methods, such as how to solve numerical problems, differential equations, algebraic equations on the machine; how to write algorithms for these numerical processes and how to convert those algorithms to programs and run them on the machine, and 3) logic of the machine and how the machine worked.

'The course had three lectures, and the most important aspect of the course was the hands-on training. We had three groups, and each group had about twenty students because we had twenty key-punch machines. The students punched the programs, and normally it came out with a syntax error in the first attempt; they went back and corrected it. After two or three rounds, they would get a program running. By the end of ten days, they were reasonably confident of using the computer.'[48]

Mahabala explains the reasons why the computer course was started in IIT Kanpur: 'Computers were not available in plenty in India. So, we had to do two things—1) teach scientists how to program these computers, and 2) convince people that problems faced by business could be solved using the computers. That's what I would call "information processing". We had to train scientists and some leading persons in business about this technique of programming. And the best way to do it was to induct them into a course. It was a ten-day course—mainly we didn't want to teach a theoretical course, we wanted people to get enough hands-on time and feel the power of computer programming.'[49]

The TA 306 and the First MTech Programme in Computer Science at IIT Kanpur

In 1965, the first MTech group was welcomed to IIT Kanpur, and two years later a computer science option for MTech and PhD students in electrical engineering was introduced. Commenting on the origins of the first batch, Rajaraman says, 'We took about twelve students in the first batch, largely because of the small faculty size. That year I went to Berkeley, taught a CS course and understudied the head of the computer centre there. So that when I came back, I knew how to run a large computer centre in a university system.'[50]

Elaborating on the course, Rajaraman says, 'Along with the MTech programme came the introduction of a compulsory course in computer programming and numerical methods for all engineering students. It was a pioneering step at IIT Kanpur. A course called TA 306 (TA stood for technical arts) was taught in the first and second semesters (of the BTech programme). Students were taught analogue computing as well as digital computing and numerical methods. TA 306, in fact, spread the news of computers to students in other departments too. Metallurgists, civil engineers, chemical engineers . . . all attended. They became conversant with using computers and were not afraid of the machines.'

A Textbook on 'Principles of Computer Programming'

As Rajaraman was teaching the TA 306, he started writing down notes for his lecture—notes on programming, numerical methods and logic. Mainly because books imported from abroad were expensive, these notes were cyclostyled and given to the students taking the course. When Rajaraman went to Berkeley, he got positive feedback from the faculty there on his notes, and that helped him expand them into a book once he returned to Kanpur. Initially, it was printed at the IIT press and sold for Rs 5 at the institute's book store. Both students at IIT Kanpur and those visiting from outside for the intensive programming course bought this book.[51]

Encouraged by his wife, Rajaraman decided to publish this as a book with a regular publisher. Rajaraman insisted that the book should not be priced higher than Rs 15; international books at the time cost in the range of Rs 300–400. He soon provided a photo-ready copy of the book to Prentice Hall India, which published the first edition using 'lower quality newsprint' in 1969. Within six months, the first edition of 3000 copies got sold out. And the second edition was printed on much better-quality paper!

Computer Culture at IIT Kanpur in the 1960s

IIT Kanpur was like an oasis in the middle of a desert. In a nondescript town in India lay an institution that was extraordinary—with good quality students, young and well-educated faculty and world-class infrastructure, thanks to KIAP. These ingredients combined to provide a compelling environment for learning. Those early days of computing in Kanpur and in India provided a solid foundation for many future stalwarts of Indian IT.

Rajaraman, commenting on some of the students who either took his TA 306 course or did their master's with a focus on computer science, says, 'Many of them reached very high levels. Bhaskar Pramanik, who later went to Microsoft; Som Mittal, who was a metallurgy student; and Saurabh Srivastava . . . they all took the TA 306. Others include Ravi Sethi, who went to Princeton; Abhay Bhushan, who created FTP (File Transfer Protocol); Raj Kanodia, who went on to work in the network group at MIT; Narayana Murthy, who went to work at IIM Ahmedabad and Patni Computers before starting Infosys; Hari Sahasrabuddhe, who continued in IIT Kanpur; Muthukrishnan, who also continued at IIT Kanpur; and Radhakrishnan, who went to Concordia and later became head of the department there.'[52]

Recounting his wonderful days at IIT Kanpur, Saurabh Srivastava, who was from the first batch of BTech students from the institute, says: 'Computers were like very prized possessions.

The computer centre was a huge place, with false flooring and lot of security. We were very proud that we had a computer. A lot of us used to hang around—we would do our programs, give them in and try to spend as much time as we could over there. A couple of my batchmates actually just spent entire nights hanging around there.'[53]

Narayana Murthy, describing his graduate student days at IIT Kanpur, says, 'When I joined, it was a master's in electrical engineering (EE). There was no computer science (CS) course then. CS came much later. However, we were the first batch in EE when a concentration in CS was introduced. What it meant was we had to take a course on computer systems organization, automata theory (a topic in theoretical computer science), switching theory (theory of circuits), software engineering, operating systems, etc.

'It was an environment of family, in the sense that there were very few students in the CS area. The CC (computer centre) was a place where we all used to meet and spend time together. We also had a plethora of languages available—Snowball, LISP, GPSS, SLIP, FORTRAN, WATFOR. It was a well-equipped computer centre. It was the only educational institution then among IITs and IISc that had a mainframe in its computing centre.'[54]

Amusing Anecdotes from N.R. Narayana Murthy's days at IIT Kanpur

Most of us know of Narayana Murthy as the doyen of Indian IT and a venerable computer professional, as a larger-than-life captain of the industry. But here are some amusing anecdotes regarding computers from his graduate days at IIT Kanpur.

My First Sighting of a Computer—by Narayana Murthy[55]

'When I went to IIT Kanpur from the University of Mysore, I had no idea what a computer looked like. One of my batchmates at IIT Kanpur says he will show me the computer. He takes me to the computer centre, points to a machine which was taking in cards and spewing out printed papers, and says that is the computer. Later in the day, I was excitedly telling my friends about how the 'computer' was making a lot of noise. Then, this friend tells me that the machine I saw was actually only the printer, printing out what the computer had already produced in punched cards. It was quite ego-deflating for a young student!'

Matchmaker, Matchmaker, Make Me a Match—by H.N. Mahabala[56]

'Narayana Murthy was my student at IIT Kanpur. One day in class he asked me, rather mischievously, "Can a computer find me a match?" But it made me think a little bit. What does "finding a match" really mean? You have to collect a lot of information about a person, and apply filters to identify the right match. It is, after all, information processing. So, I told him that computers can help find a match. But I rushed to add that the job of identifying probable candidates and the process of giving weightage to different factors will have to be done by a human.'

Training Programme for IAS officers at IIT Kanpur—by Narayana Murthy[57]

'Prof. Mahabala was conducting a course on FORTRAN programming for the Indian Administrative Service (IAS) officers of the Uttar Pradesh government. I was his lab assistant for that course. One of the officers came up to me and asked why his program was not printing the answer. I reviewed his code and realized that he had not put the 'Go-To' command to the printer. The officer was puzzled and informed me, 'Prof. Mahabala just told us that computers can arrange marriages and you are telling me it cannot print on its own!' The next day I told Prof. Mahabala, 'Sir, you really create problems for us by weaving such stories in your training.'

Under the leadership of Kelkar, and with assistance from the American consortium, IIT Kanpur went on to become a torch-bearer for not only engineering education but also for computer science education in the country in the 1960s. However, there were some disappointments too for the institute, when viewed through the prism of IT. Despite being among the top two computer centres in India around that time, IIT Kanpur did not make the cut as one of the Regional Computer Centres that the government of India established. Another was the faltering of the plan for creation of an electronics park in Kanpur. In 1965–66, discussions were initiated between IIT Kanpur authorities and the Directorate of Industries of the government of Uttar Pradesh to establish an industrial park for entrepreneurs adjacent to the campus. This was envisaged along the lines of the clusters in the US, like Silicon Valley and the Stanford University, where one would have enterprises producing technology-intensive equipment in Kanpur, with the prototype design, testing and standards laboratory inside IIT Kanpur, and an ecosystem that would nurture entrepreneurs in India. The scale of investment was expected to be around Rs 5 crore within a three-year period.[58] Alas, the plan did not go anywhere. Among other things, the IIT Kanpur authorities realized rather late that the land earmarked for the electronics park had been leased to a brick-making concern. A tragic case of the brick winning over the chip!

We now sail to the south. What was happening in the 1950s and 1960s in Bengaluru, Chennai and Hyderabad?

Computing in South India: How the Computing River Gently Coursed through Bengaluru, Chennai and Hyderabad

Computing at IISc Bengaluru

The IISc was an institution of interest for computing in the decades of the 1950s, 1960s and 1970s. Around the time ISI had developed its algebraic analyser and was getting its first digital computer, the faculty at IISc were independently working on a differential analyser.[59]

V.C. Rideout, a faculty member from the University of Wisconsin, USA, came as a visiting professor to IISc and helped build India's first analogue computer, the PREDA (Philbrick-Rideout Electronic Differential Analyser). Rajaraman, who was a student at IISc in the 1950s, says, 'Prof. Rideout, who came to IISc in 1954–55, brought with him operational amplifiers, which are packaged sub-components and they are the heart of a differential analyser. He brought twenty operational amplifiers built by a company called Philbrick. By the time he left, Prof. Rideout completed a system that could solve linear differential equations up to the fourth or fifth order. My associateship thesis was to build the non-linear units to make the computer solve non-linear differential equations. The department had hardly any money. Fortunately, we had a lot of American disposal equipment (those that were left behind after wars). I went around with a solder in hand, picked up resistors (electronic components that resist flow of current), capacitors (electronic components to store electrical charge) and even an oscilloscope tube that was required. I picked these things up from the junk, and created the unit.'[60]

Some lecturers at IISc, who were working towards their PhD, used this computer to solve differential equations for transient simulations in high-tension wires or modelling vibrations of tall columns.

Prof. Satish Dhawan, after whom the Indian satellite launch centre at Sriharikota is named, was the director of IISc during

The PREDA computer, with V. Rajaraman standing next to it. Courtesy: IISc archives

two stints between 1962 and 1981. He expanded IISc significantly in new directions and oversaw the creation of forty departments, four divisions and seven interdisciplinary research centres. With outfits like the Centre for Information Processing, and School of Automation, IISc started taking firmer steps in the computing journey. By 1970, IISc had set up a computer centre with an IBM 360/44. This centre later became the Supercomputer Education and Research Centre (SERC)—the journey of which is detailed later.

Meanwhile, in the 1950s and 1960s in Bengaluru, a number of public-sector engineering and national laboratories emerged, and they started using computers in their operations. For example, a Ferranti Sirius computer was installed at National Aerospace Laboratory (NAL), thanks to the efforts of the International Civil Aviation Organization in Montreal, Canada, and funding by UNDP.[61] This computer was used not just by the scientists at NAL but also by researchers from IISc, DRDO labs and other public-sector organizations. The other computers that were set up in Bengaluru included an Elliot 803 at Hindustan Aeronautics Limited and an ICT 1903 at Hindustan Machine Tools. In fact, Bharat Electronics Limited (BEL) partnered with International Computers Ltd (ICL) and assembled forty-eight ICL computers for sale in India.[62]

The presence of an engineering cluster coupled with strong educational institutions in the region made Bengaluru a fertile ground for the IT industry to develop in the future.[63] We will see this narrative in play in the stories of how Motor Industries Company Limited (popularly called MICO) catalysed Infosys's foray into software services, and how Texas Instruments chose Bengaluru as its destination for a development centre.

Computing in Chennai and Hyderabad

For the first time in south India, an IBM 1620 was installed under the aegis of Fundamental Engineering Research Establishment at the College of Engineering, Guindy, in 1965.[64] This computer centre functioned like a regional resource, and several users from south India accessed it. By 1970, when College of Engineering, Guindy, hosted the fifth annual meeting of the Computer Society of India, its computer centre had conducted three advanced summer schools on computer programming. Other computing facilities were soon established in Chennai, at the Integrated Coach Factory of Southern Railways, at Binny and Co., and in the physics department of the University of Madras.[65]

The computer was not yet quite centre stage at IIT Madras in the 1960s. Unlike IIT Kanpur, which was heavily influenced by the MIT model of education with a big computer, IIT Madras followed a German-inspired 'Technische Lehranstalt' (Technical College) education model, which placed greater emphasis on hands-on engineering skills, especially mechanical engineering skills.[66] It was only in 1973 that a computer centre was established in IIT Madras with a state-of-the-art IBM 370, a story which we will encounter in the next chapter.

C.R. Muthukrishnan, who was a BTech student at IIT Madras between 1960 and 1965, recounts the scope of computing at that time: 'There was no computer on campus then. But the curriculum at IIT Madras was very demanding and made me ready for computer education later on. We had mathematics (partial differential equations, matrix theory, etc.) and physics in all five years. In the electrical engineering department, we had courses on vacuum tubes, semiconductor theory. My friends and I went on a study tour to

Electronics and Radar Development Establishment (LRDE) in Bengaluru. There we saw transistors, and the scientists there talked about logic gates. That created a penchant in me to go further in this area.'[67]

And what was happening in Hyderabad? The Defence Research and Development Laboratory (DRDL) under the Defence Research and Development Organisation (DRDO), from where the story of India's guided missiles began, moved to Hyderabad in 1962. Major General (Retd) A. Balasubramanian, entrusted with the responsibility of setting up a computer centre in DRDL, installed an IBM 1620 and PACE Analog computer there in 1965. He also set up Regional Computer Centres for DRDO in Hyderabad, Dehradun and Delhi for R&D.[68] DRDL successfully developed an anti-tank missile system and indigenous rockets. The computers were used for flight simulation studies.

Balasubramanian also played a key role in getting an important computing institution, the Computer Society of India (CSI), registered in Hyderabad. In 1964, he attended an international conference in IIT Kanpur, where it was decided to create a forum for discussing research and scholarly aspects of computing. Thus, the idea of the CSI took birth. Balasubramanian volunteered to help create an association and formally registered CSI in Hyderabad. Narasimhan of TIFR became its first president, and Balasubramanian its first secretary.[69]

Speaking at the first CSI Convention held in 1966 in Kolkata, Narasimhan said, 'The relevance of the computer system is clear. The immediate aim should be to make the planners, policymakers and project managers become more aware of this great revolution . . . to assist them in applying these techniques to problems that need urgent action . . . to create this awareness among the public at large.'[70]

Many Indian IT stalwarts fondly remember their association with CSI as an important aspect of professional development in the beginning of their careers in the 1970s and 1980s. One of us, Kris Gopalakrishnan, recalls his CSI association: 'Computer Society of India was the premier organization for software professionals in that period. They took on the role of educating professionals and public on programming. We needed to create a cadre of programmers in the country. I took courses on operating systems in Mumbai. There was a sense of sharing to create the workforce that was required. And that I think was very unique to India.'[71]

CSI went on to become a powerful association in the next decades and hosted an exciting annual conference where new products would be launched and exhibited. We will read more about these product exhibitions in a later chapter.

We traversed India and discovered the slow and steady progress of computing in the 1950s and 1960s. The next decade witnessed quicker progress. The number of computers in India, which was around 100 in 1970, increased 10 times to around 1000 in 1978.[72] The 1970s were defined by the impact of inward-looking IT policies of the Government of India, the boost to computing provided by government-led mission-mode computerization projects, growth of computer science education in the country, and the ingenuity of Indian entrepreneurs who battled hard to survive in that time period.

3

Emphasis on Self-Reliance and the Domestic Hardware Industry

We saw how there existed, in the late 1960s, a strong undercurrent of self-reliance in Indian IT. It got only stronger in the 1970s, spurred by the fallout of the India–Pakistan war of 1971. India was concerned that western nations would not be willing to sell their advanced military electronics and computers. India was also wary of the potential limitations that could be imposed on the end use of these technologies. It is against this backdrop that ECIL's TDC computers and TIFR's expertise in hardware design helped India successfully complete its largest computer-led electronics project of the 1970s—the Air Defence Ground Environment Systems (ADGES) project of the Indian Air Force, funded by the newly created Department of Electronics (DoE).

The DoE envisaged computer procurement for the nation through the twin strategies of selective imports and self-reliance. Mainframe computer systems had to be imported from developed nations. The DoE provided import licences to organizations committed to earning foreign exchange by means of exporting software. They decided to license the manufacture of minicomputers to the Indian private sector, a strategy that not only helped India save foreign exchange but also led to a flurry of hardware start-ups. This first wave of entrepreneurship in Indian IT also produced a niche group of entrepreneurs who focused on software products for the domestic hardware. You read that right—software products in India—and we will soon learn about these entrepreneurs.

By the time India started manufacturing minicomputers, the world was at the dawn of the personal computer (PC) revolution. The policy focus on self-sufficiency and licensing did not help us to develop a vibrant hardware industry with a focus on both exports and the domestic market. India missed an opportunity to create a world-scale hardware industry in this era.

This period also saw the emergence of some IT capability-building initiatives in India. The DoE established the National Centre for Software Development and Computing Techniques (NCSDCT) in 1972 at TIFR, which later became the National Centre for Software Technology (NCST) and was instrumental in training many Indian professionals in cutting-edge software technologies. The DoE also established the National Informatics Centre (NIC) in 1975. NIC became the nodal organization for leveraging IT for government and governance. The DoE and the Department of Telecommunications were involved in the Education and Research Network (ERNET) project that connected educational institutions in India. India's first email was sent in this decade.

Another important aspect of capability-building was done by the educational institutions—primarily in laying and strengthening the foundation for computer education in the country, and secondly in building bridges for industry to adopt computers for business applications. IIT Kanpur introduced a BTech programme in computer science, which went on to attract some of the brightest minds in the country. IIT Madras had one of the most powerful computers in Asia in the mid-1970s. It was not just the IITs that were active in computer education; IIM Ahmedabad too set up its own computer centre, which had a defining influence on the careers of many an Indian IT entrepreneur.

We will learn more about Indian IT trying to be self-reliant and intent on building its capabilities during these years.

The Air Defence Ground Environment System Project—an Indigenous System for a Strategic Requirement That Should Have Had a Larger Impact on Indian Hardware and Systems Engineering

Post the 1971 war, the Radar Communications Board, which was chaired by the Indian prime minister and which included the three defence services chiefs, projected the need for an Air Defence Ground Environment System (ADGES). This was envisaged as an automated radar system that would alert the Indian Air Force when there was a likely intrusion into Indian airspace by enemy aircraft. Given the geopolitical situation post the war, Indira Gandhi, the Indian prime minister, was not in favour of importing the ADGES system. The primary reason for this was that the manufacturers and system integrators would then be in the know of the parameters used in the ADGES and could share this information with other countries. Sarabhai, chairperson of DAE and also a member of the Radar Communications Board, suggested that TIFR should build an indigenous ADGES system.

P.V.S. Rao, who was the project lead, describes the complexity of the requirements: 'You have to track it (enemy aircraft), you have to guess which way it is headed, you have to guess the airport which launches an aircraft for a (Indian) fighter to intercept. Then you have to guide the fighter step by step till such a point that they (both Indian and enemy aircraft) are within range of each other. Then you have to put him (Indian fighter pilot) in a position which is advantageous to him in taking offensive action rather than becoming a target. And because they (enemies) send aircraft in large numbers, all these calculations had to be done not for one aircraft but for something like forty to sixty aircraft at a given point in time.'[1]

Rao adds: 'You have to do this, not from a single node (of ADGES) but from nodes spread over the borders of the country . . . If the enemy changes tactic you are supposed to change tactic too, and give revised instructions to this person (Indian pilot). And at the end of the mission, you have to take your man safely back . . . And you have to have communication between all these nodes . . . Some of them (nodes) have to be mobile, and this has to be implemented in an environment which ranges from the deserts of Rajasthan to the heights of Sikkim.'[2]

A tall order indeed! But that did not deter Rao and the TIFR team. The ADGES project, which commenced in 1972, was the largest IT project that India had ever undertaken till then. The TIFR team worked closely with the Indian Air Force and twelve other organizations. The project involved about 800 person-years of effort, and took twelve to thirteen years to be implemented in full. The key computing infrastructure was the ruggedized TDC

316 computers from ECIL. The ADGES was an important element of the Indian air deterrent strategy and ensured that no hostile incursion into the Indian airspace escaped notice.

Ideally, this programme should have had a larger impact on Indian hardware and systems engineering. But, as in the case of the TIFRAC, India built just one successful ADGES. Again, the hardware, systems engineering and product management expertise and capabilities that were gained from the ADGES project were not transferred to the Indian private sector. India once again lost an opportunity to build indigenous hardware capabilities.

In fact, realizing this shortcoming, in 1972, the DoE made P.V.S. Rao the chairperson of a panel tasked to study indigenous manufacture of minicomputers in the Indian private sector.

Government Policies Define a Decade Focused on Self-reliance in Hardware, Selective Imports and Capability-Building

The P.V.S. Rao Committee presented its report to the DoE in 1973. The report concluded that minicomputers could be manufactured in India without any foreign collaboration or technology transfer from developed countries. The committee forecast a requirement of about 1400 minicomputers for India in the next five years. As expected, this report was consistent with DoE's strategy of self-reliance and conservation of foreign exchange. But while the report was submitted in 1973, the DoE did not announce a minicomputer policy till 1978!

While the delay might seem inexplicable, there were some reasons that discouraged the DoE from announcing a policy earlier. Firstly, in 1973, the DoE was concerned that import of components for manufacture of minicomputers by Indian companies would lead to a strain on foreign exchange. So it decided to wait till India built the capability to produce those components. Secondly, DoE wanted the flux in the global minicomputer industry to stabilize. Unfortunately, it did not anticipate the catalytic impact of Moore's Law (an observation that the number of transistors on a microchip doubles about every two years) and the release of newer products with improved performance-to-cost ratio, year on year. By the time the minicomputer policy was announced, the global IT hardware industry was at the end of the minicomputer era and at the dawn of the personal computer era. Thirdly, the DoE was not sure how the minicomputer policy would impact ECIL, their flagship IT hardware PSU, and wanted to give it time to establish itself before opening the market up for private players.

By the time the minicomputer policy was announced in 1978, the DoE did a U-turn and allowed Indian companies who had licences to manufacture minicomputers to import components. But other restrictions on the licensees existed, including an upper limit on the revenue of a licensee at Rs 2 crore and an upper limit on the price of a minicomputer at Rs 3 lakh. While we may smile now as we read about the antiquated models the government adopted to control the market, they constituted a real challenge for those trying to enter the business then. Saurabh Srivastava, an IT industry veteran, reminisces about the challenges of being a minicomputer manufacturer in those days. 'The government created a manufacturing policy on computers and there was a limit of fifty minicomputers per licence, which wasn't viable to manufacture. I got together with a couple of friends in the US with a licence to make these computers. We did try to see if we could aggregate a lot of licences and make more, but there were penalties for making more than fifty computers! So, we eventually did nothing.'[3] Indian companies like DCM, HCL, ORG, IDM and later Wipro obtained licences to manufacture minicomputers in India, and we will soon see what they accomplished.

A few other committees from that time, which reviewed the adoption of computers in India, made recommendations in line with the general sentiment of suspicion towards new technologies that existed among the political class. A committee headed by R. Venkataraman and later by V.M. Dandekar in 1972 advised the government of India that agreement of labour unions be obtained prior to introduction of computers in the private sector. It also called for strict controls in introducing computers in government departments. This aligned well with the dominant view that India was a labour surplus economy and thus had to consider technology, which might make a lot of the workforce redundant, with caution. This was despite the fact that the policymakers probably understood that in the long run, computerization would lead to faster economic growth. Even today, this fear and debate continue, albeit in the context of artificial intelligence replacing the human workforce. Such was the policy outlook that prevailed in the early 1970s that it made it difficult for the Indian industry to increase computerization and provide more business to fledgling IT companies like TCS.

Things changed in 1979 with the Sondhi Committee recommendations on electronics. It was probably DoE's first industry-friendly set of recommendations. It encouraged the import of components for manufacture of minicomputers in India, did not favour the quantitative restrictions placed in the 1978 minicomputer policy, and allowed the Indian private sector to enter computer and peripherals manufacture. The Sondhi Committee also favoured easier import of large computers into India, especially against the obligation of software export. This was in continuation of the 1974 scheme of DoE where Indian companies could import computers if they undertook to use these computers to export software. In fact, it was this 1974 scheme that helped TCS import a Burroughs mainframe computer. The 1974 DoE scheme and the Sondhi Committee recommendations became the trendsetting policies that encouraged the growth of software exports from India.

Another important policy of this era, one that had a significant role to play in the growth of the Indian software industry in the next two decades, came from the recommendations of the DoE's Manpower Committee (1980), which was headed by V. Rajaraman. The key recommendations were to expand the bachelor's engineering programme in computer science to more engineering colleges and to introduce a new master's programme in India called Master of Computer Application (MCA).

Rajaraman explains the rationale behind the committee recommending the MCA programme: 'We had a huge number of students with BSc and BA (degrees) who didn't have the skill sets to be employable. So, we felt that this large resource was all quite good but didn't join engineering for some reason . . . And so, the MCA was thought of as a way of giving (them) employment opportunities. The second important aspect was that in order to write good software you don't really require an electronics engineering degree or a degree in computer science . . . You can train people to write software, particularly for applications. Systems analysis and systems design are somewhat different from hardware design and logic design, and so on. So, we thought that systems analysis and design should be an area which should get emphasis (in the MCA programme).'[4]

S. Sadagopan was a young faculty at IIT Kanpur who went on to become a faculty member in IIM Bangalore and founder director of IIIT Bangalore. He says, 'Prof. Rajaraman and Prof. Sampath (a professor of electronics who was the Deputy Director of IIT Madras and later the Director of IIT Kanpur) believed that the MBA programme was very powerful and they came up with the term 'MCA' to rhyme with MBA! The emphasis of MCA was on applications. It was sufficiently in-depth and hence a three-year programme, unlike the two-year MSc programmes.'[5]

Perhaps the most famous MCA graduate in India and the first MCA to join TCS was N. Chandrasekaran, who rose to become the CEO of TCS and the chairperson of Tata Sons.

An Era of Building Capabilities, Taking Risks, and Growth At TCS

The early 1970s was a defining period for TCS as the domestic computer services business was stagnating. Kohli described the challenging times: 'Towards the end of 1972, we really didn't know where we could go and get jobs (Indian client projects). There were no other jobs. And then in 1973, I was elected as a director on the IEEE (Institute of Electrical and Electronics Engineers) board. So, at that time I started looking (for) . . . some element for export of software. Either that, or we had to shut TCS down.'[6]

Kohli expanded on how he identified a customer who subsequently became a joint-venture partner: 'I zeroed in on Burroughs, which was the number-two computer company at that time and located in Detroit. I visited them quite a few times in those two years, and with my contacts at MIT, my contacts at the IEEE who were very senior electrical engineers, tried to convince them that they should experiment getting software prepared somewhere else for themselves and sub-contract it. And towards the end of 1974 they give us quite a big order. That set up the whole export of software and that is how the relationship with Burroughs developed. Of course, IBM was there, but IBM being the number-one company, I said that that they will be on their own. That is how Burroughs came to the country, and Tata Burroughs was formed.'[7]

S. Ramadorai, a young hardware engineer in TCS, who later went on to succeed Kohli as its CEO, describes the relationship between the Tatas and Burroughs: 'The fundamental belief was that if this country had to progress, human capital was the critical element. But then, human capital has to be enabled by technology, which was advanced and which was accessible, in spite of all the difficulties of import, including customs duties. The choice of Burroughs as a big opportunity was driven by two or three factors. One, it was a very solid computer company. It had technology, a micro-programming technology, which was absolutely state-of-the-art. Second, the IEEE connections which Mr Kohli had, resulted in Burroughs entertaining us with regard to an opportunity for long-term benefits to India. That translated into us buying a (Burroughs) computer in 1974 through the licencing (route) . . . with export obligations, which we had to agree to perform as per government of India's approval. And Burroughs agreed to train us and make sure that we could learn about the computer, the capabilities, and how to use that machine.'[8]

S. Mahalingam, a Chartered Accountant who was recruited to TCS as an information technology consultant by Kohli and went on to become its CFO, reminisces about how TCS almost became subsumed into the joint venture with Burroughs. Given the tepid performance of TCS thanks to the sluggish pace of computerization in India in the early 1970s, the management of Tata Sons was not sure about the viability of TCS as an independent division. Fortunately, that was not to be, thanks to sanguine advice from the senior members of the DoE: 'Major General Balasubramaniam, who had done a lot in terms of introducing computers to defence services, and the chairman of the Department of Electronics, M.G.K. Menon . . . when the application (for merging TCS and Burroughs in India) went to them, they said, "Why do we want to sell away this crown jewel to a joint venture and to an overseas partner? You (Tatas) developed this capability. You created this whole area of software export. Why don't you retain it?" And at that time Tatas had to take a call. In those days there was no guidance; there were instructions . . . you got to follow what the government said. It was then decided that TCS would be retained as a separate division of Tata Sons . . . Therefore, TCS had to go ahead and look for customers which were outside Burroughs, to IBM and others.'[9]

Mahalingam also shares his insight into how the core team at TCS was retained, which, on looking back, was critical to the growth of the company. He says, 'At that time, in order to staff Tata Burroughs, people were transferred. If Mr Kohli had gone to Tata Burroughs as the managing director, I think everyone would have moved there . . . Mr Kohli was retained (in TCS) at that point in time. There were some people in whom he had a lot of confidence and who could work with him. Ram (Ramadorai), because at that time he related most closely to Mr Kohli in terms of what was required from the perspective of marketing overseas and in India, deciding on technology and technological options. I had my strengths in programs and design, more importantly, as the person to sell in the UK. Therefore, I got retained in TCS at that time.'[10] As we will see time and again, stability in the core teams, at the start and in the initial growth phase of the Indian companies, was critical to the success of the domestic IT industry.

In the 1970s, TCS worked on export projects that it obtained with the help of Burroughs—for Burroughs customers who wanted to migrate applications from a non-Burroughs computer to a Burroughs system. TCS felt that with many minicomputers becoming available in the market, there would be an increased need for migrating applications and data. With this mind, TCS developed tools and data dictionaries that could be reused and which helped to modularize these projects.

By the 1980s, TCS was taking on larger and interesting export projects. Buoyed by its ability to execute large projects, TCS took the audacious decision of buying a top-of-the-line IBM 3090 computer. Mahalingam recalls that moment and says, 'At that time the gross block (worth of an asset) of the IBM 3090 was going to be larger than the total gross block of TCS . . . I did some initial calculations, being an accountant . . . I had to generate something like Rs 1,87,000 on a daily basis! Which to me was a very, very large sum, considering the rupee was 20 to a dollar then. But the main confidence was that we had made a success of our operations so far and therefore we could go ahead and get this large a computer and then really work on it and make it a success.'[11]

In the late 1980s, TCS also successfully bid for and executed a large landmark project for Swiss SegaInterSettle (SEGA), which was a new-generation real-time settlement system for equities and bonds in the Swiss financial system.

The mid-1980s saw N. Chandrasekaran, from the first MCA batch at NIT Trichy, joining TCS. Recounting his internship there, Chandrasekaran says, 'TCS used to hire batches of twenty to forty people, and typically went to the IITs to hire. When I applied for a training programme, they were willing to give me a six-month internship. I came to Mumbai and worked under Dr A.G. Rao (a TCS veteran who went on to head the learning and development function there). Those days, the cost of the machine was ten times the cost of manpower. Today it is the reverse. My internship was always in the night shift. Dr Rao gave me two projects—one was a Burroughs 5900-based maintenance project and the other was a PC-based development project. I had to understand what was going on in the 5900 and build it for the modern times in the PC.'[12]

Two months into his internship, Chandrasekaran was offered a job at TCS. But he had to complete one important activity before the actual confirmation. Chandrasekaran explains, 'They told me that I had to meet Mr Kohli, and if he okayed it they would give me an offer. So I went to his office. Mr Kohli said, "Rao tells me that you are good and he wants to hire you. I have only one statement to make. We have been hiring only from the IITs and this will be the first time we are hiring someone from outside. You have a big responsibility. I hope you do well." That is all he said. I used to kid with him about it.'[13]

As part of capability-building, and with remarkable foresight, TCS established the Tata Research Development and Design Centre (TRDDC) at Pune in 1981. Kesav Nori, who headed software research at TRDDC, recalled its first project: 'Citibank was facing problems with an incompatible time-sharing system, which was programmed for ASCII[14] or EBCDIC[15] based terminals, and which fell flat when other types of terminals were introduced. I designed a compiler for this.'[16] Similarly, when companies began to migrate software from IBM mainframes to newer machines, TRDDC worked on language translators and automation tools to manage such migrations, later extending its work to tools for database and OS (operating system) conversions.

TCS also worked on an IBM research project that had an extreme requirement of zero error rate. TCS completed this project successfully, and in the course of the project developed a process-rigorous software engineering methodology to meet this stringent quality requirement. And this was before quality models became popular in software engineering—a subject we will examine later.

Tales from TCS—F.C. Kohli Shapes Its Culture

An MIT-educated engineer, Kohli was a patriot and decided to come back and help build an independent, modern India. Kohli was initially with Tata Electric Company before he moved to TCS, where he was at the helm of affairs for about three decades. He helped build the company and became a father figure for TCS and for the Indian IT industry itself.

Kohli at TCS[17, 18]

The grand old man of Indian IT recalled how he joined TCS: 'When I joined Tata Electric Company, the first point was to see, using the same quantity of water, how much more power I could generate. And we could get almost 10 per cent more power by managing the head losses in the pipelines and the stations which should control the frequency, and so on. It meant a lot of calculations, a lot of training of the people. Since I had some experience in computers . . . I was a very strong member of the IEEE and so I knew what was happening in the electrical and electronics fields . . . The people in the Tata

---

hierarchy knew that I knew computers so that is why I was sucked in to look after TCS and build it.'

At first, Kohli was reluctant to move to TCS, but his love for new technology and the challenge made him accept a posting as general manager in the company. He and TCS were destined for something much bigger.

Kohli remembered his early days at TCS: 'Whatever little we had—we didn't have enough money at the end of the month to pay salaries. I was the first general manager. We had to see that TCS builds up—builds up people, builds up equipment, and builds up clients. I had a very strong connection with educationists both here and abroad and that helped a lot.'

Getting the Syntax Right in Three Attempts—by S. Mahalingam[19]

'Mr Kohli used to really control this—we used to have a rule that we can't take more than ten attempts or ten compilations before a program started working as part of a system . . . And in order to control the ten, he would say that in three attempts you had to get the syntax right. There could not be any syntax errors. What if it happened (one exceeded the prescribed number of attempts)? You had to go to Mr Kohli for approval . . . None of us liked to do that, and therefore there was a phenomenal amount of discipline that really came into the organization. One was in terms of being able to utilize that resource very well as the organization was expanding. I think these rules were critical for us to be able to do that. The second thing was that, as I related to it much later, projects did not get delayed.'

Kohli, a Task-master and a Professional—by S. Ramadorai[20]

'I think he was a very thorough professional with an ability to understand implementation on the ground. Professionals who were willing to put in that extra effort were very, very important to him. Growing up professionally meant you had to earn your promotions or your salaries through showing what you could do, what you were capable (of) . . . he was pushing you as a professional, enabling you to perform the best, teaching you and correcting you wherever you made certain mistakes.'

IBM quits India, forced out by regulations

While TCS was on an upward growth trajectory, IBM in India was going through a tough phase.

As we saw earlier, IBM installed its first computer in India in 1961 and began dominating the Indian computer market with its refurbished 1401 computers. By 1971, IBM had phased out the 1401 in the western markets, but it remained the flagship model sold in India with about eighty installations, which included installations at Indian Railways and TCS.[21] Some Indian computer experts felt that IBM was overcharging Indian customers who had bought or leased the 1401. To be fair, IBM India did provide excellent service and programming support to its customers.

IBM successfully introduced other computers in the Indian market, like the IBM 1620. We saw them earlier in the context of

IIT Kanpur. Soon, IBM 1620s were installed in Delhi University, Roorkee University, Ahmedabad Textile Industries Research Association, in Defence Laboratories and at the Physical Research Laboratory in Ahmedabad. IBM's closest competitor in the Indian market was International Computers Ltd (ICL), a British company. ICL had a joint venture with the PSU Bharat Electronics Limited (BEL) to manufacture the 1901A computer in India and had a market share which was about half of IBM's.[22]

IBM was operating as a 100 per cent subsidiary in India. In 1973, the government of India passed the Foreign Exchange Regulation Act (FERA) with the primary aim of reducing foreign exchange outflow. An important clause in this act necessitated foreign companies, other than those considered 'essential', to dilute their foreign equity to a minority 40 per cent and to cede to Indian partners the majority 60 per cent stake. This was unacceptable to IBM, and the company tried to present different proposals to the government in lieu of retaining 100 per cent stake in IBM India. ICL, on the other hand, agreed to dilute its ownership and provide majority stake to Indians. IBM proposed to set up a 100 per cent export-oriented printer manufacturing operation in India, use the foreign exchange earned from it to import computers for sale in India, and also invest 26 per cent of the profits from its export-oriented operation for global R&D in India. In fact, this was the first time that an IT MNC had considered India as an R&D destination, an idea that came to fruition only much later.

There were protracted talks between IBM and the government. Ultimately, in 1978, when it was clear to IBM that the government wanted nothing else but a dilution in equity on its part, it decided to leave the country. To maintain continuity of service in India, an arrangement was worked out between IBM and the DoE. The operations at the IBM factory which was refurbishing the 1401s stopped. A company called International Data Machines (IDM), formed by ex-IBM India employees, took over the data centre operations and punched-card manufacturing business of IBM. A majority of the employees of IBM India joined Computer Maintenance Corporation Ltd. (CMC), a public-sector undertaking set up by the DoE to take over the maintenance and software operations of IBM. The spare parts inventory that IBM had in India was transferred to CMC.

While some saw IBM leaving India as a setback, there were others who believed that it was a blessing in disguise. The late 1970s was a time when computer technology was turning away from mainframes to minicomputers. The combination of IBM quitting India and the Indian computer policy fuelled the manufacturing of minicomputers in the country. Companies like PSI and Wipro Systems in Bengaluru, DCM Data Products (DCM) and Hindustan Computers Limited (HCL) in Delhi, ORG Systems in Baroda, Patni Computers in Pune, and IDM and Zenith Computers in Mumbai, started manufacturing computers. In fact, this era saw India become a hotbed of entrepreneurship. True to the nature of a nascent industry, there were entrepreneurs covering all computer-related segments—hardware of different types, systems software, application software, enterprise software and software services. We will look at some of these companies that went on to define the industry or were the first of their kind in the country.

HCL—Starts with Calculators and Moves to Computers and Finally Software

The genesis of modern Indian hardware probably dates back to the dogged attempts by Vinay Bharat Ram of DCM, an Indian conglomerate, to manufacture electronic calculators in India between the late 1960s and early 1970s. The Tatas and BEL too were interested in making electronic calculators during this period. Those were interesting times for electronic calculators since Intel, which was then a memory chip manufacturer, had introduced a 'calculator on a chip', the 4004 microprocessor chip. The 4004 was pathbreaking, since it was the first of the microprocessors from Intel which, in the matter of a single decade, would shape the PC era of computing. The DCM story was important, since it was the fountainhead of things to come.

DCM's application to the government of India for a collaboration with Sony to manufacture electronic calculators was turned down. DCM then decided to make them in-house and put together a team of young electronics and electrical engineers and set them on the job, carving out a DCM Data Products division as part of the textiles business. The first indigenous DCM calculator launched in 1972 was a bulky, four-function (addition, subtraction, multiplication and division) calculator. The second model launched in 1974 was a programmable calculator, which was followed by a microprocessor-based computer in 1975. Shiv Nadar, one of the young engineers in the DCM Data Products team, made his mark as the sales and marketing head, as did other team members like Arjun Malhotra and Ajai Chowdhry.

The marketing strategy was to sell the products to companies where there was just one decision maker. Chowdhry recalls how he sold DCM calculators to sugar mills in Maharashtra: 'You would wait till you actually met the chairman, because he was the only decision maker in the sugar mill. So, you had to hang around and wait at the guest house, till you could have a chance to meet him, whatever be the time, five in the evening or seven in the evening. And once you were able to convince him, it was a pretty quick decision made by the chairman himself. But the challenge used to be getting back from the sugar mill at night. There would be no buses to get back. The only way to get back was to climb into a truck going to Mumbai!'[23]

Nadar was not happy with the focus DCM Data Products got from the parent company. So, he and a few others, including Malhotra and Chowdhry, quit to start Microcomp, an electronics calculator company, in 1974. They formed a sales partnership with Televista, a TV and electronics manufacturer, to sell the latter's calculators. The Microcomp founding team persuaded their engineering colleagues from DCM Data Products to join them. They also managed to stitch a joint venture with the Uttar Pradesh Electronics Corporation Ltd. (UPTRON), which made it easy for them to procure a licence to manufacture and sell computers.

This joint venture, formed in 1976, was called Hindustan Computers Ltd (HCL). Chowdhry recalls the rationale for this name: 'Once we figured that there was a licence available with UP Electronics Corporation, we met the chairperson at that time, Col. Rai. And it somehow worked out that we agreed to go forward and form a joint venture company. Now, we came with a lot of background from DCM Data Products; we had already done calculators, we really had a good idea about how to design and manufacture a computer. So he was quite impressed with the whole concept of what we had in our minds and with the team especially.

And, looking at the team, he said, "Okay, we will invest 26 per cent, you bring in 74 per cent," and that's how a computer company would be formed.

'But then there was the whole issue of naming the company. And, I think, one of the big decisions that we took was to use the name "Hindustan" at that stage. The name was used for a very specific reason, so that it would position us very high. It would make us larger than life in a manner (of speaking). And in those days, "Hindustan" was only used by large companies or government-owned companies. Now, we were a joint sector company and we had some government ownership, and that's how we got the name, Hindustan Computers Limited.'[24]

HCL's first product was a computer, the Micro 2200, based on a PPS-4 microprocessor[25] manufactured by Rockwell International. Chowdhry describes the touch-and-go nature of the first sale by HCL: 'The initial breakthrough came from IIT Kharagpur, who actually agreed to buy our first lot of products, and that was really the beginning of the whole adventure. Soon, because of that decision, one after the other, different IITs started to buy. And then the research institutes started to buy. The interesting part was that all of them said, "Look we want to see your computer sometime, can you show it?" And we would tell them to come to our labs in Delhi. So, those days you could not actually simulate a computer. What we did was to show them a bread-board model, which would be laid on two or three tables, with all kinds of wires all over the place. And we would show them some calculations that we would do on the system. That's how we initially got going, and the challenge was that everyone said, "You must deliver the product by 31 March because that's the financial year end." And we barely managed to deliver by even 27 or 28 of March to various places in the country . . . So, that's how HCL got started. Actually, if we hadn't delivered by 31 March, there would be no HCL!'[26]

The first blockbuster from HCL was the 8C microcomputer, launched in 1977. It was among the earliest computers in the world to use the emerging 5.4-inch floppy drive. Another innovation in the 8C was that it could use a car-battery power back-up, which was novel and an extremely useful feature in India, where power cuts were so frequent. Rajendra Pawar, who was heading sales in the western region for HCL, describes the disruption that the HCL 8C caused in the Indian computer market: 'We launched the country's first microprocessor-based commercial system which we called 8C—8 for 8-bit and C for commercial . . . I remember that we launched the product on the dimension of price, which was never done, (as) computers were priced up in the sky. So, the HCL 8C at Rs 83,500 was at a decent price point and the market responded well beyond our expectations . . . There was a lot of interest from the early customers of IBM and ICL. And we also thought that it would be our main segment. But this price point actually opened the floodgates. We saw large numbers of mid-sized companies (showing interest), who had never even thought before that they could own a computer. This was opening a window in the minds of people—that computers were within reach and they could actually get a new-generation device.'[27]

To put the 8C in perspective, Apple 2 was introduced in 1977 and IBM introduced its personal computer (PC) in 1981. And that was not all, the 8C had an operating system, BASIC interpreter, and a sort-application developed by HCL's software R&D team. Microsoft had developed its first BASIC interpreter for Atari in 1975. The HCL 8C was an incredible Indian achievement for its time. One of the innovations by HCL was to sell a computing solution around the 8C, though this was challenging. Pawar says, 'Since many customers were first-time users of computers, we thought the next big breakthrough would be to think about presenting a package. That we will sell you a payroll package, and we will sell you a sales invoicing package. The computer box they did not quite understand . . . but the package solution they did . . . And we thoroughly underestimated what would it take to sell the package. We were selling it for Rs 5000, including implementation. And, of course, it took blood, sweat and tears for us to honour our commitments. But there was a huge learning.'[28]

With the advent of IBM's PC, many other manufacturers started using PC architecture based on Intel's 8086 microprocessor chip for their hardware and the licensed Microsoft Disk Operating System (DOS) that powered IBM's PC as their operating system as well. HCL too launched its PC—the BusyBee—in 1984. However, HCL developed its own operating system, probably based on the Control Program for Microprocessors (CP/M) operating system, whose source code HCL bought. Reports suggest that it ran the two most popular PC software—Lotus 123 (a spreadsheet) and Word Perfect (a word processor)—faster than the Microsoft DOS did.

In fact, HCL's entry into software services was serendipitous. HCL had attempted to set up an American subsidiary in the late 1980s to sell Magnum, its top-of-the-line symmetric multiprocessor-based computer running UNIX. However, this venture had teething problems and was not successful. When HCL wanted to shut down the American subsidiary, it realized to its surprise that its customers were very impressed with the quality of HCL's support engineers who were migrating their existing applications to the Magnum multiprocessor system. So HCL decided that instead of selling computers, the American subsidiary would sell software services.

Chowdhry recalls the turn of events: 'We had great capability in UNIX. So, what we did at that stage was that we took a whole bunch of engineers from our R&D, who were actually working on UNIX, and we placed them within R&D departments of different computer companies and technology companies to do UNIX work there. Because UNIX was a very big deal those days. And as result of that, it was a sort of beginning of our first venture into software. In a manner, we pivoted from hardware to software.'[29]

We now look at Wipro, a contemporary of and competitor to HCL in hardware. The younger generation today rightly thinks of HCL and Wipro as large IT services companies, but, as we are discovering, their genesis lay in hardware.

Wipro—Minicomputers to R&D Services

In the 1970s, Azim Premji was running his family's vanaspati and soap business, Western India Products (Wipro). Premji was entrepreneurial, and in 1976 diversified into manufacturing hydraulic and pneumatic cylinders from a factory on the outskirts of Bengaluru. Ashok Narasimhan, an alumnus of IIM Ahmedabad, was Wipro's general manager. Premji and Narasimhan decided that computers were a promising bet for the future. Wipro applied and got a licence to manufacture minicomputers. In 1980, Wipro Information Technology was established.

With a licence under its belt, Wipro had to build a team with experience of building minicomputers. Their choice was Dr Sridhar Mitta, a hardware professional working in ECIL. Mitta had a PhD from Oklahoma State University and an MTech from

IIT Kharagpur. Mitta had worked on a skunkworks project in ECIL to build its first microprocessor-based computer. Mitta describes the project: 'A few engineers took the initiative, got a few chips and started making certain systems using (Intel) 8008, using core memory and other peripherals already available. One thing good about the public sector was that nobody would stop you from doing anything you wanted to do. So, in that way a band of engineers did this system more as a hobby rather than as a project. Every year, ECIL, when they announced the annual results, also announced their new products. In 1978, the management came and saw the working microprocessor system, named it Micro-78, and introduced it as India's first microcomputer, costing under one lakh of rupees!'[30]

While Mitta was keen on entrepreneurship, Narasimhan convinced him that the Wipro offer was as good as it got since Mitta could launch a start-up with someone else's money. Mitta and his team got working on designing a computer around Intel's 8086 microprocessor and collaborated with IISc's Centre for Electronics Design and Technology (now called Department of Electronics Systems Engineering) to design Wipro's first computer, the Wipro 86.

Premji recalls its launch: 'When we started making computers, we created a big wave in the industry when we unveiled Wipro 86 at the Annual Convention of the Computer Society of India. Everyone was surprised with how latest the technology was. Wipro 86 was the first non-mainframe system to have multiple terminals and facility for multitasking. In those days, the multitasking user concept was very new. In an era where databases used to be separate from the system, Wipro integrated the database into the operating system, called the DBOS. This led to interactive management of data and entering of data in a real-life format. We also ported the UNIX operating system for servers. This was an absolutely new technology for India.'[31]

Wipro simultaneously built an ecosystem of hardware and software suppliers. Since the Wipro team had a strong R&D approach, they helped the partners with the design of various hardware sub-systems, like multilayer printed circuit boards, power supplies and terminals. Wipro also licensed its operating system from a company in the US and licensed COBOL, FORTRAN, Pascal and BASIC compilers from Indian companies, including Softek, an interesting start-up we will discuss later. The partner model at Wipro was similar to what the world would witness a few years later when PCs became mainstream. Mitta puts it succinctly: 'What Wipro did was to create this ecosystem of companies who were able to support and help us expand pretty fast. So, in turn, they also did work for other computer companies. But that is good.'[32]

Wipro's moment of crowning glory in hardware came in 1985 when it designed an Intel 80386 microprocessor-based computer that could run the UNIX operating system. Ashok Soota, who was the CEO of Wipro Infotech at that time, recalls an anecdote: 'It gave us multiprocessing capability and I think to everybody's pleasant surprise we suddenly found that we were now addressing the super-mini range (a higher-end minicomputer), and which at that time was considered the exclusive preserve of proprietary architectures like the VAX and IBM. We were very cost-effective against them because we were now based on standard open systems. And it was a huge thing for Wipro and it opened out a completely new segment for Intel . . . We were certainly among the first two in the world to do it and we got a letter of appreciation from Dr Andy Grove (co-founder and at that time CEO of Intel).'[33]

Wipro Series 386 minicomputer based on Intel's Intel 80386 microprocessor. Courtesy: Wipro archives

Wipro also focused on software products. Premji says, 'In 1983, Wipro Systems was formed with a charter to develop software products. We managed to create a highly successful project management software which was called InstaPlan. It sold very well in the US. It was truly a world-class product, giving neck-to-neck competition to the Harvard Project Manager in the early days. In fact, Harvard Business School started using InstaPlan for a couple of years in their project management courses as well. It was only due to certain archaic foreign exchange regulations in India that InstaPlan could not survive over the years. In those days, the Lotus-123 Spreadsheet Software was very famous. We created Wipro-456, a software similar to Lotus-123. We also sold major software products from other software vendors like Microsoft, Lotus, Borland, Symantec, etc.'[34] By the mid-1990s, Wipro merged its hardware and software businesses.

In the late 1980s, when it became easier for hardware MNCs to sell in India, Wipro decided it was time to diversify beyond hardware and into services. Since Wipro had built up a strong team that was aware of both Intel architecture and UNIX, this became the basis for its R&D and engineering services. Mitta expands on the journey of this new service: 'Initially we started with Intel, then we went to Tandem computers, then to NCR and to many companies. When we initially set up the Tandem Development Centre, it was a very difficult decision to make (for Tandem). So, Tandem sent a set of people to various countries and companies and finalized on Wipro. Tandem was the world leader in fault-tolerant computers which are used in stock exchanges, banks and missions that don't fail. And we were going to design and support their most important sub-system, the communication sub-system.'[35]

There were some lighter moments in this arduous journey of selling R&D services. Subroto Bagchi remembers a funny anecdote when he was Wipro's salesperson in Silicon Valley and was trying to open the Sun Microsystems account. Bagchi first met with Walt Brown, who was leading Sun's efforts to build a worldwide support network for its Solaris operating system, and later with his team member, Tom Best. 'His opening statement was—"Let me tell you something, I don't even know where India is!" . . . So, I kept my briefcase down, looked around, and there was a white board. I walked up to it. No hands had been shaken and no visiting cards exchanged yet. I picked up a felt pen and, completely ignoring him, I started drawing the world map. He was very curious with this strange kind of perseverance. As I started drawing the world map and came to Singapore, Tom said, "I know where that is." So, I turned back and said, "Tom, if you know where Singapore is, then this is India." Tom then looked at the world map, looked at me and said, "You draw the world map rather well." And that was the starting point of our building a relationship with Sun.'[36]

After establishing itself in R&D services, Wipro also entered the enterprise services domain in the 1990s. Simultaneously, Wipro started a strong focus on software engineering and quality certification processes. This focus on quality continued, and Wipro was among the first companies in the world to be certified at the Software Engineering Institute's Capability Maturity Model (SEI CMM) Level 5, the highest level, in 2002. Wipro grew to become one of India's largest IT services and R&D services companies.

Was Wipro the first IT start-up in Bengaluru? Let us find out.

Minicomputers and Other Hardware from PSI—Genesis of the IT Industry in Bengaluru

Processor Systems India (PSI) was a company started by V.K. Ravindaran, V.K. Harindran and Vinay Deshpande in 1973. Our research has led us to believe that PSI was possibly the first IT start-up in Bengaluru. For those interested in Bengaluru trivia, PSI's office continues to exist in a nondescript building on Richmond Road, and not in any of the city's current IT hubs.

PSI's focus was computer and related hardware. The first product was an electronic telex-exchange monitoring system for Western Union. PSI did the hardware design manually and had draftsmen do the PCB layout. But PSI had a tough time getting an SSI (Small Scale Industry) certification as a hardware manufacturer.

The officers wanted to classify them as a drafting company instead, since no category existed for computer and related hardware for SSIs.

PSI was among the first in India to produce, in the mid-1970s, a computer using a microprocessor, which was used in a sonar (sound navigation ranging) system. PSI also went on to build a successful DEC PDP-11 clone called Omni, which stood the Indian defence establishment in good stead, at a time when they faced import restrictions on technology from the US.

When foreign computer players were allowed in India, PSI formed a joint venture with the French computer maker Bull to manufacture computers in Bengaluru in the mid-1980s. Later, the Aditya Birla Group bought out Bull's stake, and it became a software company, PSI Data Systems.

Bengaluru region's hardware story extended into the early 1980s. Gopal Srinivasan, a scion of the TVS family and an MBA from the University of Michigan, started TVS Electronics. The company made dot matrix printers that were ruggedized to work well in India's hot and dusty conditions.[37] So far, we have looked at hardware start-ups. When there is hardware, can software be far behind? Let us now look at the story of an Indian software product start-up Softek, which focused on compilers and productivity software.

Softek: Making Systems Software Products

HCL's R&D team included a bright systems software expert, Diwakar Nigam. He recollects making up his mind to work only in systems software, right from the time of his MTech days in computer science at IIT Madras: 'Placement came into the picture and many people went to Tata Burroughs and TCS. I think there were only one or two exceptions and I was one of them. I didn't want to do COBOL programming. In fact, I avoided it like the plague in my class also. It was offered twice—in the first year and the second year. So, I skipped the TCS interview. When Prof. Mahabala saw me, he asked me where I was during the time of the interviews. I said I had been sleeping. He said, "No problem I can put you there." And I replied, "Sir, I really don't want to go"!'[38]

Nigam joined HCL. He was responsible for developing systems software and utilities for HCL computers. Nigam soon realized that he wanted to focus on building systems software for not only HCL products but also for other computers. He decided to start Softek in 1979 along with a few other IIT alumni. Softek focused on compilers initially, including a successful COBOL compiler that was sold for computers from ORG Systems, ECIL, Wipro and DCM. This was followed by a FORTRAN compiler. To place Softek in the global context of that era, Microsoft was making BASIC interpreters for home computers in the late 1970s.

Softek also developed a personal productivity suite—consisting of Softwords (word processor), Softbase (database) and SoftCalc (spreadsheet). During that period, Softek also developed a blockbuster product that was a first of its kind—Akshar, a word processor for the Devanagari script, which could be used on a PC. Nigam fondly recalls its story and says, 'There was a very large number of people who were using the Akshar software . . . Then we built Akshar Laser Composer for the composing industry, where the fonts were very important. In developing this product, we also worked together, first with IIT Kanpur and then with C-DAC, on building multilingual keyboards for computers. It was a great product and I think it was the most pirated product after Microsoft products! The typesetting industry (Hindi) sitting in places like Meerut and Allahabad were using it.'[39]

The proliferation of PCs in the mid-1980s in India also saw the advent of software piracy, which made it difficult for Softek to operate. Not surprisingly, when the National Association of Software and Services Companies (NASSCOM) was formed in 1988, Nigam was at the forefront of its anti-piracy initiatives. Softek slowly moved towards the enterprise application domain with its Softek Integrated Management System, which could do general ledger, payroll, sales and inventory management for enterprises. Softek and Nigam did what start-ups do, day in and day out, today. They pivoted in the early 1990s to focus on enterprises and business process management solutions, with some innovative work for Citibank and its loan processing operations in India.

We have looked at some fascinating developments in the creation of the fledgling Indian IT industry. This period also witnessed some important developments in IT capability-building for the country, to which we turn now.

―――

National Centre for Software Development and Computing Techniques (NCSDCT), and the Story of India's First Postgraduate Diploma Course in Computer Science

In the first two decades after India's independence, computers were primarily considered in the context of research and scientific advancements. But the policymakers were also clear that the influence of computer science and technology should go beyond these domains and impact the economy as a whole. Prof. M.G.K. Menon said, 'When I was the chairman of the Electronics Commission and Secretary, DoE, UNDP asked me what projects in electronics needed to be taken up in India. I suggested three projects in the field of information technology: three major computer centres in the country. One to deal with the area of software techniques and computing technologies, the second to deal with management information systems and the third to deal with engineering solutions. They denied funding for the third centre, which was supposed to be at the National Aeronautics Laboratory, because they did not want to fund a large computer for work that they thought had some defence connotations. But UNDP approved the other two. Thus the first became NCSDCT at TIFR. The second became the National Informatics Centre (NIC). The first was headed by Prof. Narasimhan and the second by his disciple, one who worked with him closely, Dr N. Seshagiri, who helped build NIC.'[40]

Supported by a US$2 million funding from UNDP, TIFR created in 1972–73 an autonomous unit called National Centre for Software Development and Computing Techniques (NCSDCT). They acquired a DEC 1040 computer to replace their CDC 3600 and initiated several software technology projects. Commenting on the genesis of NCSDCT, R.K. Shyamsundar, who was the founding dean of the School of Technology and Computer Science at TIFR, says, 'NCSDCT mainly started with three–four projects. There was an advisory committee which was chaired by Sir Maurice Wilkes (a British computer scientist). Bill Wulf (an American computer scientist) came with his team to develop an operating system and a concurrent language. Another project that was started was around graphics. R.F. Sproull (an American computer graphics expert) visited and S.P. Mudur drove that project so that computers could be used for virtual and 3D modelling. Later, a diploma course in software engineering was initiated.'[41]

S. Ramani and his colleagues at NCSDCT at TIFR created what was probably India's first postgraduate diploma course in software engineering. Recalling that effort, Ramani says, 'We bought an ECIL 316 and I started building a computer network on these machines with the help of my colleagues, Anant Joshi and Vinod Kumar. I was excited about educational applications of the computer. The idea was to build a remote station software and to put the TDC 316 at VJTI (Veermata Jijabai Technological Institute), an educational institution 20 km from TIFR, connect the computers in TIFR and VJTI and use it in real education. We were excited about the idea of an "open university", an inexpensive method of training working professionals who paid for their own education. These were low-cost solutions for education. Eventually, the remote station connected to the DEC 1040 at NCSDST. Students at VJTI could thus connect with the TIFR computer.'[42]

In its second batch in 1979, the course had a young engineer from Brihanmumbai (Bombay) Electricity Supply and Transport (BEST) enrolling. That was Shibulal, co-founder of Infosys. He recalls with fondness the diploma course: 'TIFR wanted to evangelize computer science. They started a CS course and I was in its second batch. I think they had about seventy or eighty people in that batch. They were teaching computer science and it was very different from the training I had at BEST. The BEST course was focused on the business side, on how you would develop business systems. Whereas TIFR was teaching the fundamentals of computer science—operating systems, compiler theory, database, networking, time-sharing, memory management . . . along with a bunch of languages like FORTRAN, PASCAL and Assembly Language. The languages were a means to experiment with, besides the theoretical learning on computer science. That was a fantastic opportunity for me to learn the 'science' side of computer science. We had fantastic teachers—Dr Ramani, Dr Mudur, Ms Joglekar. The course was held in two places. The actual classroom was in VJTI in Matunga and we were allowed to use the computer at TIFR. All of us had accounts on the DEC 10. It gave many of us a great learning platform.'[43]

NCSDCT evolved and became the National Centre for Software Technology (NCST) by 1984. S. Ramani became its founding director in 1985 when NCST was set up independent of TIFR.

Commenting on the focus of NCST, Ramani says, 'Our research encompassed computer graphics, databases, networks and knowledge-based computer systems. We carried forward many traditions from TIFR into NCST. One of them was the running of a large computer centre, running it 24/7 round the year and making it available to everyone in the country. We also made sure that we charged people for use of the computer. At NCST, our job was to take software industry professionals who never had a formal education in computer science and give them an equivalent of a university-level education. We still ran part-time courses, but at a much larger scale than we did at TIFR.'[44]

NCST was also a nodal centre for an important initiative—ERNET—which was responsible for developing India's academic computer network and bringing the Internet into the country.

The Education and Research Network (ERNET) Project, and the Story of India's First Email and First Internet Connection

In 1985–86, the ERNET project, which networked the premier educational and research institutions in India, began with the help of funding from UNDP. The government brought eight institutions to collaborate on the ERNET project—the five IITs, IISc, NCST and a small team headquartered in the DoE. Quite remarkably, the official consultant to UNDP for the ERNET project was Dr Vint Cerf, Turing Award winner and co-designer of TCP/IP protocols.

NCST was well positioned to support the project for two reasons—its big computer, a VAX machine with the ULTRIX operating system, and its proximity to telecom infrastructure and sea cable lines. Also, Ramani had been tracking the rise of academic networking, particularly the ARPANET in the US, from his post-doc days at the Carnegie Mellon University. He says, 'Here was a network that did not need good infrastructure—a poor telephone network, a noisy network, a network that broke connections, often was adequate, because it was using a computer to manage all the deficiencies of the communication network. I realized that this was a technology that would be of immediate value to India.'[45]

UNDP made it clear that all the ERNET progress reports had to come over email and precipitated the first email going out of India from the DoE servers. Later, the gateway at NCST connected with Centrum voor Wiskunde en Informatica (CWI) in Amsterdam, marking the first Internet connection in India. The ERNET programme soon got leased line connections to all the IITs, and then connected educational institutions in remote locations in India using the VSAT network.

ERNET, which started as a computer networking project, actually prepared the country for the broader Internet revolution. Sadagopan says: 'Perhaps for the first time, all the IITs came together. We found that the Indian scientific community, even in the IITs and IISc, was somewhat disconnected. The traditional post used to take too much time, and through emails we could easily connect with our fellow professionals. Earlier, we could not be reviewers or sub-editors for journals because we were not connected. Those opportunities opened up. More importantly, the core team involved with ERNET could contribute to the evolving Internet protocols. A whole range of master's theses could be done on this topic. The software services industry also benefited from the STPIs (Software Technology Parks of India) that got connected to the ERNET. The ERNET created a core team of high-tech communications professionals who could become part of the Indian IT industry. In PASCAL language, we typically declare—thus, INT 'ERNET' becomes Internet!'[46]

Early Email Exchanges in India

First Email in India, Sent between NCST and IIT Bombay—by Deepak B. Phatak[47]

'Our activity started (in 1985) even before the official ERNET project began. Dr Ramani from NCST and I wanted to have an Indian email mechanism. We decided to do some experiments on the UNIX machines which had just come to India.

'Those days, if you were to attach a modem to the computer, you required a clearance from the P&T (Post & Telecom) department. For every modem they would take fifteen days to approve. In our experiments, we were struggling with the UNIX environment and the new modems. After two to three cycles of such approvals, we decided to complete the experiment without seeking upfront approvals. Soon, we celebrated the first email between NCST and my software lab at IIT Bombay. Of course, we got the approvals post facto.

'Much later, at a CSI event, when I narrated this incident and said we could have gone to jail for our infractions, Mr F.C. Kohli wryly remarked that Ramani and I would have become freedom fighters of "free India for IT liberalization".'

ERNET's Positive Influence on the Human Interest Front—by S. Sadagopan[48]

'ERNET provided Internet for the first time to people in the IITs, both faculty and students. I remember how a chemistry professor at IIT Kanpur complained about the ERNET project and said we were taking away all the funding from the government. And a year later, he was all appreciative of ERNET because his daughter had gone to Berkeley and he could still stay in regular touch with her, through emails, twice a day.'

The readers, especially the younger lot, should pause for a moment to mull on these anecdotes. We live in an era where email and instant communication are a given. We encourage you to remember your first encounter with the email or talk to the elders in your family about theirs!

National Informatics Centre (NIC), and the Story of the Asian Games, Micro-Earth Stations and Grassroots Connectivity in India

As we saw earlier, M.G.K. Menon's efforts led to the creation of a second centre that looked at leveraging computing for national development. The backstory to the establishment of this centre starts with N. Seshagiri, who earned his PhD from IISc Bangalore in microwave telecommunications engineering. He joined TIFR in 1966 and worked on satellite communications and spacecraft design. Recognizing the intellectual spark in him, Prof. Menon pulled Seshagiri into the core team to help set up the Electronics Commission in 1971. The Commission came out with a report titled 'Perspective Plan for Growth of Electronics Industry in India' and, based on it, the central government set up the National Data Centre. By 1976, the Commission decided to infuse informatics-led information systems to aid the government departments in their decision-making. With the help of a US$4.4 million funding from UNDP, the National Informatics Centre (NIC) was set up in New Delhi, with Seshagiri as its first founding director general.

The charter of NIC was to develop computerized information systems for government departments. It owned the domain name 'nic.in', which was allocated only to Indian government entities. These days, NIC allocates the domain name 'gov.in'. In its initial years, NIC actually competed with computer centres of other government departments in the provision of computerization services (Inter Data 8/32 system at the Department of Statistics and the Burroughs 3800 system of the Planning Commission)![49] In 1980, NIC commissioned a Cyber 170/720 CDC system, which was probably the biggest computer installation in India at the time.

NIC finally gained momentum, thanks to a lucky break it got with a marquee project, the IX Asian Games held in New Delhi in 1982.

This sporting event is popularly remembered in India for precipitating the introduction of the first colour television sets in the country. What is lesser known is the stellar work that NIC put in to design, develop and implement the Computerised Asiad Information Systems (CAIS) for the games. NIC installed interactive terminals at over a dozen sporting complexes and stadiums across the country. These terminals were connected to a host computer through leased lines and radio frequencies. Interestingly, the NIC network allowed for an information inquiry service covering different aspects of the Asiad Games results, through free-format questions that could be handed to the NIC terminal operators. Indian newspaper readers were thus treated to some refined sporting analysis.

One of the most important initiatives of NIC was establishment of the Nationwide Computer Network (NICNET) in 1987. Commenting on the origins of NICNET, Seshagiri said, 'My biggest achievement has been the setting up of the NICNET network using VSAT (Very Small Aperture Terminal) bandwidth at a time when the term VSAT was not even coined. VSATs were called micro-earth stations then. I had seen research papers in IEEE and communication journals about a new technology with very small apertures that was arriving. That appealed to me, as I thought that it is one path by which we can have low-cost communication. I then went to the DoT and told them about it. The DoT officials told me that it was not possible, and they worked out the numbers to say that a VSAT network would cost Rs 480 crore. When I worked out (the costs), the same network came to Rs 75–80 crore.'[50]

The design philosophy of NICNET was to depend almost entirely on satellite and wireless-loop technologies, bypassing the terrestrial cable networks as far as possible. Despite opposition from DoT, NIC successfully implemented the VSAT network, which became the third such network in the world, after the two VSAT networks that were then in operation in the US.

The NIC team developed a predominantly query-based decision-support information system for the Indian government.[51] NIC developed more than 5000 databases in coordination with twenty-six government departments like agriculture, employment and industry.[52] Using NICNET, NIC helped the government collect various types of information, such as on weather and crop yields. Distributed geographic information systems were also developed on the network. In order to maintain these large databases on a national scale, NIC installed four very large computer systems (S-1000s from NEC, Japan) at Delhi, Pune, Bhubaneswar and Hyderabad, to act as the four nodes of NICNET, with a CDC computer as the main host.

NICNET offered email services and Internet access through a direct high-speed link to Sprintnet of the US. It also created COURTNIC for litigants/advocates, providing the status of pending cases at the Supreme Court; MEDLARS (Medical Literature Analysis and Retrieval System) databases in the area of biomedical and healthcare; and, through DISNIC (computer networks at the district level), set the stage for an e-governance programme in the country. NICNET and ERNET were communication networks created for entirely different target audiences, and there was no direct link between them. Was this a missed opportunity in facilitating academic research on copious amounts of government data on India?

Another feather in NIC's cap was its ushering in of video-conferencing technology to India. It happened when it facilitated a lecture on 4 December 1996, which was made in London and viewed by industry leaders sitting in Hotel Maurya in Delhi.[53] Seshagiri proudly recalled the effort: 'The government is supposed to be backward in its views. So, I thought, why not bring the latest technology to those most backward in their views? That's how I was responsible for the entire computerization of the government.'[54] Much later, in 2015, NIC developed the PRAGATI (Pro-Active Governance And Timely Implementation) platform, combining digital data management, videoconferencing and geospatial technology.

Now, to turn to the places where capability was being built for Indian IT—the educational institutions and their computer science education programmes, especially at the IITs and IIMs.

Computer Science (CS) Education at IIT Kanpur and the Runaway Success of Its CS BTech Programme

As we saw in the previous chapter, IIT Kanpur was the fountainhead of computer education in India. Through the 1970s, students from various walks of engineering were kept captivated by the computers on campus. Bhaskar Pramanik, who went on to head software giants Oracle and Microsoft in India, fondly recalls his time at the computer centre and says, 'In my final year (of electrical engineering), I decided to do my BTech thesis on design of logic circuits using NAND and NOR gates. Now, you have to understand the context, because this was in 1971. And it was actually only in 1972 that Intel came out with the 4004 microprocessors (that made use of gates)! I was very fortunate because IIT Kanpur had just imported an IBM 1130 and, basically, I had this computer all to myself. This got me interested in computer sciences and I decided that that was really something I wanted to pursue as my career.'[55]

The CS courses were started for master's students at IIT Kanpur in the late 1960s. In spite of the resounding success of the MTech programme, the CS discipline was not considered mature enough to be started as an undergraduate programme. That changed in 1978. Commenting on the deliberations that led to the first BTech programme in computer science at IIT Kanpur, Rajaraman says, 'First, the Senate debated it. It was accepted somewhat grudgingly . . . we will not start a department but we call it a programme . . . So, the programme was started with twenty students . . . civil engineering, metallurgy, chemical . . . each department contributed a few seats. When the results of the Joint Entrance Examination (JEE) came out, we found that rank forty was the last to be admitted to those twenty seats. Everyone was very surprised. They thought that very low ranks would choose the computer science programme and that the mechanical and electrical engineering courses would be the ones attracting the best students. But we attracted the best students because the perception (about the course) outside was somewhat different.'[56]

It was remarkable that the top-ranking students realized the innate potential of the emerging field of computer science. It was estimated that eighteen of the twenty students of the first batch went abroad (mainly to the US) for further studies. Commenting on how the emigrating students proved helpful to IIT Kanpur and the Indian IT industry in later years, Rajaraman says, 'I asked myself why I went through all the trouble to just export the guys to the US. But they did help. Rajeev Motwani, who went abroad, did very well there (Rajeev was an early adviser and supporter of companies like Google and PayPal). Unfortunately, he passed away, but his family donated a building for the computer science department in Kanpur. Similarly, many of the students who went there became professors, entrepreneurs and so on. And when India reached a stage in the 1980s when it was able to export software, it helped. The fact that these students had done very well there gave confidence to the Americans that Indians could also write software. It increased confidence in India among the people who gave jobs to Indian companies. So many of our good talented people were there and they became ambassadors for the Indian software industry in their own way.'

The IIT Kanpur students joined the Indian software industry too, and TCS was probably the largest recruiter of MTech CS students from there. Soon TCS started to increase the numbers it recruited from all IITs, including BTechs from non-CS backgrounds. This constituted a challenge, since these recruits did not come with exposure to programming and software design. Kohli, with his good connect with IIT Kanpur, requested Mahabala to do a detailed course on programming and systems design for TCS's college recruits.

Mahalingam says: 'In this course they would teach programming. Very intensive thing . . . I think it went on for about two months in terms of classroom lectures. And because we didn't have the use of computers at that time, it had necessarily to be done in the classroom. So, this was the first introduction to computers, and that system which Prof. Mahabala and I established continued for a very long time.'[57] TCS soon had its own experts anchor the course.

S. Sadagopan, who joined as faculty in IIT Kanpur in the late 1970s, explains why the CS programme there came to be highly regarded: 'We were the first to teach various computing languages in India—PASCAL, C, and then, later, Java programming. We also participated in some of the larger projects in the country, like ERNET, AI and computational linguistics projects. Through the 1970s and 1980s, IIT Kanpur and its computer science department were the most preferred in India.'[58]

Around this time, a concatenation of events led to a new dawn in computing in the south of India. We head to IIT Madras to catch that computing sunrise.

Computer Science Education at IIT Madras, and the Story of a Computing Workhorse and Figurative High Priests at the Altar of its Computer Centre

As we saw in the previous chapter, IIT Madras was rather subdued on the computing front till the end of the 1960s. That situation changed dramatically in 1973 when it acquired the IBM 370, making it possibly the largest computer installation in Asia at that time! It also helped that teaching talent in the form of Prof. H.N. Mahabala, Prof. C.R. Muthukrishnan and others migrated from IIT Kanpur to IIT Madras around this time.

Commenting on how the computer came to IIT Madras, Muthukrishnan says, 'There was a tight policy about importing computers. One could not get a computer worth the name to serve an institution for anything less than a couple of crores (in Indian rupees). At that time, the annual budget of IIT was only around (Rs)

6 crore. So, you are talking about over 30 per cent of the annual budget for a computer!'[59]

Recalling his role in selecting the computer, Mahabala says, 'Everyone was surprised that IITM wanted to go in for an IBM 370. The Germans (who were funding the purchase of a computer for IITM with a grant) were also surprised and questioned us as to how we would build up usage for such a large computer. But I was somehow strong in my persuasion that we have moved away from computers as calculators and that we will soon be solving complex problems for industry using the computer. The Germans were half-minded (about the choice) but agreed.'[60]

The IBM 370 computer came by sea to Chennai port and from there was taken by bullock cart to the IIT Madras campus. Once again, the humble bullock cart features in the saga of Indian computers! Describing the computer, Muthukrishnan says, 'It was a powerful computer at that time, although its configuration will look ridiculous now—512Kb of memory, four platters of removable disks of 100 MB each. At that time software was bundled with hardware. The computer could service both scientific and industrial applications. We had to run this centre because the maintenance charges from IBM were quite high.'[61]

IIT Madras smartly hired one of the IBM engineers, S. Srinivasan, an alumnus of the institute, who helped instal the IBM 370 there. Recalling his days at the computer centre, Srinivasan says, 'Since I installed the machine, it was a sort of homecoming for me. This system had many packages, like simulation packages, optimization packages . . . It was a nice way for industry to handle complex problems. I helped ONGC, Indian Oil and other organizations.'[62]

Inauguration of the IBM 370 at IIT Madras. Faculty members H.N. Mahabala (seated, extreme right), S. Sampath (seated, extreme left). Courtesy: IIT Madras Heritage Centre

Indeed, this aspect of supporting industry became the one defining aspect of the IIT Madras computer centre. Commenting on this collaboration, Mahabala says, 'When we got that computer, we were in a position to convince businesses of larger establishments to use computers for their work. The interesting aspect was that they had all heard of the computer and the great things it could achieve, but didn't know how to go about using one.'[63]

The IBM 370 at the IIT Madras Computer Centre— Some Interesting Anecdotes

Professors Mahabala and Muthukrishnan were the figurative high priests of computing at the IIT Madras computer centre. The IBM 370 was a money-spinning workhorse and was in operation till the early 1980s. The professors remember some stories from the computer centre with great relish.

GE's Illumination Project for the Asian Games—by H. N. Mahabala[64]

'GE India had taken the contract to illuminate the stadium at the Asian Games. They were not sure if the lamps they were using and the locations where they were placed would do an adequate job. So they wanted a computer simulation for that purpose. Their bid for the Asiad would be accepted only if the simulation was verified by computers. This was something totally new.

'I went back to my physics basics. I learnt that each lamp threw a concord of light on the floor of the stadium. And we had to find where the intersections were and whether they overlapped and covered every portion of the stadium. And we did it—my research student and I were able to complete the illumination project. People back in GE did not believe that such work could be done in India.'

Blowing the Thermal Trip—by C.R. Muthukrishnan[65]

'Around 1978, the air conditioner for the computer came into some great difficulty. It was not delivering sufficient cooling. There used to be a thermal trip—the system would simply shut down when the internal temperature went up to 56 degrees Celsius. We would wait for some time for the system to cool down and we would turn the machine back on.' Spare a thought for the IBM 370 enduring a midnight thermal-trip!

> **And There Was Fun Too**
>
> It was not a case of only work and no fun at the computer centre. Aficionados of Tamil cinema will be delighted to learn that the IIT Madras computer centre was featured in thespian Kamal Haasan's movie *Vikram*, released in the mid-1980s.

The MTech Course in Computer Science at IIT Madras

It was clear that the institute could attract good-quality people who could support the IBM 370 only if they ran a computer science programme offering an MTech degree. Muthukrishnan recalls the context around opening up this programme to MSc students: 'We realized that CS engineering was a developing field and it must be opened to people from varied backgrounds with some amount of mathematical and physical sciences. Five seats from the MTech programme were allocated for MSc students.'[66] One such MSc student who benefited from this allowance is one of us, Kris Gopalakrishnan! He says, 'I was lucky to get into the MTech programme. This was the first time they were allowing MSc students with a background in maths and sciences to enrol in the programme. I think the focus of IIT Madras was on software, and that's the reason they allowed it.'[67]

In fact, it was a rather serendipitous incident during his MSc Physics days at IIT Madras that led Kris Gopalakrishnan firmly down the path of computing. Kris recalls that incident: 'One day I was going from the library to the hostel on my bicycle. I was carrying three books on the cycle carrier. Someone behind me, and on a cycle himself, stopped me to inquire about the books I had. These books were on computers. IIT Madras had a very large computer and I was trying to understand what computing was all about. He suggested that I take a course on FORTRAN programming, which was offered free on the campus. And if I took that course, I would get access to the computer centre, he said. I took the course, got interested in computers and, luckily, got admission for the MTech in computer science. That person was Prof. Mahabala, and what a lucky coincidence it has been for me.'[68]

Kris found himself immersed in very interesting computing work. He says, 'The focus of the MTech programme was on software. We were asked to design a complier, end to end. There was a language called PLC, which was a subset of the language PL1. We were asked to develop a compiler for that as part of the programme. This allowed us to understand the intricacies of programming, and how programs would be interpreted by the computer. Some of the work required me to program in assembly language. My project also included developing a command line interpreter. The IBM 370 at that point was primarily a batch system. We would write the programs on cards; data would be on cards and the system would read those programs and work. My project was to create a command line interpreter so that we could interact with the computer on a real-time basis. Of course, the interpreter had only a minimum set of commands. We just wanted to prove that it could be done.'[69]

One of the labs had a PDP 8 computer that was used for a brain-scanning project. Kris signed up as a candidate for brain scanning and also programmed on that computer to print out the scans. Perhaps his participation in this brain project was prescient of things to come—much later, in 2015–16, he would fund three chairs in the Center for Computational Brain Research at IIT Madras.

The Story of 'Kolam' Patterns and the Birth of Indian Parallelism

In the 1970s, IIT Madras also undertook some early research projects in the area of theoretical computer science. Kamala Krithivasan, who joined as a faculty member in IIT Madras during that period, recounts her early encounters in this research area: 'I joined Madras Christian College (MCC) in 1970 under Rani Siromoney as her PhD student. The first topic we considered was parallel context-free languages. The area started when Noam Chomsky gave a formal definition of a grammar.'[70]

The MCC researchers proved for the first time in the world that there were context-free languages, like the Dyck set, which could not be generated parallelly. Their paper appeared in the *Information and Control Journal* in 1974, and Arto Salomaa of the University of Turku, a veteran theoretical computer scientist, termed their finding 'Indian Parallelism'. Kamala Krithivasan turned her attention to array grammars and on generating *kolam* patterns (kolam is a traditional Indian folk art consisting of decorative patterns drawn or painted in the courtyards in front of typical south Indian homes) using formal grammar. Narasimhan of TIFR, who was working on generating pictures using grammar, was clued into MCC's work. It was he who gave an impetus to theoretical computer science research work in India by conceptualizing an international conference in 1981, the Foundations of Software Technology and Theoretical Computer Science (FSTTCS).

While many of the developments in India's computer education journey took place in the IITs, an equally interesting development was taking place in the leading business school of the country, the Indian Institute of Management Ahmedabad (IIM Ahmedabad), which was using computers to teach management information systems to students, and to analyse data for research by its faculty.

The Computer Centre at IIM Ahmedabad—the Story of How They Built One of India's Most Sophisticated Computing Facilities

Similar to the way the computer centre at IIT Kanpur was set up with the help of American universities and funding, one at IIM Ahmedabad too was established with part sponsorship and collaborative support from American institutions like the Ford Foundation and Harvard Business School. It was set up to conduct research and impart training in business management in India. By June 1970, the Ford Foundation made a grant of US$2,21,000 for purchase of computer equipment at IIM Ahmedabad.[71]

J.G. Krishnayya, a pioneer in the use of simulation, geographic information systems and computer graphics in India, joined as faculty and played an important role in the computer journey of IIM Ahmedabad. He did a study of the available computers in the market and decided to go for a time-sharing system based on a microcomputer. The Ford Foundation team concurred, advising him to consider the HP2100 system—a computer that had already been successfully installed in the business schools at Harvard and Stanford. Krishnayya was assisted in this computing journey by N.R. Narayana Murthy, who joined the IIM Ahmedabad computer centre as its chief systems programmer after completing his master's at IIT Kanpur.

Narayana Murthy, recollecting that important decision he made in life, says, 'Around this time, when Prof. Krishnayya came to IIT

Kanpur to recruit, Prof. Rajaraman asked me to speak to him. Prof. Krishnayya wove excellent magic around the kind of computer he was getting at IIM Ahmedabad—the first time-sharing system, and an opportunity to understand the operating system because he was getting the source code for the system. I asked him what the salary would be and he said it would be around Rs 800—slightly less than half the salary all my colleagues got. I spoke to Prof. Rajaraman, and he said that this was a fantastic opportunity to learn a lot. The salary might be low but I would never regret it. It would be an extraordinary opportunity to be ahead of my colleagues in learning. I sent a telegram to my father . . . he was a teacher, and he said that I should take the job that provided me an opportunity for learning.'[72]

Narayana Murthy believes that choosing IIM Ahmedabad was the best decision he made in his life. 'We had a wonderful time. The opportunity to work there was for nearly twenty-four hours a day. We were supposed to help the students from 7 a.m. to 10 p.m. We had to do our work from 10 p.m. to 4 a.m. We developed a basic interpreter for an ECIL machine, we wrote a simulator on the HP2100 system, we tinkered with the operating system quite a lot and understood it very well—the scheduler, the interop routines, etc. IIM had higher per-capita books on computer science as compared to other institutions in India.'[73]

After three years at the IIM Ahmedabad computer centre, Narayana Murthy moved to Paris. Based on a paper that he and Prof. Krishnayya wrote on information retrieval for a conference in Italy, he got a job offer from the chairperson of the conference session, who, incidentally, was also a senior manager at a French technology firm called SESA. The Paris experience was a source of great learning and personal transformation for Narayana Murthy. He realized at the end of his French sojourn that the only way a country could grow was by creating jobs, and the only way to ensure that jobs were created was by enabling more entrepreneurs. The seeds of entrepreneurship had been sown in his mind!

Another person whose entrepreneurial spark was lit in the corridors of IIM Ahmedabad was Ashank Desai, who went on to found Mastek, an IT services company. Recollecting his days at the institute's computer centre in the late 1970s, Ashank says, 'The idea of my company, Mastek, came from the course we took that taught us how to use computers for management applications. We could simulate various processes of queuing and scheduling and come out with outputs. We had software packages available on the HP machine. That changed my outlook on using computers for real-life applications. We were at that cusp of this evolution where software was becoming an important part of IT. I realized that sitting at IIM Ahmedabad.'[74]

The number of computers in India which was less than 1000 in 1978 increased to 80,000 in 1990. Similarly, software exports increased from an insignificant amount in the 1970s to US$128 million in 1990–91.[75] While the action in the 1970s was in hardware and capability-building, it shifted to software and the government's mission-mode IT projects in the 1980s.

Growth of Software Services and Mission-Mode Government IT Projects

The entrepreneurship wave of the early 1980s was dominated by software start-ups, each of which, interestingly, focused on a different domain in the IT sector. For example, there was Infosys in software services exports, Mastek in IT solutions for the domestic market, FutureSoft in niche telecom software, IIS Infotech in offshore-based software services, and Tally in software products for the enterprise. The spurt in demand for programmers at software companies, and for business managers who could leverage IT systems (hardware and software) in end-user companies, provided an opportunity for training start-ups like NIIT. The success of the established software companies and the start-ups soon got international attention, and we saw the first trickle of MNCs, such as Texas Instruments (TI), setting up their software subsidiaries in India.

New IT industry associations emerged. The Manufacturers Association for Information Technology (MAIT), bringing the computer manufacturers together, was formed in the early 1980s. The software companies, faced with a growing tussle in finding their voices among the dominant Indian hardware companies, came together in the late 1980s under the umbrella of National Association of Software and Services Companies (NASSCOM).

The 1980s witnessed some watershed decisions by the Indian government, leading to important policies and mission-mode computerization programmes. The New Computer Policy announced in 1984 initiated liberalization of the Indian computer industry. The licencing requirements to manufacture computers were eased, and software was now recognized as an industry. The Computer Policy of 1986 allowed companies to import computers duty-free for developing software for export. These policies played an important role in spurring the growth of export-oriented software services.

These government policies nurtured a fledgling Indian software industry. These policies were different from the licence-control and self-reliance focus of the policies that governed the manufacturing of minicomputers.

During this time, the government of India initiated some of the most impactful IT projects. For instance, the Railways Passenger Reservation System project, initiated in this era, still remains one of India's most iconic IT projects to impact the common man in a significant way. Another landmark was the Rangarajan Committee's banking mechanization project, which made banks more accessible to the general public. And, in order to assuage the bank unions, 'computers' were euphemistically referred to as 'advanced ledger posting machines'.

Similarly, with the aim of keeping abreast of cutting-edge technological advancements and to develop India's national capability, the government of India undertook three important programmes in the 1980s: it established the Centre for Development of Advanced Computing (CDAC); approved the setting up of a National Supercomputer Education and Research Centre (SERC) in IISc; and kick-started the Knowledge Based Computer System (KBCS) initiative, which heralded India's first foray into artificial intelligence.

Overall, Indian IT had set sail in both domestic and international waters. We will now follow its magnificent journey.

The 1984 Computer Policy and the 1986 Software Policy: The Foundations of Indian Software Exports

We saw the labyrinthine world of India's computer policy in the 1970s in the previous chapter. At the dawn of the 1980s, when the Rajaraman Committee suggested creation of a Master's of Computer Application (MCA) programme, it built a strong foundation for developing an exceptional cadre of IT professionals in India. In 1981, another committee headed by Rajaraman recognized the importance of promoting software exports and recommended that genuine exporters be allowed to liberally import computers for creating software in India.

In November 1984, the government of India announced a Computer Policy to enable and simplify manufacture and procurement of computers. Within a year, the number of computers produced in India increased by 100 per cent and computer prices declined by 50 per cent.[1] While the computer policy of 1984 was focused on hardware, it was the first to recognize software as a separate industry segment.

These ideas were cemented in the Software Policy that was released in November 1986, which focused on computer software exports, software development and training. This policy eased import of computers and software tools and made them duty-free to facilitate software exports from India. The only condition was that the importer was expected to export software and earn 250 per cent of the cost of the imported computers within four years. A forward-thinking aspect of this policy was that it allowed Indian software exporters to use CMC's network of IBM 4342 mainframes at a subsidized tariff. This illustrates the ability of our policymakers to incentivize technology-driven entrepreneurship in an era when the Indian economy was not yet liberalized.

The most fascinating aspect of the 1986 policy was its innocuous wish-list clause. In hindsight, it proved to be a master stroke— software developed in India could be exported using communication systems such as satellite and cable. This provided the bedrock for the growth of offshore software services. Not surprisingly, this policy nurtured start-ups focusing on software exports. From insignificant software export earnings in 1978, India realized US$131 million in software export earnings in 1990.[2]

We take a peep now into the world of some of India's start-ups from this era.

Infosys—Export-Oriented Software Services

The world today celebrates the story of Infosys and of its intrepid first-generation entrepreneur-founders. But how did it all begin?

Here is a quick snapshot of the work experiences that shaped Narayana Murthy to the point of founding Infosys.

After completing his MTech in IIT Kanpur, he had a knowledge-deepening first job managing the computer centre at IIM Ahmedabad. He then had a stint as a software professional in France, which profoundly influenced his thinking, especially about entrepreneurship. On his return to India, he worked at Systems Research International, a Pune-based think-tank. By the late 1970s, Murthy was heading the software division of Patni Computer Systems (PCS). Narendra Patni, an alumnus of MIT, and his brothers had founded PCS after a decade of experience at their successful start-up, Data Conversion Inc., which focused on offshore-based typesetting services for leading publishers. PCS's primary business was as a sales partner to Data General Computers, a leading American minicomputer company in India. To fulfil the export commitments that came along with its import of computers, PCS would use some of the computer time of the machines it sold in India to develop software for Data General. This prompted PCS to hire Murthy, who in turn recruited an A-team of programmers. Murthy's team of software professionals included N.S. Raghavan, Nandan Nilekani, Kris Gopalakrishnan, S.D. Shibulal, K. Dinesh and Ashok Arora.

Soon Murthy was raring to found a start-up himself: 'As I completed three or four years at PCS, I was itching to become an entrepreneur. I had decided when I was leaving Paris that the only way societies could solve the problem of poverty was by creating jobs, and the only people who could do this were entrepreneurs. Therefore, I wanted to become an entrepreneur and I was waiting for such an opportunity.'[3]

Murthy elucidates four trends in the world of IT that came together to create such an opportunity in IT services[4]—

(1) availability of super minicomputers like the Data General MV/8000, DEC VAX-11/780, and availability of minicomputers from Prime that provided computing power almost as good as the IBM mainframes. They were cheaper too. Murthy believed that companies would buy these minicomputers in large numbers; (2) availability of the Relational Database Management Systems (RDBMS) and a relational model of data[5] on the minicomputers, which made it easier to query and maintain a database, making them efficient for enterprise applications; (3) transaction monitors that checked if a transaction was completed as per the business rules, and which were available on the Data General and VAX minicomputers at a small fraction of the price that IBM used to charge; and (4) plentiful availability of bright engineers from IITs and other institutions, who had hardly any employment opportunities in India. So, there was a demand for high-quality jobs to absorb these engineers.

Thus, Infosys was established by seven engineers in Pune, India, with an initial capital of US$250 in 1981. All the co-founders of Infosys were young professionals who were starting their careers and had decided to give the entrepreneurship opportunity a shot. Kris Gopalakrishnan reminisces about those days: 'Murthy decided that he will set up his own company, Infosys, and he talked to me, Nandan and N.S. Raghavan, and subsequently to Shibulal, Dinesh and Ashok Arora. All of us, of course, said yes. In my case it was a simple decision to make at the age of twenty-five. I didn't think too much. It was an opportunity to work with an interesting team. It was an opportunity to create a business, and if things didn't work out, I could, of course, go and join somebody else. That was my thought process at that point in time.'[6]

All the co-founders of Infosys had exceptional technical capabilities in different aspects of programming. Shibulal reasons why he was picked by Murthy: 'I believe I was asked because of my knowledge of business applications and the systems side. Generally, there is a Chinese wall between the COBOL program and the assembler program. I was one of the few people who could actually do both.'[7]

Interestingly, Murthy could not join Infosys right at its start. 'I had given my word that I would complete two critical projects with PCS before I left them,' he says. 'One was the installation of an advanced real-time system for Bombay Electricity Supply and Transport undertaking, and the second was a user-acceptance of a complex distributed process control system at Rourkela Steel plant. Even though I had resigned from PCS on 29 December 1980, I walked out of it on 18 March 1982. And that's when I joined Infosys as a founder-employee.'[8]

Infosys's first customer was Data Basics Corporation. The Infosys team, while at PCS, had developed for it the Comprehensive Apparel Manufacturing Package (CAMP) on Data General computers. When Data Basics knew that this team was starting up, they asked Infosys to help in customizing CAMP for various customer installations. Infosys soon added GE to its list of notable clients. Raghavan says, 'Many were surprised (that GE chose Infosys) because we didn't have an IBM mainframe machine. We had to use simulators and develop the system. But still, GE thought we would be able to do that, and that was the confidence we created.'[9]

While the initial projects that Infosys undertook were executed mostly onsite, it started work on a game-changing idea, the global delivery model (GDM). This was a mission of Murthy and his co-founders. Murthy says, 'As we sat down in 1981 in my apartment in Mumbai to discuss what Infosys should do, it was very clear that our aspirations were to add value to our customers from India.

Somewhere around 1984–85, we wrote down what we termed the 'global delivery model'. Even though it became popular only around 1991–92, the formal document was written earlier. Basically, the global delivery model recognizes the principle of globalization. Globalization is all about sourcing capital from where it is cheapest, sourcing talent from where it is best available, producing where it is most cost-effective, and selling wherever the markets are, without being constrained by national boundaries.'[10] The idea of GDM was being put into practice even at Infosys's first client. Kris says, 'For Data Basics, we developed the next version of software from India, sent it via two or three magnetic tapes with different couriers, which would take fourteen days to reach the client. And then we would go to the US and instal the software, and support and maintain it.'[11]

Infosys chugged along at a sedate rate through the 1980s. In 1983, Infosys acquired a Data General MV 8000 computer in order to train its employees and do software delivery from India. But it did not need the computer full time and found a willing client in MICO (now Bosch), who not only agreed to instal the machine but also took on Infosys as a software vendor. Infosys consequently shifted its operations from Pune to Bengaluru. In 1987, Infosys established a marketing presence in the US by establishing a joint venture with Kurt Salmon Associates, a premier management consulting firm to the retail and consumer products industries.

But the Infosys founders soon found themselves facing an existential question. Kris recalls that moment and says, '1989 was a milestone or a kind of traumatic time for Infosys. Because, in eight years of operations, we had not grown much in terms of revenue, in terms of employees. There was an offer of about US$1 million to buy Infosys. But we decided, of course, not to sell at that point. We gave ourselves three years—to actually invest in

The Infosys team, including N.R. Narayana Murthy (extreme left, front row), N.S. Raghavan (3rd from left, front row), Kris Gopalakrishnan (4th from left, front row), S.D. Shibulal (extreme right, front row), and Ashok Arora (extreme right, back row, behind Kris) with the Data General MV 8000 computer. Courtesy: Infosys Archives

the company and grow the company. So, 1991 was an opportune time for us. Luckily, the government opened up the economy and we were able to now invest in the company, invest in sales and marketing, invest in other aspects of the business. And thus started the journey of laying the foundation to create a scalable organization.'[12] The team's self-belief and commitment to build an organization for the long term helped Infosys move on to its golden era of the 1990s.

Nandan Nilekani succinctly summarizes the thinking at Infosys at that time: 'In the early 1990s, before we went public, we realized that the Indian market was going to be very competitive for human capital. As India liberalized, large global companies would come in and they would all compete for the same graduates, from the same colleges and IITs. We realized that we have to be a very distinguished and attractive brand for people—to become the best employer in the country, which meant attractive stock options, creating world-class infrastructure where people constantly learn new things, and have opportunities to travel abroad.'[13] Infosys needed capital to fulfil this aspiration.

Infosys was the second entrepreneurial Indian software company after Mastek to go public on the Indian stock exchange in 1993. Infosys is probably one of the best performing stocks in the Indian stock market. It has given investors who bought the stock in 1993 about 2000 times in returns after twenty-five years of its listing! In fact, Infosys's ESOPs (Employee Stock Options) programme has become part of the folklore of Indian industry.

Raghavan tells the story of how the ESOPs were conceptualized: 'I was discussing with Murthy that we should come out with ESOPs. The quantum didn't matter, but (an employee) got a feeling of ownership of the company. Then we had arguments about who should receive them and how much. Ultimately, he said okay. We reserved some percentage of ESOPs for the star performers—that was the chairman's quota. The rest we distributed among all the employees . . . That's how ESOPs were started. There were no rules and regulations governing what the value of ESOPs should be. We were able to give ESOPs at Rs 100 or something similar, irrespective of what the value of share was. I think that was a great deal; it helped us create several millionaires and it was a good scheme. And I was really proud of it.'[14] Another moment of glory for Indian IT came when Infosys listed on the NASDAQ in 1999, a first for an Indian company.

Infosys's Start-up Days

In its initial years, the founders of Infosys were all techno-managers and were leading from the front in client projects. The early days entailed an intense focus on developing technical capabilities, fine-tuning project management, creating a new business model, establishing value systems and building a world-class company. This was the secret sauce that positioned Infosys on the growth path, making it one of the most successful start-ups of all time. Outside of work, the founders took on some interesting responsibilities!

A Techno-Manager Rolls up His Sleeves—by N.R. Narayana Murthy[15]

'When we installed our data centre in the early 1980s, we were supposed to provide a 1401 simulator on the Data General MV/8000 computer. Shibulal and I were responsible for that, but we didn't have a machine in India at that time. So, we sat down and wrote the code on a piece of paper. It was about 15,000 lines long. Then I took it to New York, where we got a free machine between 10 p.m. and 6 a.m. at the office of Data Basics Corporation, and I tested the whole thing. For me to get that free machine I had to work at Data Basics on their projects between 4 p.m. and 10 p.m. So, the point I am making is, by getting into the technical details of a project I could lead from the front.'

Aspirations for Good Corporate Governance and a Global Brand—by Nandan Nilekani[16]

'We were all working together under the leadership of Narayana Murthy, and we felt that the time had come for the company where people with technology backgrounds and software skills themselves should be growing it. Our goal from day one was to create a very professional company that recognized merit, that had high standards of corporate governance, that was sharing wealth with employees, that pursued the highest (standards of) quality, and that had a global focus. We wanted to create a global brand. So, all these ambitions, or desires, or aspirations, were part of the founding team when we set up Infosys in 1981.'

Hardware and Product Ideas at Infosys—by Kris Gopalakrishnan[17]

'We decided to do something in India, and two initiatives were taken—one was to venture into manufacturing and hardware, and the second was to develop a software product for the Indian market. That software product became the banking software product Finacle, in later years. On the hardware side, we chose the telex machines, which were imported those days. We said we would use PC platforms and develop a telex machine for the Indian market. We developed the product and sold it to the Department of Telecommunications, which managed the post offices. And we successfully installed several of these systems, which remained operational till recently, when telegrams were discontinued in India. But from an Infosys perspective, we found that having just one client, the government, was making it difficult, and so in the 1987–89 time frame, we sold the business to another company.'

Value Systems—by S.D. Shibulal[18]

'Mr Murthy and I were doing a testing in MICO, and he found one digit different. Not even a digit, one character was placed a space away. He said, "Shibu, why is this happening?" And, in the middle of the night, he called up Mr Venkatrajan, who was the CIO of MICO at that point in time. He (Venkatrajan) was not very happy (since he was requested to come over to the office) . . . He looked at the issue and laughed. And told us, "This is happening because there is a bug in the original software, and has nothing to do with you guys." The next morning, they (MICO) were supposed to start the testing and user-acceptance of the system. Mr Venkatrajan comes in at eight and tells us, without any testing, "I am accepting it now because these guys are so diligent. No point in spending much time testing it all over again." So, value systems matter quite a lot, in fact a whole lot!'

Technical Capability—by K. Dinesh[19]

'We couldn't be just good only in application software, we also had to be good in systems software associated with application . . . Data General came out with its new hardware in a 32-bit architecture. So now, routines which were in assembly language (for a 16-bit machine) wouldn't work in 32-bit architecture. So, we had to go to their offices in Orlando and make sure that all these routines worked in 32-bit before the application could be ported to a Data General 32-bit operating system . . . That was the strength of Infosys, we could bring the application knowledge, system knowledge and business knowledge to deliver solutions to the clients.'

A Chef in France—by N.S. Raghavan[20]

'We had this project to develop a distributed management application package for Reebok, France. Murthy and Dinesh were the first to go. They took an apartment in Paris . . . a small apartment . . . it had only one bathroom and one room. Murthy used to cut the vegetables for our meals and Dinesh used to wash the vessels. I was the chef mixing all the ingredients, and I used to make sambhar with some sabji. We worked very hard and we all had a very good time.'

Start-ups Find their Own Unique Domains of Operation

In the 1980s, we saw start-ups emerge in various IT domains, differentiating themselves by focusing on different geographies (with an India, US or Asia focus), or on their unique offerings (IT services, solutions or products). Infosys started as an export-oriented software company right from the beginning. TCS was a software services company focused on the Indian market, and later went on to focus on exports. HCL and Wipro were hardware companies that pivoted to software services exports. We now turn our attention to the stories of other start-ups, like Mastek, FutureSoft, IIS Infotech, Tally and NIIT.

Mastek: Enterprise Solutions

As we briefly saw earlier, Mastek had its origins in the dormitories of IIM Ahmedabad, where its founders Ashank Desai, R. Sundar and Ketan Mehta did their MBA. Mastek, a name derived from 'management and software technology', was formally incorporated in 1982. Ashank remembers their first project: 'We went to Richardson Hindustan, now Procter & Gamble, because they had a very unique problem of production planning for Vicks (a cough and cold medicine). In the rainy season, the requirement for the product was high, but their production capacities were low, and so they had to stock it. It was one fine operations research problem.'[21] In fact, Gurcharan Das, then CEO of Richardson Hindustan, encouraged the Mastek team, telling them that they would be given a bonus if they delivered on time, but fined if they got delayed. The Mastek team did win the bonus for the project!

As an Indian software start-up, Mastek did things differently. It had a management solutions and product soul in its initial years, and developed an enterprise resource planning (ERP) product called MAMIS in the mid-1980s. Mastek's first international expansion was to Singapore, and not to the US, as was the case with other IT companies. In fact, Mastek's move to software services came in a serendipitous way when a Singapore customer had an urgent requirement for IBM RPG (a high-level programming language) programmers. Ashank was so confident of his team's can-do spirit that he agreed to the requirement without even knowing what RPG meant! He managed to buy from a pharmaceutical company in Mumbai some computer time at night on their IBM System/36, on which his team practised and mastered RPG in a couple of weeks. The team also managed to wow the Singapore customer with its RPG skills. Ashank says, 'This is a story of the Indian programmer— he learns (a program) in fifteen days, many times learns a language on a flight. The Indian programmer can pick up pretty fast and do something he or she has not seen before.'[22]

Another feather in Mastek's cap was that they became the first Indian software company to go public in 1992. Mastek transitioned into an enterprise software services company with industry vertical solutions from the mid-1990s. Much later, in 2005, the Mastek team created Majesco, an insurance software product company, which went on to become the first Indian product company to get listed on the New York Stock Exchange.

FutureSoft: Networking and Telecom Software

Not all Indian IT entrepreneurs were engineers, or from an IIT or an IIM. K.V. Ramani, a physics graduate, got into IT after completing an IBM training course in the early 1970s. He started as an unpaid trainee for a couple of years, before becoming a programmer in the computer division of Shaw Wallace. He cut his programming teeth developing and deploying ERP-like software programs, first for the agriculture division of Shaw Wallace and then for the Malaysian Sime Darby trading conglomerate.

By the mid-1980s, Shaw Wallace started work with a Danish company, Christian Rovsing, and the European and the US markets for software services, and Ramani got exposed to core technology areas like computer networking. This coincided with some macro-shifts happening in the IT market. As Ramani explains, 'AT&T, which is on the telecom side, acquired NCR . . . they wanted to fight the threat of IBM coming into communications by getting into computing. Computers and communications were merging . . . Therefore this was great place to get into. That's how I started FutureSoft in 1985.'[23]

FutureSoft's first project was for Christian Rovsing, which was developing a computer networking software for its client,

American Airlines, to help the airline seamlessly communicate with its partners. Ramani, trying to take advantage of an Indian policy that allowed computer equipment to come into India without payment of any duty, requested Christian Rovsing to ship the testing equipment on loan to FutureSoft for the duration of the project. But the customs department, which came under the finance ministry, did not recognize the import policy promulgated by the commerce ministry and did not clear the equipment.

Ramani then had to park himself in Delhi and coordinate between the commerce and finance ministries. This involved some action that would have done a Bollywood thriller proud. Ramani says, 'So, I went to my hotel, put on my best European suit and rented the best car I could get in Delhi. And I told the driver, "Go straight in front of the back gate and jam the brakes, as if a VIP is coming." The ministers typically used this gate to enter. I walked past all the security guards and police, and they saluted me. The funny thing is that at the front gate they would not have given me a pass. That's how I got in.'[24] And customs did release the equipment. Think again if you believed that Indian entrepreneurs did not have chutzpah!

FutureSoft was the first in India to develop communication stacks (software that allowed a computer to implement a particular communication standard). Ramani says with pride, 'When we went to a COMDEX show or a CEBIT show, we were not in the software pavilion, but in the datacom and networking or telecom pavilion. Our neighbours used to be the giants like Alcatel or NEC. We used to be selling software and we were the only Indian company in the pavilion. At one point in time, we were the world's largest protocol stack owners.'[25]

In 2004, FutureSoft merged with Hughes Software Services India to form Flextronics India, which after subsequent acquisitions became part of Capgemini in 2019.

IIS Infotech: Focus on Offshoring Projects, UK and Specific Industry Domains

Saurabh Srivastava started International Informatics Solutions (which was subsequently renamed IIS Infotech) in 1989, after successful stints with established companies like IBM and Tata Burroughs. IIS Infotech was a software services company with a different strategy. It had a novel business model with a focus on specific geographical markets and industry segments. Srivastava says, 'Firstly, (I realized) my competition would be Tata Unisys or TCS; they're much bigger. In the next three years I couldn't be among the top three software services company (if I competed directly). So, what could I be in the top three? Most of the work being done by the big companies was 'body-shopping' (simply providing IT professionals on contract). In those days Tata Unisys had about 15 per cent of employees offshore, about 150 people. And that was it. I could scale to 150 people and manage that as offshore services. So, my first focus was on being offshore, doing full project life cycles. The second thing was, everybody (other Indian software companies) was in the US and I wanted to go to the UK. It was harder to do business there, but if you got it right, you were protected. And the third thing was focusing on financial services. I had a very clear strategy of how we wanted to focus IIS Infotech.'[26]

The offshore services focus of IIS Infotech presented some challenges. While the typical model essentially consisted of selling the expertise of the Indian software professional who would work on client projects onsite, an offshore project meant selling a promise of delivery quality from India. This meant that IIS Infotech had to invest a significant portion of its profits in its early years to obtain an ISO 9001[27]/ TickIT[28] certification, which would boost its clients' confidence in the offshore delivery model. In doing so, IIS Infotech became a pioneer among Indian software services companies in following the quality management and certification path. In fact, from the 1990s, Indian software services companies were the exemplars worldwide in obtaining the highest SEI CMM (Software Engineering Institute Capability Maturity Model) certifications.

IIS Infotech did well, and was sold to the F.I. Group, a British software and systems company, in 1997. It merged with other portfolio companies of the group and was renamed Xansa.

Tally Solutions for Accounting: Enterprise Software Products for the PC Era

Bharat Goenka latched on to programming after listening to a lecture on FORTRAN by a professor from IISc, and started Peutronics, a software training company, in the early 1980s. This was also the time when Goenka's father, who was running a textile factory, heard from computer sales executives about how a computer could help his business. Goenka remembers his father's approach towards the computer—it was business-oriented rather than technical: 'When I buy a car, I want to be a driver and not a mechanic. When I buy a computer, I want to run my business and not become a computer expert,' he would tell Goenka.[29]

Armed with a PC that he got for his birthday, Goenka decided to help his father's factory keep accounts. His father's words motivated

Goenka to innovate on what he describes today as 'noiseless and codeless software'. Codeless, because a business user did not need to know programming or use codes to access the software. For example, users should have the freedom to name an account head 'Travel Allowance' rather than use a code like 'T001'. Noiseless, since the software should allow business users to enter data as they would without a computer. For example, they could enter a date either as '1 Jan 2020' or '1/1/2020' and the software would recognize that they were the same. This in-house accounting package was the genesis of an accounting software called PFA (Peutronics Financial Accounting). When Goenka hired an advertising agency to launch a campaign for the software, the agency suggested a new name, 'Tally'. Bharat and his father were initially not keen on the name, but to their surprise soon found 'Tally' rolling off their tongues easily.

The launch of PCs in India in the mid-1980s and its quick adoption by companies gave Tally a standard hardware platform to ride on. But it was not an easy journey. Goenka says, 'The product industry (in India) remains glamorous on paper but it doesn't remain glamorous in the market. It is not an easy market to sell due to the absence of a strong sales ecosystem.'[30] As did Diwakar Nigam at Softek, Bharat too faced the challenges of software piracy and the lack of a software sales ecosystem. The modern software product start-ups in India should thank these intrepid product warriors for their toils. By the late 1980s, Tally became well engrained in the accounts departments of Indian companies, where it continues to be popular even today.

With hardware and software available, and latent demand emerging in different industries, computer adoption was limited primarily by the capability of the human resources in user-organizations to leverage IT. Most employees in Indian organizations had not even seen a computer, let alone know how to use one. It was seeing this opportunity that NIIT was started—to make it easy for everyone to learn to work with computers.

NIIT: IT Training for Software Professionals and MIS Managers

Rajendra Pawar was among the earliest employees of HCL. From his vantage point in its corporate planning function, he had a ringside view of the Indian computer market. Pawar believed there were two constraints that came in the way of Indian companies realizing the benefits of IT. First, a shortage of talent to write programs and run the computer infrastructure. Second, the knowledge gap among the corporate leadership teams on how to adopt IT in their companies. Pawar and his IIT Delhi friend, Vijay Thadani, decided to take the entrepreneurial plunge to address these gaps in the Indian market and launched National Institute of Information Technology (NIIT) in 1981. Pawar says, 'It was about bringing people and computers together successfully, and people here were not just youngsters who wanted to learn computers but also leaders who had to embrace technology and leverage it.'[31]

They launched NIIT at the CSI Annual Conference in Chennai in 1982 with the tag line, 'An idea whose time has come'. They licensed video-based instruction materials in the IT domain from a company that Pawar had met at the National Computer Conference in the US. Quickly, NIIT expanded from its first centre in Mumbai to other cities. They also tapped into their alma mater and brought in PhD students from IIT Delhi to train NIIT students. NIIT, much like start-ups today, realized early on that attracting the best talent was the key to growing a profitable business. Pawar says, 'In 1984 we were the largest recruiters of MBAs (from IIM). Out of the nineteen people who majored in systems that year, we hired eighteen. We could hire the talent because people were interested in the field. We were in both the learning business and the consulting business (of IT).'[32] Apart from bringing in courses on computer programming and information systems, NIIT is credited with introducing innovative programmes on information systems planning for corporate leaders.

NIIT pioneered the franchisee model for centres, especially in smaller towns. This was an answer to the challenge of expanding pan-India without diluting quality. NIIT preferred to provide franchise opportunities to young professionals working in good companies in the cities who were willing to go back to their home towns. In the mid-1980s, NIIT also started a software services division, which in 2004 was spun off into a separate company, NIIT Technologies.

Pawar reflects on NIIT's impact and says, 'We created hundreds of entrepreneurs, who ultimately went to many countries. And that model of building a very strong control on process, using a lot of technology and methodology, intensive training of people, and right choice of partners . . . I think that helped us scale and sustain. And build computer literacy at a societal level . . . preparing society to embrace technology.'[33] Education is still the focus of NIIT's founders. In 2009, Pawar and Thadani started NIIT University, which is one of India's premier private universities today.

Inspired by the emerging vibrancy of the software industry, IT MNCs, especially from the US, took baby steps to set up software subsidiaries in India. Let us look at the advent of Texas Instruments (TI) in Bengaluru.

TI's Software Subsidiary Inspires Other IT MNCs to Explore India for Talent

TI was one of the dominant semiconductor companies in the 1980s. It realized the potential Asia held, both as a market and as a talent hub, and wanted to set up an R&D subsidiary in the region. Srini Rajam, an alumnus of IISc, was among the first employees of TI in India, and later went on to become its head. He recounts TI's decision-making process in identifying India as the destination of its Asian subsidiary in 1986. 'The leadership for that came from Dr Mohan Rao who was an executive president at TI and also in charge of advanced product development. He was working very closely with the chairman of TI at the time, Mark Shepherd. They started at a region first, looking at many countries as options—China, Philippines, others . . . and then chose India. Then, many cities in India were considered, and finally Bengaluru stood out in terms of the educational environment, proximity to institutions like the IISc and also the ecosystem of R&D that was already in Bengaluru through the government R&D institutions and companies here. It was a great selection process that lasted about twelve months.'[34]

TI's Bengaluru R&D subsidiary primarily worked with the global teams of TI in their core engineering related to product development using software tools for Very Large Scale Integration (VLSI) design. It was sophisticated work and TI ensured that the Bengaluru office was suitably equipped for this collaborative work. TI installed a state-of-the-art satellite communication system, an earth station, in its Millers Road office in the heart of Bengaluru. Rajam elucidates the reason behind this arrangement: 'The R&D centre in India had to be equal to any R&D centre around the world in terms of infrastructure, in terms of the capabilities. The only way (to achieve this) was to have a dedicated station, a dedicated communication system that would provide the same bandwidth to the engineers that they would get anywhere in the world. Immediately, there was an article in *Newsweek* that had a picture of the station as well as all the engineers standing around it . . . saying we were equal to the rest of the world in terms of capability.'[35]

One of the clauses in TI's licence from the Government of India to operate this earth station mandated the stationing of an officer from DoT at its Bengaluru office. The only role of this officer was to ensure that no official government secrets or sensitive India-related information were sent via satellite communication!

The R&D subsidiary model of TI became one that other IT MNCs like HP and Motorola would emulate. Rajam recalls, 'This was a proof of concept of something that was not only viable but strategically very important for the corporation. And TI was willing to share its experiences and stories with other MNCs. And help them get started in terms of the infrastructure or in terms of going about things in India. TI thought that this was something you did to build the multinational R&D community in India, which in turn would help everybody.'[36]

This feeling of helping everybody when it came to the common aspects of setting up shop, especially with policy and infrastructure, was not only present among the IT MNCs but also among the Indian software companies. They were coming of age and genuinely felt that they had a very different set of issues from what the domestic hardware industry had. The time was ripe for the Indian software industry to have an industry association of its own.

Genesis of NASSCOM: Software Industry Emerges from the Shadows of the Hardware Industry

As we saw earlier, Computer Society of India (CSI) was the first Indian association for computer professionals. It comprised members predominantly from academia and government, and, in the 1970s and 1980s, was the largest in the field in terms of membership. The annual conference of the CSI was like the Comdex of India, and saw computer product launches.

Over time, the management information systems (MIS) professionals and hardware manufacturers found themselves in a state of tension, with the research and public sector dominance in the CSI and decided to form the Manufacturers Association for Information Technology (MAIT) in 1982. Bhaskar Pramanik, who was then working for NELCO, a Tata Group hardware company, recalls attending the meeting that resulted in MAIT: 'I remember very clearly. It was in the Taj Mahal Hotel and it was convened by Mr Prem Shivdasani from ICIM. He had invited Mr Azim Premji and Mr Ratan Tata, and I accompanied him. He had also invited Shiv Nadar and others. Vinay Bharat Ram from DCM was also there. He was talking about the dynamics of the IT industry and the fact that nobody was really making very much money. I remember everyone talking about how to develop the market, collaborate and ensure that the customers got the best value.'[37]

In the latter part of the 1980s, CSI continued to be focused on new technology, research and skill development. MAIT was busy lobbying the Indian government to retain the protectionist policies that would help domestic hardware manufacturers keep the MNC hardware vendors at bay. While the software industry was a part of MAIT, the software companies felt that they were not given a rightful hearing at that crucial juncture. The fledgling software industry, especially software exporters, wanted to make a focused representation to the government of India on issues like India's branding in overseas markets, challenges in setting up data communications infrastructure, and in finding professionals who were trained in the current technologies. They realized that an industry association for software companies was an idea whose time had come.

Saurabh Srivastava recalls how the idea of NASSCOM was sown one wintry evening in Washington DC: 'The kind of reception we got abroad was people saying, "Software from India? Are you serious!" We had to mend this together . . . get together as a group, start to market ourselves as an industry. We started what was called Software India Seminars in those days. Except for TCS and Tata Unisys, everybody else was a start-up. We didn't have money, and so we got the Department of Electronics to help subsidize some of it . . . Fifteen to eighteen of us would go to these seminars. On one of these trips . . . I think a seven- or eight-city tour in 1988 . . . When we finished it, we all got together and we said we need to create an industry body.'[38]

Harish Mehta, who was with Hinditron and later founded Onward Novell, and was also a founder of NASSCOM, reminisces about how the idea for a separate association got stronger: 'There were some thirty to forty of us . . . Saurabh, Nandan, Ashank, Ramani and others . . . who were involved in the software business. We all had similar issues. Saurabh and I discussed this and said, "Let us form an association." We went around the country—to Bengaluru, Delhi, Kolkata—we met whoever was in the software business and we decided to form the association. Whether it was Narasimhan at Wipro, or Joe Cletus at DCM, or Nirmal Jain at

TCS, they were all coming together (with us). Some of them had a hardware piece also. So they were very reluctant to officially go against the government position. Also, MAIT was strongly opposed to NASSCOM taking birth. And their thought process was that more associations would fragment (the industry) and government would exploit the multiple voices. We said no, we had to create an identity for software, and it had to be done only through a separate identity like NASSCOM.'[39]

Ashank Desai brings out an important aspect of NASSCOM's culture, that of subsuming individual interest for the greater good of the software industry: 'We (NASSCOM) told the government to help us import software at a low cost so that we could train many people. They (DoE) said, "You are asking zero per cent duty (on software imports). How are you going to protect yourself?" Some of us may have suffered, but it was required for the industry. We (Mastek) were producing MAMIS; zero duty meant that all other (imported) packages would come at low price. We could not take that view as a company, but (took the view of) what was good for the country and industry. The kind of debate and consensus we had was the foundation of NASSCOM. We had a culture of trust and informality, of working together for the betterment of the industry.'[40]

K.V. Ramani highlights two reasons for NASSCOM's success in its early years: 'One, we had a consistent policy of staying together as an industry. We would collaborate and cooperate in NASSCOM, but as individual companies would go out and compete . . . Even today that is a success factor of NASSCOM's. And the second reason was Dewang Mehta (president of NASSCOM), who was an outstanding personality. He was a media person, he was an articulate speaker, he was a writer, he would do a fundraiser—everything that was needed to make this industry succeed. Foreign governments and agencies used to seek his help to replicate this model.'[41]

NASSCOM grew from strength to strength as a pre-eminent industry association in India, and its work in setting the strategic agenda and shaping policy for the IT industry became well known. One of its moments of crowning glory came at a very difficult time for the industry, when it helped to quickly resurrect Satyam Computers in 2009, a fascinating story that we will look at soon.

While the 1980s saw a slew of software start-ups, MNC software subsidiaries, and an association for software companies emerging in India, it also witnessed the struggles and successes of a few mission-mode government computerization projects—projects that impacted the average Indian citizen and helped computers gain widespread acceptance in India.

The Indian Railways 'Passenger Reservation System' (PRS) Project: The Story of the Common Man and Computers, and How It Inspired an Attitudinal Change in India

'Let it now be the glory of Imperial Britain to confer on the same people a boon of inestimable value in the form of a work of the greater extent and utility which the world had yet seen; a work, which, by its facilities of intercommunion and rapid conveyance of the super bounding products of an exhaustless soil to the great emporia of commerce shall help to arouse the dormant energies of millions . . . and exalt her to her rightful position as one of the most magnificent empires under the sun.'

This is an extract from the 1844 proposal of Rowland Macdonald Stephenson of the East Indian Railway Company for large-scale railway construction in India.[42]

Since the plying of the first passenger train in India in 1853, Indian Railways today has become the third largest rail network in the world, running 21,000 trains and ferrying 23 million passengers every day.[43] Its Passenger Reservation System (PRS) project, implemented in the mid-1980s, remains one of India's most visible and successful government-led IT projects. Let us discover how general elections in India, robots in a factory in Japan, a three-hour delay at the reservation counter for a CEO of an Indian IT company, and some good old-fashioned project and risk management led to the success of the iconic PRS project.

The PRS Project: An Introduction

The modern reader, being used to the comforts of online ticket booking, might not fully appreciate the challenges of making a railway reservation in the manual-ticketing era. Can you imagine having separate counters at the railway station for each train? Can you imagine standing in queue overnight to buy a train ticket (and not for the latest iPhone)?

Subroto Bagchi, co-founder of Mindtree, says, 'Railway computerization was triggered by the fact that the average commuter had so much difficulty buying a ticket, so much difficulty getting a berth. It was like going on a pilgrimage. And if you couldn't get a ticket, then you probably had to deal with touts in the railway ticketing system. So, against this backdrop comes the idea that you could bring speed, efficiency, transparency, cut the middleman out . . . there was a groundswell of support for anything that could make an ordinary person buy a train ticket easily.'[44]

The PRS project, though, was not the first instance of computerization at Indian Railways (IR). Through the 1960s and 1970s, IR had been using IBM 1401s in their zonal headquarters and at the Railway Board for payroll and freight accounting applications. A 1977 railway task force identified two key areas for computer applications—freight operations and passenger reservations. But the PRS was not considered financially viable unless it was developed along with the freight IT system.[45] A few years later, a team comprising officials from IR, ECIL and CMC went on a study tour evaluating five railway systems around the world (France, UK, Germany, US, and Canada). The study team realized that the IR context was rather unique, given its size, complexity and transaction volumes. For instance, in 1984, IR handled over 5 million passengers who travelled on over 600 long-distance trains, with around 50,000 reservation requests.[46] They concluded that a buy option was not suitable and that only an indigenously developed PRS might work for India. The Railway Board warmed up to the idea of implementing the PRS independent of the freight system. Some positive winds were blowing for the PRS project in the political circles too—the general elections were due in 1984 and the PRS was seen as a potentially people-friendly project.

Commenting on the back-channel machinations that led to approval of the PRS project, Ramani says, 'In 1984, at a dinner table, P.P. Gupta (MD of CMC) sat next to Madhavrao Scindia (then railways minister) and sold him the idea. Scindia suggested that it be done for Northern Railways first and be implemented in Delhi. Within ten months, CMC delivered the PRS to them. The moment it started working in one city, people's representatives stood in Parliament and started demanding the reservation system for their cities. We should hand it to the research lab in CMC and to P.P. Gupta's team which implemented all of that.'[47]

The PRS Pilot Project and beyond

Indeed, by the time Indian Railways (IR) tendered for development of the PRS in 1984, CMC became the front runner for implementation of the project. It had developed a prototype PRS with a single train, and had an informal arrangement with IR at Secunderabad to study the railway systems and obtain feedback on its prototype.

Fifteen personnel each from IR and CMC spent the next fifteen months, sometime in 1984–85, finalizing the specifications for the system before they undertook the pilot. Such an elaborate preparation proved crucial to the project's success. The software for the pilot project was written in FORTRAN, used a flat-file data structure to enhance speed, and was implemented on a Digital Equipment Corporation (DEC) VAX-11/750 system. According to V. Rajaraman, it was the first time in the world that such a system was developed for online transaction processing on a VAX cluster. IR rolled the PRS prototype into service in November 1985 on two trains—the Tamil Nadu Express and the Grand Trunk Express, both running between New Delhi and Chennai. And computerized railway reservations became a reality in India.

By 1986, IR created an autonomous organization called Centre for Railway Information Systems (CRIS) to develop and manage its important IT systems. CRIS first implemented the next version of the PRS, called Integrated Multi-train Passenger Reservation System (IMPRESS), and then began work on the Countrywide Network of Computerized Enhanced Reservation and Ticketing (CONCERT) system, leveraging leased lines and satellite communications technology to make railway reservation accessible even in remote areas in India. CONCERT was implemented first in Secunderabad in 1994, and by the year 2000, fifteen years after the modest start of the PRS project, Indian Railways achieved the goal of providing 'from anywhere to anywhere' reservations.

Recounting the technology efforts that his DEC team put into the PRS project, Som Mittal says, 'Digital was a major technology provider for the PRS project. The system was distributed, and so you had to go for minicomputers. VMS (VAX operating system) was a very stable software on which the application was built. The biggest problem came when I had to buy a ticket from Mumbai for a train not originating there, say a ticket from Delhi to Chennai. We couldn't do that because the databases were not updated. We then used a robust technology called RTR (reliable transaction router) which would ensure that when a transaction took place in one region, all databases across regions were updated simultaneously, because we could not issue the same ticket twice.'[48]

In 2002, the PRS journey reached a momentous milestone when it became available over the Internet. The Indian Railways Catering and Tourism Corporation (IRCTC), a public-sector organization under the ministry of railways, developed the web front-end on the BroadVision software platform and integrated it with the PRS. This was one of India's earliest and now largest e-commerce sites—it has witnessed a phenomenal growth journey, from a sale of twenty-nine tickets on its first day to 7.78 lakh tickets daily and accounting for 70 per cent of reserved tickets sold in 2018–19.[49]

The Passenger Reservation System had truly arrived in India. Commenting on the far-reaching impact of IR's PRS, Som Mittal remarks, 'If the system went down for some reason, I used to get a call from the Railway Board, informing me of questions raised in Parliament and the two-kilometre-long queue at the station! I was stressed about receiving calls from two of my customers—the Railways and the Bombay Stock Exchange, because both systems touched the lives of maximum citizens.'[50]

What explained the success of the PRS project?

The Exemplary Risk-Management of the PRS Project Led to its Success

Rather than formulating the entire PRS as a single large networked application connecting all stations in India and costing Rs 100 crore—a proposal that surely would have been stillborn—the IR management conceived it as an application covering just New Delhi and costing Rs 10 crore at first.[51]

From a project management perspective, the PRS team built sufficient redundancies into their plan in order to de-risk the implementation. For instance, the sufficiently long time (of fifteen months) allocated for the project-scope definition permitted several refinements of the requirements document and resulted in a pilot implementation that did not require much reworking. In another instance, during the pilot-release phase, the team had a parallel-run for fifteen days, during which the reservations made by the PRS system were compared with the manual ones to ensure accuracy. The Indian IT companies embraced this philosophy of 'de-risking' as they rapidly grew in later years.

From a human capital perspective, IR undertook significant risk-mitigating measures. IR assured its labour unions that the PRS project would not lead to any retrenchment. The Railway Board cited the case of use of robots in the Japanese auto industry.

Between 1979 and 1984, about 10,000 robots were used in the Japanese automobile industry, replacing 7000 workers. At the same time, about 60,000 new jobs requiring higher-order skills were created in the industry.[52] IR put into practice what they promised. And even though the accounting workload decreased post PRS-implementation, IR retained the number of reservation counters at its stations, and the counter and back-office staff were given the benefit of working six-hour shifts rather than eight-hour ones. The redundant typists, who used to prepare reservation charts manually, were redeployed as ticket-checking staff. IR also placed a lot of emphasis on training the reservation office staff to operate the computer system.

The PRS project was an outstanding success. Based on a study of the Delhi PRS, mean waiting time for a customer reduced nearly threefold to twenty-four minutes and led to an estimated annual saving of Rs 10 crore to the economy. The employees were not adversely affected from the job perspective. Some post-implementation studies indicated that IR needed 33 per cent more staff to handle the additional workload at 1985 service levels.[53]

The Indian Railways 'Passenger Reservation System'—Anecdotes and Perspectives

Developing a Railway Reservation System Demo—by S. Ramani[54]

S. Ramani from NCSDCT, P.P. Gupta, managing director of Computer Maintenance Corporation (CMC), TIFR and Hemant Sonawala, founder of Hinditron, an early IT services company in India, collaborated on the first international network conference in India in 1980.

Ramani says, 'PPG (P.P. Gupta) had personally gone through a bad experience of standing in a queue (at a railway reservation counter) for several hours one Sunday. He found that experience frustrating. He said, "Computers are not just meant to run payroll sitting on the sixteenth floor of some building in Nariman Point (a business hub in Mumbai). They should impact the quality of life of common people." As the head of a high-tech public-sector company, he asked what we could do about it.'

So they all developed a railway reservation system demo for the conference and later presented it to the chairman of the Railway Board.

Funding for the PRS Project Nearly Stopped—by S. Sadagopan[55]

'In 1989–90, we had an interesting railway minister, George Fernandes, who happened to be a union leader (in his early years). He thought that the railway reservation system was serving only the rich and not the common man. And he was seriously reconsidering the continued funding for the passenger reservation system project.

'I went with a couple of others to meet the minister and ended up discussing how technology and society have to work together. I said, "We as officers can afford an assistant to stand at a railway reservation counter and buy our tickets. But by making the reservation system available outside office hours, on weekends, it will benefit the assistants when they want to book a ticket for themselves. A daily labourer stands to lose a day's wages if he stands in the queue for a long time. In some cases, he may even lose his job just waiting at the reservation counter. So, the reservation system is not just helping the officers and the rich people, it is helping the common man."

The minister remarked, "I hate you guys but you have a point." The meeting started off on a negative note, but by the end the minister had changed his mind and the funding for PRS continued.'

Importance of the Indian Railways Passenger Reservation System—by Kiran Karnik[56]

'I would say that a very good example of a mission-mode project is Indian Railways computerization. This was something many people experienced. It was really a revolution. It was a very (well) directed attempt and an effort, saying we will computerize the (ticket reservation) process and get it going. Keep in mind also that it was not just a technological challenge, or a challenge of creating a software. It was also a major challenge in terms of the societal context, of asking—Would computers really displace people and would they lose jobs? It required a lot of political skill and willpower to get it going. And I contrast that with the banks in India, which were very slow in adopting computerization.'

The PRS project was an eye-opener and caused an attitudinal change among the general public and blue-collar workers in India about computerization. Somewhat inspired by the success of IR's PRS project, some bank unions even accepted limited computerization, overcoming their earlier resistance. But the banks initially failed to manage the human resource aspect well. In contrast to the PRS project, the banking computerization initiative floundered for several years before ushering in the necessary transformation.

History of Banking Computerization in India—the Story of Unions, Euphemisms and the Inevitability of Computerization

It is believed that State Bank of India (SBI) obtained for data processing a unit record machine from ICT (International Computers and Tabulators) in the 1950s and installed it in Kolkata. This was probably the first instance of automation in Indian banking. Soon, SBI's demand for computing power outgrew the capacity of the ICT unit record machine. In the 1960s, SBI migrated to an IBM 1401 electronic computer, which was the workhorse of computing in India then.[57] These machines were used for inter-office reconciliation and statistical analysis.

While Indian banking was taking baby steps in adopting IT, the late 1960s and early 1970s were marked by a tumultuous time in India, dominated by wars and socialistic thinking. The Dandekar Committee Report (1972) prescribed controls for the use of computers in government and industry. The committee's recommendations made it mandatory for organizations to obtain formal agreement from labour before introducing computers. This ensured that rapid bank computerization took a back seat. There was another event in that era that greatly transformed the Indian banking industry in particular—all private-sector banks were nationalized in 1969. The banking sector underwent a metamorphosis post-nationalization—from being just 'money lenders' to being 'agents of development'; from 'banking for the privileged' to 'banking for the masses'. The Government emphasized lending to small businesses, agriculture and weaker sections of the society, and the banking industry witnessed unprecedented expansion. By 1983, the banks had seen a nearly 5 times increase in number of branches and a nearly 12 times increase in the quantum of deposits.[58] While the number of branches, transactions and services increased, the banking systems and processes remained more or less the same, and this put the Indian banking industry under tremendous stress. While the bank managements realized the need for computerization, the employee unions, especially after bank nationalization, adopted a strident view against it.

It is in such a context that we should view the multitude of commissions and committees that the Reserve Bank of India set up towards banking transformation. Computerization proved to be a banking-Sisyphus in this time period.

The Rangarajan Committee (1984) Recommendations and the Advent of 'Advanced Ledger Posting Machines'

The topic of computerization of the banking industry came into the limelight again in 1983–84, when a committee to present a computerization roadmap for the banking industry was set up by the RBI. Dr Manmohan Singh, who was then governor of RBI, asked Dr C. Rangarajan, then deputy governor of RBI, to chair it. Given the tremendous increase in the activities of banks and their geographic spread, the committee observed that a certain degree of mechanization was essential for banks to efficiently perform functions like customer service, housekeeping and data generation for control and monitoring.

Mechanization was envisaged at various levels—branch, regional or zonal office and head office—with varying emphasis for each level. For instance, at the branch level, mechanization was to be implemented as either 'model I' or 'model II'. In model I, a standalone electronic ledger posting machine with an attached memory module was to be installed to perform dedicated functions at different counters. In model II, a single microprocessor-based system was to be installed in a branch.

Recalling the importance of computerization of bank branches, Rangarajan commented in later years: 'Changes in computer and communication technologies have revolutionized the way in which banking is being done. The customers of banks have also become demanding . . . They want the services to be performed very quickly, that is why in the process of computerization, which we had envisaged some years ago, importance was attached to branch-level computerization. The branch provides the greatest interface between the bank and the customer.'[59]

The trade unions were quick to respond, and they declared 1984 as 'anti-computerization year'. As the story goes, the Rangarajan Committee was aware of the trade unions' stand, and the word 'computer' was rarely mentioned. The committee was officially called the Committee on Mechanisation in the Banking Industry (1984). Commenting on how a euphemism for the word 'computer' emerged, Subroto Bagchi says, 'The bank clerks and the unions were up in arms that they would not let computers come in. It was a pervasive perception that computers would take jobs away. Then somebody had a smart idea of not using the word 'computers' and instead calling them 'advanced ledger posting machines (ALPM)'. So, a funny acronym called ALPM came in, and it is interesting how words have a life of their own! And the union leaders also would rather have computerization come in through the back door.'[60]

The Dighe Tribunal of 1982, appointed by the government to adjudicate the dispute between RBI and its employees, empowered RBI to use minicomputers for its operations, provided that there was no retrenchment or displacement of labour of more than

10 per cent. Subsequently, the Indian Banks Association (IBA) entered into a mechanization agreement with the employees' union in 1983.

The banks accordingly undertook various steps, including the setting up of a separate computer policy and planning department, the electronic data processing (EDP) cells in each major bank, empanelling manufacturers of ALPMs, and standardizing hardware and software. The emerging modern computing technology in the form of minicomputers was considered adequate for the volume of work at the branches, and the mainframe, which provided better security features, faster data transmission and message-switching facilities, was chosen for the head office.

How did this period of banking transformation fare? It proved to be a case of a mountain in labour producing a measly mouse. The first reason was the unrelenting attitude of the labour unions against computerization. When they realized that the ALPMs were nothing but computers, their positions hardened. The banks realized that they could not go far without roping in the buy-in of the unions. The second reason was the unpreparedness of the computer vendors. While the vendors pursued the banking gold rush with glee, they were unable to deliver the large number of machines required. One estimate suggested a nearly 40 per cent shortfall in supply of ALPMs.[61] The vendors were ill prepared on the software front too— they had little understanding of actual banking needs and there was little pre-testing of their software. At one bank, over 77 per cent of the ALPMs supplied were not in working order on account of lack of appropriate software and support![62] The final reason was the lackadaisical approach of the bank managements—their frenzy to acquire machines seemed more to meet RBI goals than to achieve bank automation. There were even cases where the machines at the branches were used for playing software games like chess!

Besides the branch-computerization efforts, there were some successful computerization efforts undertaken at the Reserve Bank level. Soon, some winds of banking change began to blow by the turn of the decade.

Computerization in Reserve Bank of India, and a New Committee on Computerization

The Reserve Bank undertook two successful initiatives in the 1980s—computerization of the clearing houses, and the building of a telecommunications network among banks. The cheque-clearing operations were voluminous, repetitive, of a routine nature, and eminently suited for computerization. RBI created a National Clearing Cell in 1983. In the first phase, operations at nine major RBI centres were computerized. To facilitate cheque sorting and to cut delays, high-speed reader/sorter systems driven by a mainframe, the IBM 4381, were installed at each of the four original Indian metros—New Delhi, Mumbai, Kolkata and Chennai.

Under the second initiative, the RBI Committee on Communication Network for Banks and SWIFT Implementation (Society for Worldwide Interbank Financial Telecommunication) recommended, in 1987, the setting up of BANKNET to facilitate interbank fund transfers within India. The ingenuity of the committee was evident when they suggested that the four IBM mainframes in the metros doing the cheque-clearing operations be also used as the hubs for the BANKNET network. The committee also recommended that India should join the international SWIFT network and use the same security and messaging protocols used in SWIFT.

While the 1984 RBI Committee on Mechanisation in the Banking Industry hogs the limelight, the RBI Committee on Computerisation in Banks of 1988 (again chaired by C. Rangarajan) is often missed out in discussions. The phrase 'computerization in banks' was used without apology by this committee. It made an important recommendation that paved the way for digital banking. It endorsed the introduction of credit cards with widespread acceptance across merchant establishments in India to reduce the load on cash and cheque transactions. This committee also recommended the setting up of a network of ATMs in Mumbai as a pilot.[63] It also suggested modalities for implementing online banking.

In the early 1990s, the economic liberalization of India, coupled with the infamous securities scam, hastened the transformation of the banking system. It led to the establishment of the Electronic Funds Transfer (EFT) system and the addressing of several technology issues in the banking industry. The 1990s saw the advent of newly licenced private banks in India which were technologically savvier than the nationalized banks. This transformation of the banking industry also led to the creation of home-grown and world-leading banking software products, which are described later in this book.

While the computerization at Indian Railways and banks impacted the quotidian lives of the average citizen in India, the 1980s also witnessed the country taking on more esoteric computing battles, ones that were fought in the exalted and technological corridors of educational, research and defence-related institutions in India. These were battles that would usher in supercomputing and AI to India.

Laying the Foundation for Supercomputing in India— the Story of the Cray, Computational Fluid Dynamics and the Call for India's Self-Reliance

The seeds of supercomputing were sown in the early 1980s when the Indian Institute of Science (IISc) was planning its seventy-fifth year celebrations. Recounting the discussions that led to this, N. Balakrishnan, who was a young assistant professor at the time and who went on to head the Supercomputing Education and Research Centre at IISc, says: 'Prof. Ramaseshan was the director and he formed a committee with Prof. Roddam Narasimha as the chairman, with Dr Seshagiri and Dr Mathai Joseph as two external experts, and me as a picker boy in the team, to come up with a plan for supercomputing. We soon submitted a proposal to the government (Department of Science and Technology). Things blossomed back again when Prof. C.N.R. Rao took over as the director and Prof. Rajaraman joined IISc (to head the computer centre).'[64]

Balakrishnan, who was part of a supercomputer study team from IISc that visited the US and Europe, says, 'We went to Minneapolis; we went to the offices of Cray and Control Data Corporation; then we also saw machines in Florida and in the UK. A scientist in the UK warned me about supercomputers and said, "Be very careful before you enter into it. Even if the computer doesn't have a job, I can't switch it off." We realized that the supercomputer was an awesome machine, even when it came to consuming power.'[65] The IISc team suggested an onion-layered configuration for the supercomputer—a very large per cent of the people on the outer periphery of smaller machines, a smaller percentage that would go slightly deeper, and an even smaller percentage of the users going to the supercomputer.

But the institute faced tremendous difficulties in procuring the supercomputer from Cray. The US government put in place an onerous process for obtaining export clearance for the supercomputer, which included surprise inspection of the use of the computer and the source codes of the programs being run. The US government was also worried about misuse of the supercomputers on campus for India's defence applications. Balakrishnan says, 'We were initially talking to them about the Cray X-MP. The negotiations kept going and it became the Cray Y-MP. And we realized that it just wasn't coming!'[66] Finally, the institute cancelled the order given to Cray, and bought instead a Cyber992 computer, the fastest CDC mainframe at that time, along with two CDC 4360 superscalar computers and a VAX 8810 from DEC.

Meanwhile, there was a growing consensus that India should become self-reliant in building and using supercomputers. C.N.R. Rao, who was also the chairperson of the Science Advisory Council to the Prime Minister (SAC-PM), formed a committee, with V. Rajaraman as chairman, to recommend the way forward. The committee discussed the need for a high-performance computer for solving complex computational fluid dynamics problems in areas like aerospace, atmospheric sciences and weather/monsoon prediction. It also studied the changing technological scene globally with respect to supercomputers. Scientists worldwide were looking for alternatives to vector supercomputers (like the ones from Cray and CDC), which consumed enormous amounts of power and required special cooling. They were exploring the possibility of building supercomputers using parallel processing of several microprocessors. The committee felt that such an approach offered a less risky (the US did not place any embargos on the export of microprocessors) and much cheaper option for India to develop its own supercomputer. Accordingly, the committee submitted a report in February 1987 to the SAC-PM, titled 'Technology Mission to Develop a Parallel Computer'.[67]

The committee also realized that the potential hardware speed of parallel computers could not be utilized unless new algorithms tuned to the parallel structure of these computers were developed. Thus, it placed an emphasis on developing research in parallel algorithms in the academic institutions. It recommended the formation of a national mission for parallel computers with a budget of Rs 32 crore. The Department of Electronics established the Centre for Development of Advanced Computing (CDAC) in April 1988 at the campus of the University of Pune. In the next chapter, we will look at the outcomes of India's supercomputing research efforts.

Supercomputing was not the only high-tech area that got India's attention in the 1980s. Artificial intelligence did too.

History of Artificial Intelligence Research in India

It is difficult to find a modern discourse or even a casual conversation on technology without a reference to Artificial Intelligence or Machine Learning. AI seems to have become ubiquitous in our daily lives—in the curated news articles and entertainment videos we consume digitally, or in the product recommendations we see when we buy online. But, have you ever wondered where and how the AI journey began in India?

The first course on AI in an Indian educational institution is believed to have been introduced in IIT Kanpur in the late 1960s, when H.N. Mahabala returned from his sojourn at MIT, US, where he had interacted with Marvin Minsky, one of the early pioneers of AI.[68] Early research in AI was started by R. Narasimhan at TIFR, where he built upon his seminal work from his Illinois University days on syntactic pattern recognition and visual perception in computers.[69] The Machine Translation for Indian languages project at IIT Kanpur, and the Optical Character Recognition project at ISI Kolkata, in the 1980s, may have been some of the earliest AI/ML research projects in India.

In 1986, the DoE, with assistance from the UNDP, decided to support AI in a systematic fashion through a five-year project, the Knowledge-Based Computing Systems (KBCS) project, as part of the Indian Fifth Generation Computer Systems (FGCS) research programme.[70] The KBCS project focused on emerging developments in areas like intelligent man-machine interface, knowledge-based processing and management function, problem solving and inference making function and the development of parallel processing platforms for KBCS. A key technical goal of the KBCS project was to develop a state-of-the-art computer (AI) programming environment in which major R&D efforts could be carried out.[71]

The nodal centres under KBCS included CDAC, the central government's DoE, Indian Institute of Science for parallel processing, Indian Institute of Technology Madras for expert systems for diagnosis, Indian Statistical Institute for image processing, National Centre for Software Technology for expert systems and natural language processing, and Tata Institute of Fundamental Research for speech processing. During the period 1986–95, each nodal centre received a total of Rs 1.5 crore and collectively produced fifteen PhDs.[72] This period also saw what was probably India's first AI/ML conference. The KBCS 1989 conference was organized by NCST and was attended by researchers from across the world. The main topics addressed at the conference were expert systems and knowledge representation, logic programming and reasoning. The conference also included one-day tutorial sessions on various aspects of AI, like task-specific architectures for construction of knowledge-based systems, language processing and computational vision.

Early Examples of AI Applications in India

Mahabala of IIT Madras believed, even in the 1980s, that AI had been oversold in its early years and that it had delivered only in the area of expert diagnostic systems. His team in IIT Madras developed Eklavya, a qualitative and multimodel diagnostic system, which was a knowledge-based program designed to support a community health worker in dealing with symptoms of illness in toddlers. NCST produced Vidya, an intelligent tutoring system for Hindi. It was a remedial system aimed at enhancing student performance. NCST's natural language understanding efforts combined information retrieval techniques with machine-assisted English-to-Hindi translation.

TIFR too was focused on natural language processing, with a special emphasis on speech synthesis and recognition. TIFR demonstrated its speech synthesis system in the context of a railway reservation inquiry application. Other AI systems that were developed in India included the flight scheduling expert system Sarani (developed at CDAC, Mumbai), an image processing facility using AI and computer vision techniques (developed by

IISc under sponsorship from ISRO), and Nipuna, an expert system for monitoring the health of radars (developed by the Centre for Artificial Intelligence and Robotics of the Defence Research and Development Organization, an AI research centre established in 1986).

While the success of initiatives like KBCS and FGCS were mixed, it provided the nucleus to nurture future AI/ML research in India, a subject to which we will return in a later chapter.

⸻

The Indian IT industry expanded its wings and began soaring high in the 1990s. Software exports increased from US$128 million in 1990–1991, crossed the milestone of US$1 billion in 1996 and reached US$4 billion by 2000.[73, 74] The government supported the IT industry with policies like the Software Technology Parks of India. This facilitated the global delivery model—where software was developed both in India and the client location—to become dominant. In order to manage its hyper-growth, the Indian IT industry embraced processes and systems for quality and human resources practices.

5

The Rapid Growth of Indian IT Services

L ike a teenager taking the seemingly inexorable steps towards adulthood, often with enthusiasm and at times with uncertainty, the Indian IT industry was finding its feet in the world. Let us put the industry size in perspective. In 1990, the Indian IT industry was just over US$100 million.[1] In fact, a 1992 World Bank report made a bold prediction about the industry reaching US$1 billion 'soon', a milestone that was achieved in 1996.[2]

NASSCOM (National Association of Software and Service Companies) represented the IT companies forcefully in the political corridors. It found a kindred soul in N. Vittal, secretary of the Department of Electronics, who adroitly moved the government machinery to support and provide a fillip to the Indian IT industry. Under his leadership, the game-changing Software Technology Parks of India (STPI) programme was launched. STPI and NASSCOM were two truly unique factors that played an important role in the rapid growth of the Indian software services industry.

The industry adopted the global delivery model (GDM), scaled up its HR practices, and set up systems to handle large-scale recruitment and training. The industry embraced the quality movement wholeheartedly—first with ISO 9001, and then with the Software Engineering Institute's Capability Maturity Model (SEI CMM) by Carnegie Mellon University (CMU). By 1999, six of the twelve SEI CMM Level 5 companies in the world were from India.[3] The Y2K (Year 2000) opportunity materialized, and the Indian IT industry lapped it up.

Indian IT companies began to list in the Indian capital market from the early 1990s. In a first for an Indian company, Infosys listed on the NASDAQ in 1999. The capital markets focus introduced an era of outstanding corporate governance and reporting in the industry. With the capital raised, the software industry began building impressive office campuses.

In this decade, MNCs like IBM came back to India, often in joint ventures with Indian partners. Large-scale offshore development centres (ODCs) emerged, pioneered by the efforts of companies like GE and Nortel. There was a second wave of entrepreneurship in the 1990s, and companies like Cognizant, Mindtree and Microland were established.

In 1995, the average Indian citizen had her first brush with the Internet, as Videsh Sanchar Nigam Limited (VSNL) made it available for public access. From a national computing capability-development perspective in this decade, we witnessed the launch of India's indigenous supercomputer, the PARAM. In terms of computer science education, the Kanwal Rekhi School of Information Technology was established in IIT Bombay.

The US$400-Million Horse that Flew and the US$1-Billion World Bank Report

A successful collaboration between two organizations—NASSCOM, representing the IT industry, and DoE, representing the government—contributed significantly to the growth of the Indian IT industry in the 1990s. Dewang Mehta, as executive director of NASSCOM, began to amplify the voice of the software services industry with great gusto. He coined a new mantra, '*Roti, Kapada, Makaan* (Food, Clothing, Housing) and Bandwidth',[4] a play on the traditional political slogan that promised the electorate food, clothing and shelter. It succinctly captured the growing importance of IT in India and the influence it was beginning to have among policymakers. Harish Mehta says, 'We (NASSCOM) had a list of 300 policies and processes which were strangulating the industry. So, we presented it to the DoE.'[5]

N. Vittal, who became secretary of DoE in May 1990, immediately took the industry demands to a meeting of the Committee of Secretaries. He recalls that meeting: 'Mr Bimal Jalan, finance secretary, said, "What is your export now, US$100 million dollars? Assuming that I agree to all the concessions you asked, how much exports can you make next year?" I said US$300 million, he pushed for US$500 million. Finally, I suggested that we agree on a middle figure of US$400 million for the subsequent financial year.'[6]

It was with this background work done that Vittal next attended the annual event of NASSCOM in New Delhi.

Narayana Murthy, who was vice-president of NASSCOM during 1990–92, recalls that occasion and says, 'We had been discussing with Mr Vittal about providing us with tax exemption as well as communication capabilities to access the computers of our customers. He said, "I can do all of these for you provided you guarantee that you will quadruple the revenue." There was deathly silence when he made that suggestion to the huge gathering.'[7] Clearly, the IT industry was jolted by the stretch goal that the DoE secretary was suggesting. S. Mahalingam recalls a humorous story narrated by Vittal to explain his rationale for the aggressive goal that had been set: 'Due to some annoying circumstance, Akbar (the Mughal emperor) decided to end Birbal's (his witty minister) life. But he agreed to hold off for a year because Birbal claimed he would make the king's horse fly. When asked why he said such an unbelievable thing, Birbal explained that one of three things could happen in a year—the king could die, or he (Birbal) could die, or the horse could fly. Much later, Vittal said the horse (Indian IT industry) indeed flew.'[8]

The DoE soon commissioned a study, funded by Japan through the World Bank, to foster and direct export of Indian software services. Vittal invited NASSCOM members to be part of the committee, and they seized the opportunity to leave their mark on the report and its recommendations. The report submitted in 1992 suggested that with coordinated action, the Indian IT industry could grow from US$164 million in 1991 to US$1 billion in 1996. It recommended several actions to be taken in the areas of marketing and distribution (such as opening liaison offices in the target-market countries), training and education (such as establishing centres of excellence for quality management), financing (such as obtaining sweat equity and issuing IPOs) and infrastructure (such as developing wide-band datacom networks for software exporters).[9]

The cover of the World Bank-funded report that first forecast the US$1-billion potential of Indian IT. Source: Pradeep Gupta

The US$400 million horse soon became a US$1 billion steed. The report seemed to break a psychological barrier for the Indian IT industry. Pradeep Gupta, founder of Cybermedia and the person who led the market research activities in India for the report, says, 'When Jack (Jack Epstein, principal consultant for the report) and I used to go and make this presentation all over the country, people would say US$1 billion was not possible. But, as I said, NASSCOM members were very much part of the steering committee and these guys really built upon that (report recommendations), giving the industry a great amount of confidence, and the rest is history.'[10]

Let us turn our attention to the creation of the game-changing STPI policy.

Software Technology Parks of India—A Government Programme that Unleashed a Wave of Indian IT Services Companies

Surprisingly, the inspiration for the software technology parks idea came to Vittal from a successful stint he had as commissioner of the Kandla Free Trade Zone in Gujarat in the mid-1970s. He had helped businesses there overcome the stifling scrutiny of customs officials and grow. Vittal, recounting how he applied those learnings to the IT industry, says, 'If you want any effort to succeed, you should be able to free that industry from the customs problem. I said why not, just as (in the case of) the Kandla Free Trade Zone, try to do (the same) for the electronics industry. Because software is not visible, it is not like producing a garment from a closed area, it is something which can be done by communications (technology).

I said that you can create software in a technology park, from even your own bedroom.'[11] Thus, Software Technology Parks of India (STPI) was set up as an autonomous body by the DoE in 1991 to promote software exports from India, and technology parks were established in several cities.

R. Chandrashekhar, a former Indian bureaucrat and a past president of NASSCOM, appreciates the light-touch policy interventions and single-window clearance mechanisms that Vittal effected at STPI, which made them more business-friendly than the Export Processing Zones (EPZ) in India. He says: 'Vittal realized that regulation was a big factor. In the EPZs, it was a very strict regime, because nothing could come in, nothing could go out. If you look at the paperwork or even the physical logistics of the whole transaction, clearly it would not have enabled the IT industry to grow. At STPI, he made it very simple and easy.'[12]

STPI opened up new vistas for the Indian IT industry. Saurabh Srivastava says, 'What was limiting growth was infrastructure. You could only get tax exemptions if you set up an export-oriented unit or zone. And the government wasn't building enough of them and so we couldn't grow. The biggest aspect of the STPI scheme was it was both real and virtual. It basically said I could take this building and call it an export zone.'[13]

STPI Provides IT Infrastructure and Communications Support

Not only did STPI allow IT companies greater flexibility in opening up offices, it also provided them the necessary infrastructural and communications support. STPI Bengaluru set up an IBM AS/400 and an IBM ES/9000 system in their facility and made them available to IT companies as common infrastructure.[14] We saw earlier how TI had set up an earth station in Bengaluru for its global connectivity. STPI followed suit in the 1990s. Subroto Bagchi says, 'STPI invested in the satellite system and earth stations and made them available free of cost. Neither Infosys nor Wipro, TCS . . . none of the big companies of that time could have afforded an earth station. I can still remember that when we started in 1990 at Wipro's Global R&D, we had dial-up modems!'[15] Vittal re-allocated Rs 12 crore meant for the Semiconductor Complex in Mohali to establish base stations for STPIs in six cities.[16]

Vittal also ensured that STPIs were created as administrative units with autonomy and the capability to implement the regulations. Every STPI was served by one of the erstwhile ERNET engineers. Thanks to their technical chops, the STPI team in Bengaluru developed innovative solutions to extend the reach of the earth station to far-flung areas of the city. B.V. Naidu, who was a research engineer at ERNET and later became director of STPI Bengaluru, says, 'During those days, mobile networks were not there. We put up the first multipoint network using radio links in all the buildings (which housed software export companies). At one point in time, I think we had 180 towers in Bengaluru having the radio point network connecting to the gateway in Electronics City. To identify whether a building had a software company or not, you just had to look up—if the building had a tower, there was a software company in it.'[17]

STPI and VSNL—A Communications Turf War

When it came to providing communications technology, STPI and the IT companies had repeated run-ins with VSNL, a public-sector enterprise that provided overseas communication services.

STPI and VSNL, though both government organizations, did not seem to be cut from the same cloth. Saurabh Srivastava says, 'VSNL was a monopoly and they would charge you horrendous rates. You applied to them and you didn't even know when they would reply.'[18] VSNL nearly scuttled STPI's earth station plans. Srivastava recalls the timely intervention by the DoE and says, 'It would not have happened except for two guerrilla tactics—one, Mr Vittal himself becoming industry aggregator to negotiate (infrastructure and rates with VSNL) and two, Roy Paul (from Vittal's team in the DoE) creating a competitive vehicle (threatening to form a government company called Satcomm that would have competed with VSNL).'[19]

Another communications battle between STPI and VSNL was over provisioning of IPLC (international private leased circuit) lines, which were used by the IT companies for Internet access and business data exchange with customers outside India. When STPI tried to build a business relationship directly with US telecom carriers who had established business links with VSNL, it met with reluctance and refusals. Eventually, STPI brokered a deal with a much smaller player called IDB Systems. B.V. Naidu says, 'When our IPLC traffic was growing and IDB Systems was getting more business in the US, AT&T, Sprint and MCI got the jitters. One by one they came, without the knowledge of VSNL, and signed up with us. By 1998 or so, we became one of the largest data communication carriers, carrying IT industry traffic out of Bengaluru. That is when VSNL came forward to build a relationship (with STPI).'[20]

STPI Helps IT Industry Thrive

How the industry triumphed during this period is a telling example of the power of collaboration, of the influence of NASSCOM, and of the unflinching support the industry received from STPI, Vittal and his DoE machinery.

The IT industry embraced the STPI programme enthusiastically. S. Mahalingam says, 'You could really proliferate centres, not these large campuses that needed to be built for export activities, but we could do smaller ones. I think it was a phenomenal initiative for growing many companies.'[21] Ashok Soota too concurs: 'It also gave a level playing field to small players. It created hundreds of software companies, letting hundreds of flowers bloom.'[22]

Two unlikely heroes—in the form of Dewang Mehta and N. Vittal—emerged in this blockbuster script involving NASSCOM and the DoE; unlikely because neither was a technologist, and both went beyond their traditional job descriptions, both delivering outsized impact on the industry. Harish Mehta recalls a conversation with (the late) Prof. Sumantra Ghoshal, who said that 1000 years of the downward spiralling of India had been arrested by the IT industry of the country: 'And the IT industry has grown, thanks to NASSCOM as a catalyst and Dewang as a *sutradhar* (orchestrator) of NASSCOM.'[23] Narayana Murthy, recalling the yeoman services rendered by Vittal to the industry, says, 'If there is one person in government who should be credited with the success of the Indian software industry, it has to be Shri N. Vittal.'[24]

Let us dive deeper into this story of dramatic growth of the Indian IT industry in the 1990s and its tryst with operating models like GDM, quality models like CMM and opportunities like Year 2000, aka Y2K. Let us look at R&D services, an important sub-domain of the Indian IT services industry. Here we will find answers to the question many readers will have: Why and how did the Indian hardware companies like Wipro and HCL transition into software services?

———

Policy Environment and Technology Capabilities Power the Serendipitous Genesis of R&D Services

The short answer to the question why Wipro and HCL transitioned into IT services is, government policy. Successive policies in the 1980s made it easier for Indian organizations to import computers. The 1984 computer policy allowed the import of fully assembled motherboards with processors. Not only that, the import duties on these components were reduced. This led to reduced prices and hence the proliferation of computers, especially PCs, in India. However, the policy was detrimental to Indian hardware companies and benefited the large MNC hardware companies. India never became a global player in computer hardware manufacturing, and eventually the Indian hardware companies formed JVs and became marketing and sales partners for the MNCs in India. Wipro tied up with Sun, Hinditron with DEC, HCL with HP, and PSI with Honeywell Bull. When some of the Indian hardware companies began to feel that they were playing a secondary role in the JVs, their ingenuity ensured that they positioned themselves as software R&D service providers to the MNC hardware companies.

More often than not when we think of software services, we assume it is software that powers business functions like sales and marketing, manufacturing and operations, finance and human resources. This segment of software is formally referred to as 'enterprise software services'. In contrast, the services required for product development and R&D for software products, hardware products and telecom equipment are referred to as 'R&D services'. In short, it is the CIO of the client firm who makes decisions on enterprise software services, and the CTO of the firm who makes decisions on R&D software services. Let us now look at how Wipro—one of the largest software R&D services companies in the world today—made its mark in this domain.

Azim Premji says, 'In 1992, when India's doors were opened to the likes of HP, IBM and Dell, Indian (hardware) players felt the heat. We were left with two options—either completely close the R&D, or provide competencies in the form of R&D services to the international market. We chose the latter. Our first customers were our own technology partners—Intel, Tandem, Novell, Sun, etc. The prowess that we developed out of our experience in making and servicing various types of machines is what evolved into an R&D service capability for us. This (the hardware business) led to four major competencies getting developed in the organization: (1) high-performance hardware systems, (2) chip-design competency, (3) core operating system and device drivers, and (4) embedded and device programming.'[25]

Sridhar Mitta, a pioneer of R&D services in India, expands on the genesis of the services line at Wipro: '(The Indian) Government allowed foreign (hardware) companies to come into India. It dawned on us that when the door is open for somebody to come in, it is also open for us to go out. Firstly, there was a perception in the US that Indians are good in software. The second thing we found was that UNIX was moving from a laboratory and university phenomenon to a commercial phenomenon. Fortunately for us, we had been using the UNIX source code for quite some time and we had the expertise. Using these two trends, we went to the US and offered our engineering services as unique software services.'[26] Wipro acquired multiple customers for its R&D services, which, by FY2001, contributed to 50 per cent of its global IT services revenue of US$382 million.[27]

Mitta recounts some of the non-IT, yet important, challenges in setting up ODCs in R&D services: 'When I went to understand the work at Tandem, they took me to their lab which had hundreds of computers, including huge mainframes. It was an intimidating scenario . . . We were going to have some smaller subset of these in our place (Tandem ODC in Wipro). When the machines came, they were so heavy that there was no crane in Bengaluru which could lift them and put them in. And so, we had to break walls. Then we had to keep the generator in the basement. The office was in the middle of the city, so neighbours started complaining about the noise. We had to invent an acoustic enclosure. Everything was a problem at that time . . . It was a lot of fun!'[28]

Another person who had a lot of fun in discovering and catalysing the rise of Indian R&D services was Diju Raha, senior executive at Nortel, the Canadian telecom equipment company. He says, 'The advent of digital technology demanded a lot of software expertise in telecommunication systems, which was not necessary in the (case of) electro-mechanical systems. Secondly, Nortel Telecom had a tremendous ambition to be the world leader in digital telecom, which demanded software expertise. We came to the conclusion that we just didn't have enough resources in Canada to do that. And hence we were looking the world over, on how we could tap global software resources.'[29]

Ashok Soota, who was CEO of Wipro when Nortel came knocking on Indian doors, says, 'Nortel had the ability to visualize that engineering work could be done here. They were the first large engineering player to come and give us a lot of work, and they engaged multiple of us (Indian software services companies) in their process . . . Diju Raha conceived and brought the programme to India.'[30]

How Raha did some cool sleuthing on the Indian software industry in the late 1980s is an interesting story in itself. He says, 'Just about that time, I happened to see a television programme called *Computer Chronicle*. There was a two-and-a-half-hour documentary there called 'Third World Software', which was mainly based on Indian software, and it opened my eyes. I went to meet Mr (Stewart) Cheifet (the producer of the documentary) in Harrisburg, Pennsylvania, and I bought all his tapes . . . about thirty hours of tape that he did for the two-and-a-half-hour programme with all the associated material. I went through the material and became an instant expert on the possibilities of doing things (software) in India!'[31]

Nortel perfected its offshoring model with many innovative practices that made it a reference model. Nortel had ODCs in three large Indian software services companies—TCS, Wipro and Infosys. The Indian software services companies were called Nortel's 'partners' and not 'vendors'. The ODCs in the Indian software services companies were designed to look and feel like any internal Nortel lab. The software professionals working in these ODCs had Nortel ID cards that provided them entry into any Nortel lab in the world. Nortel also did periodic employee-satisfaction surveys of their ODC employees to get first-hand knowledge of what was going well and what was not. Nortel worked with the Canadian and Indian governments to ensure their employees and partners had a smooth visa application process. The success of Nortel's ODC model paved the way for other ODCs in both R&D services and enterprise software services.

Sharad Sharma comments on his experiences during the setting up of an R&D global in-house centre in 1993 in India for AT&T, the US telecom major. 'We selected four partners at that time—Infosys, Wipro, Future Software and Data Matrix. By 2006, we came up with a set of principles that are now considered to be conventional wisdom in terms of running ODCs—think of partnering; creating a sense of ownership and belonging to a product roadmap; making matrix performance assessment work. So that systematization, I think, was very helpful in the R&D context.'[32]

Kris Gopalakrishnan, commenting on the history of MNCs in India, says, 'When IBM left India, it created a vacuum, and the first wave of Indian start-ups emerged. Then MNCs like TI, and subsequently General Electric, Nortel, etc., came, and these were the early pioneers who truly saw the capability of Indian software professionals and helped us establish the global delivery model. In 1993, when the economy opened up, IBM came back to India and embraced GDM.'[33]

We will turn our attention next to the story of the return of IBM to India.

IBM Returns to India and Makes up for Lost Time

Even after IBM left India in 1978, its computers were being bought by both Indian government and private organizations. Notably, a high-end IBM mainframe was cleared for sale to the Aeronautical

Development Agency of India to help in the design of its light combat aircraft. This deal, which was sealed at the level of the president of the US and the prime minister of India, was among the many confidence-building measures undertaken by the two countries to mend the strained relations of the 1970s. As we saw earlier, TCS made a big bet in the 1980s by acquiring an IBM 3090 mainframe, the worth (gross block) of which was higher than all the other assets at TCS then![34] Among the computing infrastructure that seeded the National Supercomputing Centre in IISc in the early 1990s were nine IBM RS6000/580s, connected in parallel with a fibre-optic network and forty-eight IBM RS6000/340 computers.

By the late 1980s, IBM was active in India, marketing and providing direct services in the country from their office in Singapore. In 1992–93, IBM re-entered India as Tata Information Systems Limited (TISL), a 50–50 joint venture with the Tatas. This was primarily to sell their computers in India and to develop and support software products for IBM. By the turn of the decade, IBM bought out Tata's stake in TISL and established IBM's Global Services organization and IBM Research in India. Though never explicitly acknowledged by IBM, many industry observers suggested that by the mid-2010s India had the largest headcount of IBM globally and a representation of all its major divisions. A high point for IBM was when it signed a large IT outsourcing deal with Airtel. According to reports, this deal was the first billion-dollar-plus outsourcing deal from an Indian company for an IT MNC.[35]

From being accused of selling obsolete and refurbished IBM 1401s in the 1970s, IBM now had its India operations becoming the second largest contributor to its worldwide patents list in 2020.[36]

And that is not all. Arvind Krishna, the current chairperson and CEO of IBM, is an alumnus of IIT Kanpur, which is where Indian capability in computer programming started with an IBM 1620 computer.

By the time IBM returned to India in the 1990s, the Indian IT industry had evolved and software services had become the dominant segment. Indian software services companies like TCS and Infosys, which were focused on software exports, were on the ascent. And Indian hardware companies like HCL and Wipro pivoted to R&D services first, and later to software services.

Let us now look at what propelled Indian software services companies to redefine the global IT outsourcing industry.

Building World-Class Software Services Capabilities

The Indian software services companies developed fine-tuned capabilities along their value-chain—in recruitment, training, delivery operations, quality, sales and finance—which provided the momentum for their rapid growth. For example, Infosys grew at a CAGR of over 75 per cent between 1993 and 2002. A strong capability in professional services, sales and marketing, and in targeting Fortune 500 clients, was built in this era. The software services industry introduced the concept of ESOPs (Employee Stock Options) programmes in India, and software services companies were among the first Indian companies to list on the NASDAQ and NYSE.

Talent Management Focused on Recruiting, Training, and Nurturing

Talent management was and is the bedrock of Indian software services companies. The only real asset that software services companies have is their employees. It has been famously said by Narayana Murthy that Infosys's most important assets leave its premises every evening![37] N.S. Raghavan, co-founder of Infosys, was responsible for its human resources function. He felt the Indian labour market had an acute shortage of programming and software engineering skills that the company could recruit directly. He also realized that the general selection process of the clients then—of asking for detailed résumés of the service-provider employees before accepting them for a project—would easily identify these shortcomings.

Raghavan strongly believed that the bright engineers graduating from the Indian universities could be quickly taught the relevant programming and software engineering skills required by the clients. 'I realized that we have to spread our net wider and go after people who are not necessarily computer science or electronics graduates. The question is, how will they do a software job? I needed to have a strong education and research department which would ensure the basic content (and skills) would be taught to the fresh college recruits and make them ready as quickly as possible. Maybe in three or four months. This way I will be able to meet and scale up with demand.'[38]

How did the Indian software companies identify the engineering students who would be quick learners of programming and other skills? Raghavan explains how they devised an entrance exam: 'The question was, how do we test those people and determine that they are suitable. So, I was looking at GRE, GMAT, CAT and other tests . . . That is how I came up with two kinds of tests. One called the arithmetical reasoning test and another called the analytical thinking test.'[39]

Once the best engineering college undergraduates were recruited, they were put through a rigorous training programme in the software services companies. Mahalingam was closely associated with developing a new training programme for college recruits at TCS. This programme had its genesis in the late 1980s and was first developed with Prof. Mahabala of IIT Madras: 'We created this software engineering training programme. We felt that we couldn't really judge the success (of the programme) unless these people (trainees) worked on systems. They had to be trained to document, test and bring a system together. The initial concept was that they do the theory in about nine months and the practical (learning—lab sessions on programming) in about nine months, with the students getting back to theory intermittently. We piloted that and we realized that we didn't need eighteen months, we could bring it down to twelve months. So, the next couple of batches were essentially (trained) for twelve months, where for six months they were on a real project . . . Over a period of time, we essentially brought the twelve months down to a programme of four months, since the undergraduates came with increased programming skills. This training programme helped TCS for a very long period of time.'[40]

Not only recruitment and training, but also the entire gamut of talent management or human resources function in Indian software services companies was inspired by global best practices. The workplace was professional and congenial. Raghavan recalls how an oft-remarked aspect of Infosys developed: 'I felt that a lot of value should be given to an organization's culture, where self-esteem is never hurt, where people are respected for their differences of opinion, respected for what they contribute, transparency, and fairness . . . I made sure that I always had this small placard on my desk which said, "You can disagree as long as you are not disagreeable".'[41]

Not surprisingly, the human resources and other functions at Infosys became subjects of Harvard Business School (HBS) case studies. Probably the first HBS case study on the Indian IT industry was written in 2001 and it focused on the question, 'How did world-class software services companies emerge from India?' The abstract for the case study says, 'Creating and sustaining a third-world-based technology company to compete globally (i.e., in the first-world) poses many challenges. Such challenges are examined through the genesis and progression of Infosys Technologies Ltd.'[42]

Ability to Deliver Good-Quality Projects as per Requirements Time and Again Powers the Revenue Engine

Delivery operations are at the heart of a software services company. Delivery ensures that software projects are completed as promised in the contract the company has signed with the client. As the Indian companies grew in size, the heroics of their employees to salvage a project took a back seat and robust project management practices were put in place. Being in the business of automating business functions for clients meant that it was only a matter of time before the Indian software services companies brought IT into their own operations. Raghavan fondly recalls an automation project that was a rudimentary ERP (enterprise resource planning) system at Infosys: 'Murthy was very concerned about billings, the revenue we were generating every month, and he was not willing to wait till the end of the month to find out how much billing was done. He said, "Raghavan can you develop a system?" What I did was make a simple spreadsheet and ensure that all the project leaders (and sales leaders) kept updating it every month. Once in the middle of the month, and once towards the end of the month, Murthy would look at it. If he realized that a large billing hadn't come in for whatever reason, he would take it up with the sales team. The project and sales leaders also realized that they could forecast how much they were likely to bill in a month . . . it (the system) was a reliable indicator of when a payment was likely to happen.' This was the genesis of what became the famous PSPD—predictability, sustainability, profitability, de-risking—model of Infosys.

As Narayana Murthy mentioned in an interview with Knowledge@Wharton, 'A good forecasting system for sales based on data gathered from the trenches ensures predictability (although predictability of costs is also needed to have predictable profit streams). Sustainability is achieved by energetic and motivated sales people who pound the pavement and make sales happen; by production people ensuring that quality products are delivered to the customer on time; and by billing and collecting on time. Every enterprise must focus on high profitability in order to ensure the best returns for its shareholders. Indeed, the long-term success of a corporation depends on having a model that scales up profitably. Finally, the corporation must have a good de-risking approach that recognizes, measures and mitigates risk along every dimension.'[43] Today, we read about Indian Internet-based start-ups facing challenges in scaling their business profitably. They would do well to read up about the PSPD model.

Ramadorai, who was CEO of TCS in this era, talks about another critical element—the importance of collaboration among delivery and other functions in a software services company: 'Nothing short of collaboration will make it (delivery of projects) happen. Projects fail in the software industry not because of a lack of capabilities, but because of non-cooperation between capable people. I think the cultural training that is given, irrespective of the way you do it in every company, is to tell people that they need to collaborate. There are no silos where HR, finance, administration work separately, but they are integrated into the mainstream so that all know the business as much as anybody else. Training and development of professionals in software development is the way of life and that is integrated into the mainstream (delivery).'[44]

The concept of delivery by a team based both in India and onsite became popular worldwide as the global delivery model. The GDM was a business model innovation by India, by Indian companies, and was mimicked by the rest of the world, especially by MNC software services companies and by MNCs who set up their IT subsidiaries in India.

The Global Delivery Model Becomes a Game Changer

Narayana Murthy provides a lucid explanation of GDM: 'As you know, in every software project there are two classes of activities. The first set of activities has a very high level of interaction with customers. And the second set of activities has a very low level of interaction with customers. The first set of activities also requires instant availability of customers whereas the second one does not require that.

'Let me give you some examples of the first set of activities— requirements definition, making a presentation to a customer on the requirements, getting a sign-off from the customer, installing the software on their machine, training the customer on the software that you have developed and providing rapid reaction warranty, which is the warranty that you provide in the first three-to-six months of a large business software. These are all the activities that have a very high level of interaction with customers that require instant reaction from the customer and therefore they have to be taken up necessarily at the customer's side.

'On the other hand, activities like detailed functional design, detailed technical design which includes database design, programming and coding, documentation and long-term warranty, have a very low level of interaction with customers and they don't need instant reaction from the customer and therefore they can be taken up from remote, talent-rich, process-driven, scalable, cost-competitive development centres in countries like India.

'In a typical project, anywhere from 10 per cent to 30 per cent of the effort will have to be delivered at the customer's site. And 70 per cent to 90 per cent of the effort could be delivered from India. The result is, (the) customer gets better-quality software delivered on time, at very attractive costs. This is the fundamental principle of the global delivery model.'[45]

The main reason for the industry using a predominantly onsite model for software development was that there were no data communication facilities to frequently send programs from India to the client site for validation. The means to disrupt this predominantly onsite model was provided by STPI, which, as we saw earlier, ensured that Indian software services companies had access to a reliable data communications infrastructure.

Nilekani recollects the 'aha' moment when GDM became a possibility, and the subsequent impact of this on Indian software services companies: 'Suddenly we saw that there was a shift in the market from onsite development to offshore development, where people in India would use the latest computers and use telecommunications to develop software for the global markets. This led to the rise of the global delivery model. We recognized that very early and that's why we went public (IPO for raising equity funding) in 1993 and built India's first (software) campus in Electronic City. We used the money (from the IPO) to build a world-class campus and bought computers. We got on board clients like GE and others who wanted their software development done here. We came up with the concept of the global delivery model, which was a 24/7 workday, where the client could be anywhere, the development could be anywhere, and by using telecom we would collaborate.'[46]

GDM soon caught the imagination of the world. Nandan's exposition of GDM was the inspiration for *The World is Flat*, a bestseller by author Thomas Friedman, an influential columnist for the *New York Times*.

An integral component of delivery and GDM was quality management, which got special focus at Indian software services companies. The quality initiative was dovetailed with the software engineering process and helped to win the confidence of prospective clients who were taking baby steps towards offshore software project development.

Quality Certifications Help Establish the Credibility of Indian Software Services

What started off as a journey with ISO 9001 and TickIT certifications for software development soon evolved with the adoption of emerging software-industry focused frameworks, like the Software

Engineering Institute Capability Maturity Model (SEI CMM). The SEI CMM specified increasing levels for software development organizations based on the state of their software development processes. The levels varied from one to five, and the higher the level, the better the software development process.

Wipro was an early adopter of the quality frameworks, and Azim Premji provides the rationale: 'Technical capability, at end of the day, was about good programming that was ensured by good-quality processes. Clients were concerned (about) how projects were monitored or how testing was carried out or how the teams were doing every day. Quality hence was the means which reaffirmed our clients' trust in Indian software development. We adopted standards like SEI CMM, PCMM (People CMM), etc. It gave us an endorsement for the quality of the process which we followed.'[47] Wipro became the world's first software services company to get the SEI CMM Level 5 certification in the late 1990s, and after a few years became the first company in the world to receive the PCMM Level 5 certification. It also adopted the Six Sigma quality framework, popularized by MNCs like Motorola and GE.

Infosys brought on board Pankaj Jalote, a professor from IIT Kanpur, on a sabbatical to drive its quality journey. He says, 'The idea was to apply the principles that we teach people in (computer science) courses in the business context while respecting the business and client constraints. We were able to put a good-quality system in place which was grounded in software engineering concepts.'[48]

What did the CMM certifications actually mean in business terms for the IT services companies? K. Dinesh, co-founder of Infosys, who was championing quality management there, emphatically talks about the business value of quality certifications: 'Our on-time delivery went up from about 70–75 per cent to about

95 per cent. Repeat business (which is business given again by an existing client), which was around 65 per cent when we had finished the ISO 9000, went up to about 85 per cent and then further up to 95–97 per cent (with CMM certifications).'[49]

Once Indian software services companies were on the path to software delivery excellence, they turned their focus on business excellence. Infosys embraced the Malcolm Baldrige National Quality Award Framework once it became an SEI CMM Level 5 certified company. Dinesh says, 'We went with the Baldrige model because it fitted with our markets focus and it was holistic. We set up the Leadership Institute in Mysore because Baldrige (framework) asked us how we prepared leaders for the future in a formal way . . . Second was strategy—how long would current service offerings last and how would you differentiate (from competition). This is when we also started looking at how business consulting could be a service to take us further. We also started implementing a formal way to communicate our strategy to our employees. We introduced a Balanced Scorecard framework to bring a holistic way to look at the business.'[50]

The Indian software services companies realized the importance of quality and went all out to get certified. By the end of the 1990s, about 50 per cent of all SEI CMM certified companies worldwide were from India.[51]

Scaling IT Sales and Marketing Meant Opening Offices in the US and Europe

In the 1970s and 1980s, Indian software services companies like Infosys sent their founders and key officers to the US and Europe to meet with clients and market their offerings. And some of them used third-party consultants to sell their services. Companies like TCS, which were part of a larger conglomerate, placed their officers with the country resident managers of Tata Group. By the 1990s, the sales and marketing functions evolved and offices were set up in the client geographies. The focus of Indian IT companies was on obtaining repeat business and building their brands to differentiate themselves from other Indian software services companies. Repeat business was important in the context of two aspects—it ensured continuity and predictability of projects, and it reduced the cost and time for sales.

For its sales team, Infosys began recruiting experienced MBAs who had studied at the IIMs and other top business schools. These recruits, who were employed in different industries in India, went through a structured training on software and software services in Bengaluru before being placed in different regions in the US and Europe. Nilekani explains the evolution of sales and marketing at Infosys: 'For a long time, we didn't do our own sales and worked with partners. Then we realized that we had to build our own independent global brand and we set up offices all over the world. A lot of the selling involved selling India even before selling Infosys. I think the important things were quality and word-of-mouth (endorsement). This is a small industry and CIOs talk to each other. When we worked with a few companies and did an excellent job, they then referred other good companies (to us). And that's how we built a large customer base over time.'[52] Even today, more than 90 per cent of the revenue of the Indian software services companies comes from repeat business.

The Indian companies needed funding in order to support such an expansion of their business into newer geographies.

Initial Public Offering was the Preferred Mode of Funding

Surprising as it may seem today, there was no formal venture capital industry in India during the early 1990s. The funding routes open to Indian software companies which were not part of a conglomerate or a business group were the public equity or debt markets. There was a preference for the equity market since it was thought to be a cheaper source of funding. Ashank describes the challenging context of listing in India then: 'Mastek was the first Indian software services company to list on the Indian equity market with an initial public offering (IPO) in 1992. There were no analysts covering the software services industry and prospective investors had to be educated by us about the industry.'[53] Adding to this challenge was the state of the Indian stock market, which was just recovering from the infamous Harshad Mehta scam of 1992.

Infosys listed on the Indian stock exchange in 1993. The primary reason for Infosys's IPO was access to equity funding to build a world-class campus in Bengaluru. Narayana Murthy describes the other key motivations to go public: 'We had to be competitive with these multinationals (software companies that were planning to enter India post-liberalization) in their compensation. We also realized that these (Indian) software centres for these multinationals were cost centres. Therefore, they (MNCs) could afford to offer much higher salaries than us and still manage to be viable . . . That is when we decided that we can create stock options and offer it to our employees. With the stock options the annualized income of our employees would be much more than what the multinationals could provide as salaries. There was also another stream of thought, that as a company that aimed to become a multinational headquartered in India, we could not be just satisfied with an India-based stock option. These were the reasons why we took a decision to list in India first, and then on NASDAQ.'[54] In fact, Infosys was the first Indian company to list overseas in 1999. This also meant that Infosys adopted global standards of corporate governance and financial reporting. Other Indian software services companies filed for their IPOs subsequently. HCL listed on the Indian stock market in 1999. Wipro listed on the NYSE in 2000. TCS continued as a division of Tata Sons till its IPO in 2004. The compulsions of being a public-listed entity and providing guidance to investors influenced these companies' business and human resources strategies.

By now, the reader is probably tempted to think that all Indian software services companies had the same strategy. It was true that all of them were delivering custom software services to their clients using the global delivery model. However, there were differences in their business strategies, especially with respect to their focus on profitability and wealth creation for their employees.

Indian IT Services Companies' Strategies—Similar but Not the Same

The now famous General Electric (GE) negotiations bring out well the differences in strategy among the Indian software services companies. GE came to India in 1990, thanks to the thawing of Indo–US relations and a focus on strengthening the economic relations between the two countries. GE agreed to buy software from India in return for India buying their products. GE evaluated Indian software services companies and selected TCS, Infosys, Wipro and a few others. In 1995, the contracts were up for renewal and negotiations were on with the Indian software services partners.

Narayana Murthy vividly recollects the tense negotiations: 'GE had a very well-practised method of negotiating with its vendors. They sequestered the five Indian companies in five different rooms in the Taj Residency. And their officers—there was a team of ten or twelve people—were going from room to room to room and negotiating with each company, saying that we have got this better deal from somebody and now you have to match it or make it better. And when our turn came, we made a presentation to them about the kind of investments that we make in our people, our training programme, our technology investment, we assured them (as to) how we are building India's first software campus. We said all of these things cost money. There is only one entity that gives a company money, month after month, and that is the customer. Therefore, we said, if you want us to develop high-quality software for you and deliver it on time and invest in quality, technology, training, infrastructure, etc., you have to provide us adequate margins.'[55]

After the second day of negotiations, the Infosys team felt that they should walk away from the contract since the pricing was not acceptable to them. Infosys conveyed this decision to GE. And Infosys agreed that it would transition the work they were already doing to whoever GE suggested. That was not an easy decision to make, since GE contributed about 25 per cent of Infosys's revenues at that point in time. At the same time, Infosys had the conviction that GE's pricing had to include a certain margin which would help them reinvest.

Narayana Murthy decided to take this as a lesson and ensured that Infosys moved on quickly: 'I said (to my colleagues), "I am as much concerned as you all, if not more. But I know that I cannot put this organization in jeopardy by accepting terms that will force us to accept such terms with all other customers, otherwise it will be unfair to other customers." And that is when I went back to office, sat down with Sudha Kumar (who was heading planning for Infosys) and dictated a letter to form a risk mitigation council. That was the first time we (Infosys) said that we would not depend too much on one customer, one technology, one application area, one geography, etc. In some way, I think what started out as a huge negative ended up a huge positive.'[56]

At that time, Infosys was a publicly listed company and was very particular about meeting its financial performance commitments to shareholders. Other Indian services companies that were not publicly listed at that time might not have faced such market compulsions.

The other differentiator that probably caught the imagination of the world in that era was the ESOPs policy of Infosys. This was the first time that all employees of an Indian company were eligible for ESOPs, as it was among the technology start-ups in the US. Raghavan, commenting on how the company-wide ESOPs programme came into vogue, says, 'My interest was to cover the bulk of the employees. About 1 per cent to 2 per cent may be doing a fantastic job, and maybe 20 per cent to 30 per cent not doing a good job. The 50–60 per cent of the people who do good work to build a foundation for our growth . . . I need to show them that we really appreciate that work. That is how ESOPs started . . . I think that was a great deal and helped us to create several millionaires.'[57] With the prolific growth of start-ups in India, there is a wonderful lesson here for founders on rewarding employees with ESOPs and considering listing on the stock exchanges or creating ESOP buybacks to generate wealth for many more.

The Indian companies also differed in how they approached opportunities like Y2K (Year 2000), or expansion into new geographies. We will explore these differences later. As the first generation of Indian software services companies was making a mark in the global IT market, it provided motivation for the next wave of entrepreneurship in Indian IT.

Second Wave of Entrepreneurship in Indian IT in the 1990s

According to a NASSCOM survey, Indian software exports in 1999–2000 stood at US$4 billion and were expected to grow at a robust 58 per cent in the next year. About thirty-seven software companies exported software worth more than US$25 million in a year, and 180 companies exported software worth more than US$2.5 million.[58] It was clear that the Indian software industry witnessed, in the 1990s, an explosion in the number of software services firms. Let us look into the stories of Cognizant, Mindtree and Microland in this second wave of entrepreneurship in Indian IT.

Genesis of Cognizant

The story begins in 1993 with Dun and Bradstreet (D&B), a company recognized for its credit rating and information services, and its grand plans to set up captives in Russia, China and India. D&B established a subsidiary in Hong Kong with Kumar Mahadeva as its CEO, and selected Lakshmi Narayanan to run the India operations from Chennai. Narayanan started his career at TCS, cutting his teeth on a payroll system for Taj Hotels, and had risen through the ranks in TCS. He left TCS to become a regional head for D&B in India. He says, 'D&B came up with a unique model to operate their business—partner with a local IT services company, part with initial equity in order to get the expertise, and eventually buy out (that stake) and be on their own. D&B selected Satyam Computers to partner with and set up a joint venture.'[59] Dun & Bradstreet Software (DBSS) thus established primarily provided IT services to its parent company, D&B.

In 1996, the company started working with customers outside of D&B. Narayanan fondly recalls an episode from then: 'The first customer that we won really was CCC, a company in the data processing analytics space. Their CEO was visiting Chennai and perchance saw the D&B board. He tried calling us a few times but our telephone operators didn't pick up the call. He got furious because this was not the experience he had had with D&B previously and decided to come over to our office. Fortunately, I was there to receive him. We started talking about our companies and I went into a sales pitch. This was on a Thursday. He said, "Can you be in the US next week?" That weekend, a few colleagues and I flew to his office, made presentations, and he was very impressed. He had a certain bias towards D&B, which was further cemented when we reacted so quickly. And that is how we started the relationship with our first third-party customer.'[60] DBSS also won important deals with clients like Pacific Stock Exchange and Manugistics and expanded its business.

In 1996, Dun & Bradstreet spun off several of its subsidiaries, including DBSS, to form a new group company called Cognizant Corporation. DBSS renamed itself as Cognizant Technology Solutions, and by 1998 moved its headquarters to the US. Narayanan recalls the strategic decisions Cognizant took at that time when it decided to list on the stock exchange: 'DBSS had a major challenge when India exploded the nuclear device in Pokhran in 1998. We went ahead with the listing although with a lower valuation. But in order to build the company and really be credible and improve the valuation, we decided to reduce the related-party business (from D&B) from 60 per cent to under 25 per cent very rapidly.'[61]

The genesis story of Cognizant finishes with the story of how they obtained exclusive rights to the name. Narayanan says, 'There were other companies in the group holding company that shared the Cognizant name. The IT services business got an opportunity when there was a second spin-off that happened in 2002, to completely own the Cognizant brand. As part of the restructuring process, we were given a choice of owning either the corporate jet or the 'Cognizant' name. I remember I was in Connecticut to sign that agreement. From then on we started building the brand.'[62] We will revisit Cognizant in the next chapter and understand how it overcame adversity in the aftermath of the 2008 world financial crisis.

The Mindtree Story

The birth of Mindtree can be traced to two major factors—first, in the 1990s, the market demand for a new type of IT services company; and second, a concatenation of events, some intended and some serendipitous, that led a team of talented and experienced IT professionals at Wipro to band together under an entrepreneurial banner.

Krishnakumar Natarajan, who was the head of Wipro's e-commerce and software products business then, says, 'In late

1996–97, I clearly saw that in the next three–four years, the IT business might become very different from the existing model. It was becoming a much more project-driven business, which means you did a project for a customer and then you needed to move on to the next project. The customer might not give you the maintenance work. A lot of the work had to be done onsite, because in the early stages you needed to do consulting with the customer to find what the real needs were before you started building the solution.'[63]

In June 1998, Krishnakumar met his former colleague Subroto Bagchi, who had earlier headed Wipro's Global R&D business and then joined Lucent Technologies in the US. They discussed plans to create a 'next generation services company in building Internet solutions while embedding the offshore model'.[64] Swiftly, they convinced a number of their colleagues and friends, like Anjan Lahiri, N.S. Parthasarathy and Rostow Ravanan, to coalesce around their vision. Bagchi recalls the key takeaways from a brainstorming meeting they had at Visakhapatnam: 'We said we will build Mindtree, which will be in the IT services business, but it will basically do three things differently—(1) it will be a company which will create shared wealth; (2) it will do aspirational work; (3) it will be a company with a social conscience. We also identified six elements for our business—domain, tools, methodology, quality, innovation and branding. They have to be like six horses pulling a chariot in the same direction, at the same speed and at the same time.'[65]

While socializing their venture idea with the partners at the venture capital firm Walden, they were informed that another person from Wipro had put together a similar business plan for an IT services company and were advised to join hands with him.

That person happened to be Ashok Soota, who was then president of Wipro Infotech and to whom Krishnakumar was reporting. Ashok Soota says, 'As the speed of change (in the IT industry) kept increasing, newer and newer opportunities came about. For example, in the years that we started Mindtree, the change was the Internet. We came to the market as an e-systems integrator.'[66] Krishnakumar remarks on this unexpected turn of events: 'At Mindtree, even before we started, we had a merger! He (Ashok) raised the aspirations (of the team) and said that we need to think big. So, we started together and that helped us scale far more substantively.'[67]

They were fortunate to start things at Mindtree with Lucent as their first client. They also showed the plucky zeal of a hungry start-up in the manner in which they got their next customer. Krishnakumar says, 'My colleague, Joseph King, had this theory that you could not approach CIOs through just emails. You needed to call them at the "golden hour", meaning, the time when the CIO came to office but the admin (administrative assistant) was not yet there. On one call, he got directly connected to the CIO of Avis and gave a very passionate pitch about Mindtree's expertise in Internet technology.'[68]

The CIO was intrigued. He was considering building an Internet-enabled reservation system with IBM, and asked Mindtree to do a pilot. Krishnakumar says, 'Once we got that small door of entry, we really put the whole organization into that. Our proof of concept really impressed the CIO, to the extent that he gave us the job to build the whole reservation system. Soon, we got other customers like Franklin Templeton. And all of that started building our customer base.'

We now turn our attention to another IT company, Microland, one with a different service focus but filled with equally gutsy tales.

Microland—An IT Infrastructure Services Start-up

By the time Pradeep Kar decided to start a company, he had had a whirlwind six-year experience in selling computers and services in India and the US. 'I had initial experience selling minicomputers (at Wipro), then went to standalone PCs (at a fledgling company, Computer Point), and in the US (at Sonata), and saw the arrival of distributed computing and the emergence of companies like Novell Netware and Compaq. It was logical, I felt, that client server networks would be relevant for India. So, I came back to India in 1989 to start Microland.'[69]

Kar was tipped off about the India visit of the head of Novell's education business, who was apparently scouting for business partners. Kar called up all the hotels in Mumbai to discover that the visitor was at Hotel Leela Kempinski. He then fixed an appointment with the executive, printed business cards at the hotel business centre for a not-yet-incorporated Microland, and became Novell's partner in India and one of the first few companies to bring network education to India. Talk about entrepreneurial chutzpah!

In 1991, when the Indian economy opened up, Kar saw an opportunity in bringing international technologies to India. He says, 'The duty structures in India (for importing software) were 255 per cent then! But companies focused on IT services exports could import at no duty. We thought it was a good idea to identify those technologies, bring them to India, supply them to companies focused on exports and provide support.'[70]

Microland soon became the India partner for companies like Compaq, Cisco, SynOptics and Netscape. Any aspiring entrepreneur would be inspired by the stories behind each of these partnerships.

The Netscape agreement was signed in a parking lot just as the head of Netscape's international business was getting into her car. The VP of marketing at Cisco wondered why he should sign up with Microland instead of with the Tatas. Kar says, 'I told him that the Tatas are not standing outside your door. The day they come, go ahead and sign up with them. So, we made it very easy for those companies to sign up with us, and by virtue of getting all these alliances we grew rapidly. We were, I think, the first company that did Rs 100 crore in five years at that point in time.'[71]

In 1997, Bill Gates, chairman and CEO of Microsoft, visited India for the first time and spoke at an event sponsored by Intel and Compaq. His talk was titled 'Enterprise Tomorrow. Today'. Kar, who hosted the visit, fondly remembers an incident from that visit: 'In the Indian tradition, when you welcome a guest, you give a gift. So, what can you give the richest person on earth as a gift which he'll find meaningful? We found out his date of birth and drew his horoscope in silver jewellery. He wanted to understand every element in the picture!'[72]

By 2002, Microland realized that just the way application support and business process support functions were being outsourced to India, even IT infrastructure support would shift offshore, and the company transformed its business model towards remote management of networks.

The world-class capabilities that the Indian software services companies built came in very handy in leveraging the Y2K (Year 2000) opportunity in the late 1990s. Let us now take a peek into the story of the millennium bug and how two computing bytes transformed the fortunes of the Indian IT industry.

The Y2K Booster Shot for Indian Software Services Export

The term Y2K referred to the 'Year 2000' problem in the IT industry in the 1990s. In the early days of digital computers, when computer memory was an expensive resource, software programmers represented the year with two bytes rather than four. For example, they used '70' instead of '1970'. Thus, as year 2000 approached, it became clear that the year would be represented as '00' and the computer system could end up thinking that the year was '0000' or '1900' instead of the second millennium. The question of what would happen if the system interpreted the '00' incorrectly kept many in the developed world awake. The doomsday scenarios ranged from wrong interest calculations to large-scale blackouts to infrastructure damage. This scenario was a huge opportunity for the Indian software services industry. Research firm Gartner estimated the cost of Y2K remediation to be US$300–600 billion.[73]

For Indian software services companies like TCS, Y2K was a good fit with their capabilities in mainframe migration projects built over the 1970s and 1980s. Mahalingam, who was the architect of TCS's Y2K factory, explains, 'The first thing was that we needed to have the capability to automate as much as possible. So, we had the tools, looking at both the program as well as the data and then deciding what we were going to do with that. The second thing was that we needed to have a rugged infrastructure—I got on rent a textile factory at Coimbatore and set up this IBM mainframe system there with a fairly big pipe (communication link). The third was we had to have a methodology which essentially made it work like an operation. It was not software alone. We came up with seventeen steps and there would be a strict entry criteria as the programs would flow through the pipe. We would decide what path the program would take depending on the language, the computers involved. That path determined what kind of interventions we needed to make, what kind of quality checks we needed to run, and each step had an entry and exit validation, and so on.

'Another factor was how we got people (to the Y2K factory), how we got a normal TCS recruit who was an engineer from a good institution to work on this. So, we wondered if we could sub-contract it because other factories work on the basis of ancillary industries. So, why couldn't I develop an ancillary industry here, where I would teach people what exactly they had to do for each step of the process. We ran the training programmes for this and we typically recruited people with a BSc degree. I think during the period of two or three years we did something like 400 billion lines of code. So, this was a huge factory.'[74]

The strategy of Indian software services companies varied with respect to how they embraced Y2K. Infosys deliberately followed a de-risking strategy, post the GE incident, and did not want Y2K to be more than a certain percentage of the total value of projects. It also felt that clients did not want to pay top dollar for a bug-fix. Shibulal says, 'Infosys was a very metric-based organization. So, they had taken the decision that the Y2K work will not be more than 24 per cent (of its revenues).'[75]

Kris Gopalakrishnan mentions that Infosys saw Y2K more as an opportunity to establish a relationship with the client and understand industry domains: 'This was a bug. No functionality would be added. Just a fix that needed to be done. Companies (clients) decided that they would do it at the lowest possible cost. That is why they would come to India. We had a large workforce that was required and we could do this cost-effectively. Indian companies used this opportunity to establish themselves as credible players, to showcase their project management and quality capabilities. We (Indian software services companies) learnt about the business of various clients—banks, manufacturing companies, retailers, etc. At the end of (the Y2K) projects they (clients) continued to use us (Indian software services companies) for maintaining the software since we understood it. This was a great opportunity for Indian software services companies to leverage Y2K to establish the Indian software industry.'[76]

For Cognizant, Y2K came at an opportune time when it wanted to reduce its dependence on its erstwhile parent D&B. Lakshmi Narayanan says, 'We said we must get as many customers as possible. Fortunately for us, around that time, the year 2000 remediation (Y2K) gave us a big opportunity. Although it might not be very interesting work, strategically we decided to get involved in it very actively. We grew rapidly, with more customers, more remediation work. Since we had been very selective in selling to important large customers in the industry segments that we were active in, we managed to retain them.'[77]

Some Indian software services companies did not see Y2K as a fit with their business strategy and have mixed feelings looking back. Ashank is pragmatic when he reminisces about the Y2K era: 'We were culturally not very much geared to ride Y2K, which turned out to be a disadvantage in a way because it opened up doors for the Indian IT industry with the Fortune 500 companies. But we focused on Web and CRM and more around smaller sized dotcom companies in 2000 and generated good business. Although, the whole dotcom business went down in 2001 and we lost a lot of money there, it helped us to remain focused on (new) technology. I still remember we built tools for the web era, of which we are still proud.'[78]

Overall, the Indian IT industry tapped into the Y2K opportunity with aplomb. According to NASSCOM estimates, Indian engineers worked on the Y2K bug remediation for 860 companies of which 500 were overseas companies. India earned around US$2.3 billion in export revenues from Y2K.[79] To put this amount in perspective, it was more than the entire Indian IT industry's export earnings of US$2 billion in 1998![80]

While Y2K was a big opportunity for Indian IT services, the second half of the 1990s witnessed a significant IT revolution in India when public Internet services were launched in the country in 1995.

Early Days of the Internet in India

In May 2020, for the first time in India, there were more Internet users in rural areas than in the urban areas. India also had the second largest Internet user base in the world, at 503 million.[81] What a journey it has been from the Internet's humble beginnings in India on 15 August 1995, when it was first made available for public access in the country. B.K. Syngal, then chairman of VSNL, described that moment for India thus: 'The world shrank the day the Internet entered our lives. It surely was a second Independence Day.'[82] VSNL launched the Internet service in five cities in India, giving retail users forty minutes per day of Internet usage, at the rate of Rs 15,000 per annum (a princely sum in those days), and at maximum speeds of 128Kbps.[83] Modern-day Internet users would find these subscription plans unbelievable!

Internet Tales from India

The Internet and ERNET Connection[84]

S. Sadagopan, who had been closely involved with the ERNET project, which preceded the launch of the Internet, says, 'VSNL thought that there will be a few hundred users. No one thought that it will be taken up so fast, but people found a way of reusing, sharing their Internet accounts. Suddenly, TCP/IP became part of the vocabulary of housewives, because they had to tick TCP/IP or dial-up for an account.'

VSNL also faced a lot of technical challenges in providing Internet services in the initial days. Sadagopan says, 'I still remember, VSNL was buying modems in ones and twos, and putting together 100–200 modems, which were failing. That was the time we (members from ERNET) actually went and told VSNL about a modem pool . . . one box which actually gives you the equivalent of 100–200 devices. So, it is kind of interesting how the ERNET project, a networking project within the IITs, actually prepared the country for the broader Internet revolution.'

The Internet Era Begins in Indian Management Institutions with IIM Bangalore[85]

In September 1995, Prof. Sadagopan had just moved to IIM Bangalore from IIT Kanpur when he was asked by the director to explore the possibility of giving the institute an Internet presence. Sadagopan worked his contact G. Varadhan, the director at STPI Bengaluru to get an Internet account for IIM Bangalore on a priority basis. He also interacted with Som Mittal at Digital to get the best modems and hardware required. Sadagopan says, 'On 30th December 1995, we worked the whole night, and also wrote a hardcoded HTML 1.0 web page for IIMB. At 9 p.m. (on 31 December) we were actually on the Internet. The next morning, IIMB was on the front page of *The Times of India* because no other IIM was on the Internet in 1995. Post that, the IT industry took to IIMB very differently.' In 1998, IIM Bangalore launched a part-time three-year postgraduate programme in software enterprise management (PGSEM) targeting young IT professionals working in Bengaluru.

The Indya Story[86]

As part of the burgeoning Internet economy in India, Microland built several companies such as Planetasia.com, indya.com, ITspace. com and media2india.net. Pradeep Kar recalls those heady days and says, 'I was busy hiring all the people. I used to carry blank offer letters and just wrote their names, their title, their compensation, and made an offer. When AOL acquired Time Warner in the US, News Corp wanted to protect their interests in Asia. They accepted my ask of 50 million dollars for one-third of the company (indya.com).

'We released a spectacular ad on the first page of *The Times of India*. This was the first time in the history of Indian advertising that the front page was an ad, and with no editorial. It said in the centre—"Breaking 163 years of perfect tradition. Catch the headlines on the last page today." You turn the page, and it says, "India changes name" (to Indya).'

National Computing Capability Development in the 1990s

Apart from the Internet, several developments in India's supercomputing capability, including the launch of the nation's indigenous supercomputer, the PARAM, were witnessed during the 1990s. From the perspective of strengthening computer science education and application of computer science to solve real-world problems, the Kanwal Rekhi School of Information Technology was established at IIT Bombay. Let us take a peek into these developments.

Supercomputing Initiatives in India

In the previous chapter, we saw how the seeds of supercomputing were sown in IISc and CDAC. Multiple supercomputing flowers bloomed in India in the late 1980s and 1990s. Roddam Narasimha, when he took over as director of National Aerospace Laboratories (NAL), realized that its mainframe computer was not powerful enough to solve complex computational fluid dynamics applications. He constituted a team under the leadership of U.N. Sinha, which developed Flosolver, India's first parallel computer, in 1986. The team continued to improve the parallel computer and, in 1992, the Flosolver Mk3 was used for direct numerical simulation of turbulent flow for the first time in India, and later for weather predictions.[87]

The PARAM is India's most well-known supercomputer. Vijay Bhatkar, founder and executive director of CDAC, was handpicked for the role and tasked with the responsibility of delivering India's supercomputer in quick time. When Bhatkar met Prime Minister Rajiv Gandhi, he told the PM: 'I have not seen a supercomputer as we have no access to it. I have only seen a picture of the Cray! But, yes, we can build a supercomputer in less time than it will take us in trying to import Cray from the US. The whole effort, including building an institution, developing the technology, commissioning and installing India's first supercomputer will cost less than the cost of Cray.'[88] In 1991, within three years of setting up CDAC, they achieved success in producing the PARAM 8000 supercomputer.

The advantage of relying on indigenous supercomputers was beautifully illustrated in the case of Indian Space Research Organization (ISRO) developing its remote sensing capabilities by means of an airborne Synthetic Aperture Radar (SAR) system. When it used its existing mainframe, a VAX-11/780 with a vector processor to run the satellite images, it faced performance issues. ISRO needed a supercomputer. In 1998, when India conducted a second nuclear test, the US imposed severe restrictions on dual-use technologies and ISRO could not import supercomputers from the US. It then evaluated three Indian supercomputers and chose CDAC's PARAM. The transputer (series of microprocessors meant for parallel processing) used in PARAM was the British Inmos and hence not subject to the US embargo. Using an eight-node PARAM, ISRO was able to process a European Remote Sensing satellite SAR image in forty minutes as compared to the eight hours it took earlier using its mainframe.[89]

The Indian supercomputers were put to use in the defence context too. Recounting the interest that Dr Abdul Kalam showed in supercomputers for India's missile programme, Balakrishnan, who was at that time a professor of aerospace engineering and a leader at the supercomputing centre at IISc, says, 'Dr Kalam was of the opinion that for the missile programme to succeed he needed to use computational fluid dynamics. He knew that you could not go to the wind tunnel 200 times and try it out (to see if the missile designs worked). So, he began looking at the possibility of using the supercomputer. And he had the money. ANURAG (the Advanced Numerical Research and Analysis Group of DRDL) was created at that time (circa 1988).'[90]

India's supercomputing journey continued, with its highs and lows, in the coming years. Balakrishnan says, 'By the year 2008–09, the gap between India and China, the US and the European countries widened so much, it looked like we would be pushed into oblivion. It was very scary.'[91] He headed the committee to suggest a way forward, and it culminated in the creation, in 2015, of a Rs 4500-crore National Supercomputing Mission, aiming at installing a vast grid of over seventy high-performance computing facilities in the country. Balakrishnan says, 'One-fourth of the scientific manpower in the country should be touched by the supercomputers when the project is over.'[92]

The Kanwal Rekhi School of Information Technology at IIT Bombay

As we saw earlier, IIT Bombay began its computing journey with the Minsk, 'a Russian machine EC1030 which was essentially like an IBM 360'.[93] Nandan Nilekani, co-founder of Infosys who graduated from IIT Bombay in 1978, fondly recalls his experiences and says, 'We had a strong computer science department. We had a fantastic team of professors like Issac (Kurien Issac), Phatak (Deepak Phatak), Sarda (Nandlal Sarda) and S.S.S.P. Rao.'[94] In 1986, IIT Bombay got its first fourth-generation mainframe computer, the CDC Cyber 180/840.[95]

Around this time, Deepak Phatak and his CS colleagues realized the growing importance of applications of computers and wanted to create a school for information technology. Around 1994, Phatak anchored IIT Bombay's outreach to its alumni for financial support for this initiative. He says, 'Kanwal Rekhi (the celebrated Silicon Valley venture capitalist and entrepreneur) agreed to give us a US$2 million matching grant. In fact, immediately afterwards, Nandan Nilekani too agreed to match the US$2 million. That is how the Kanwal Rekhi School of Information Technology was set up. We were also able to fashion some special facilities for the faculty who would join here, in terms of research grants, travel grants and so on. We gave special scholarships to students willing to do MTech, and to faculty members across the institute who were willing to offer interdisciplinary courses, and we did make a mark.'[96]

IIT Bombay is today one of the best institutions in India for computer science research.

IT services exports continued to increase at a healthy clip—according to NASSCOM, they increased more than tenfold from US$4 billion in 2000 to US$50 billion in 2009–10.[97, 98] The IT services industry expanded through the introduction of new services like ERP package implementations and business process outsourcing. MNCs flocked to India to set up IT and engineering services subsidiaries. The industry also witnessed some big shocks, including the downturn in 2008 caused by the global financial crisis and the unsavoury saga of the Satyam scandal. India heralded the emergence of the third wave of entrepreneurship towards the end of the decade. The government showed a renewed interest in mission-mode projects that included Aadhaar, the world's largest biometric ID system.

6

Indian IT Comes of Age

The world did not come to an end in 2000, after all, as predicted by the IT doomsayers. However, one important outcome of the Y2K journey was that Indian IT companies got firmly entrenched among the large Fortune 500 MNCs. The Indian companies had shown they had the ability to manage large projects under strict deadlines and with globally distributed teams. Not only did they fix the Y2K bug, but they also came to have expert IT teams who had in-depth knowledge of both legacy and emerging IT systems. Thus, the 2000s became a golden period of expansion and rapid scaling up for the Indian IT industry.

The IT industry brought GDM into adjacent services like infrastructure management, software testing, systems integration and business process outsourcing/management (BPO/BPM) and expanded its service offerings. It also brought new capabilities into its fold, like consulting. In this decade, the IT industry also grew geographically—beyond the US and UK and into continental Europe, Latin America, Australia and other geographies. This decade also saw a rapid increase in the number of subsidiaries of MNCs in India, in the form of global capability centres (GCCs) focused on engineering, IT and BPM.

But it was not just sunshine throughout for the IT industry in the 2000s. It also witnessed some dark moments in this decade. We will explore the challenges of the 2008 global financial crisis and its impact on the IT industry, and the Satyam scandal. What was heartening was that the industry found the resilience to rally after each of these crises and come out stronger.

The 2000s also witnessed a new wave of IT start-ups and companies that pushed the boundaries of the industry; they included the likes of Genpact (in BPO), Ittiam Systems (in video technologies) and Pico Peta Simputer (in hardware devices). This period also saw the advent of new IT-enabled start-ups—B2C or consumer-facing start-ups like Flipkart, Ola and Paytm; and B2B product and SaaS companies like InMobi, Druva and Zoho. This entrepreneurial trend was no flash in the pan and continues to date.

The various governments in India, both at the Centre and the states, created forward-looking IT policies. They were at the forefront of adopting IT through impactful e-governance initiatives and transformative mission-mode projects like Aadhaar, the world's largest biometric identity system for citizens.

New Service Lines and New Markets Get Added to the Industry Portfolio

The late 1990s and early 2000s witnessed a new wave of growth for Indian IT services, including opportunities beyond Y2K and those emerging post the dotcom bust. The IT industry brought GDM into adjacent services like enterprise resource planning (ERP), testing and validation, infrastructure management, systems integration and business process outsourcing. Consequently, the industry grew more than 10 times in the decade. Companies like TCS and Infosys crossed US$1 billion in revenue each in the early 2000s, and they both went past the 1 lakh headcount mark in the second half of the decade.

'In 2001, the Internet bubble burst, and growth came down dramatically. We knew that if we had to grow, we had to create new engines of growth. We looked at adjacent services and how we can replicate the global delivery model on these services—all IT-related services like infrastructure management, testing and any service that required the use of computers, like business process outsourcing. Growth continued as we picked up new services. We (Infosys) took about twenty-three years to hit the 1-billion-dollar revenue mark, twenty-three months for the next 1 billion and thirteen months for the next 1 billion. This (the early 2000s) was a period of very high growth,' says Kris Gopalakrishnan, explaining the rationale behind Infosys's expansion into new services.[1]

From the late 1990s, there was a spurt in large MNCs redesigning and automating their business processes. The ERP software applications that helped companies achieve this transformation were made popular by software product companies like SAP and Oracle. Analysts predicted that the ERP product market would grow at a compound annual growth rate of 37 per cent between 1997 and 2002, and reach about US$52 billion.[2] This, in turn, created a multi-billion-dollar opportunity for the Indian IT services companies in porting data from disparate existing IT systems and in consulting for, customizing, implementing and maintaining the ERP software.

By the early 2000s, large MNCs required the services of IT companies to ensure that their IT infrastructure, which included PCs, servers, networking equipment and sometimes even legacy mainframes, were working 24/7 and available to users. Analysts expected the IT infrastructure management services market to grow from US$146 billion in 2004 to US$218 billion in 2010.[3] Improved global data communications networks ensured that some of these services could be provisioned from India. And services around management of IT infrastructure became another business line for Indian IT services companies. Pradeep Kar narrates how Microland rode this wave: 'The Y2K created the arrival of the (Indian) software industry. Telecom deregulation created the emergence of the BPO industry. To my mind, it was only logical for IT infrastructure to move offshore. From 2002 till now, we have focused on building remote management of networks.'[4]

While ERP implementation became popular, it did not completely eliminate the need for bespoke software. This was especially true for large MNCs who were still developing new software applications or enhancing existing ones. These applications had to be architected, tested to ensure they functioned as per their design, and integrated with ERP and other applications. Many Indian IT services companies brought the specialized expertise, methodologies and tools together, and established business units focused on systems integration and testing and validation services.

Indian IT services firms also moved upstream and entered the lucrative consulting segment. Shibulal traces the chronology of new services in Infosys: 'I had the privilege of starting our Internet consulting practice in 1997. It was about technology, architecture and security consulting, and the service line was at the right place at the right time during the Internet boom. When Y2K tapered, it was followed by the enterprise solution practice, which became a pretty big part of our revenue, which was followed by the Infosys business consulting service. Then we introduced systems integration, infrastructure management and independent validation later on in the life cycle.'[5] In this decade, Infosys also set up its software engineering technology labs and the domain competency group to bring new IT and industry-domain capabilities into its fold.

Later in the decade, the Indian IT industry felt the shock of the 2008 financial crisis. This crisis also coincided with a rapidly evolving global technology landscape and provided an opportunity for Indian IT services companies to launch new services. Lakshmi Narayanan of Cognizant says, 'After this turmoil, things were not going to be the same. A new normal would be established. So, we partnered with CMU and MIT (the American universities) and started working on the future of work. Around 2008–09, we got into newer technologies, like social media, mobility, analytics and cloud computing, popularly called SMAC.'[6] The emerging technologies proved opportune for Ashok Soota too, long-time CEO of Wipro and founder of Mindtree, to launch a new IT services company. 'When we started Mindtree, the change was the Internet. The next decade was about all the SMAC capabilities and not just the Internet. We had the Internet of Things coming up, and unified communications, and yet no company came up to say that we would like to be a large integrated player which brought these newer technologies together. And that is why Happiest Minds (Soota's start-up) came into existence in 2011.'[7]

In the mid-to-late 2000s, the Indian IT services companies realized that IT-platform-based services provided a new stream of opportunity. According to Shibulal, 'Clients were looking for services that were merged with intellectual property, whether it was a platform, a tool, or a piece of code; and which could enhance productivity, reduce the cost of ownership, and reduce the capital spend.'[8] N. Chandrasekaran, then head of global sales at TCS, says, 'In 2005, I made a presentation to the TCS board asking for GBP50 million to invest in building our insurance platform. At that time, we were a 1.1-billion-dollar company. So, it was a big investment. Today, we have a number of platforms—TCS iON is hugely successful in education assessment, in insurance, banking, life sciences and others (domains). A platform-based services model changes the risk from the client perspective, gives certainty, and everything moves towards an (business) outcome as opposed to a focus on work effort.'[9]

As the Indian IT services companies began building their business at scale, besides offering their full-services play, they started adopting a full-stakeholder play—targeting not just the CIO, but also heads of other functions, such as the chief marketing officer (CMO), chief finance officer (CFO) and chief of engineering at the client's, and also opening up offices in new geographies. In the early 2000s, Infosys opened new development centres in countries like Canada and Japan, and subsidiaries in Australia and China. Chandrasekaran recounts some of the successful growth strategies he undertook when he became CEO and MD of TCS in 2009: 'We had this slogan, "Stay close and stay relevant". Say, a client budget is US$1 billion, of which US$950 million is in the

US and US\$50 million is spread over Brazil, eastern Europe and China. One approach is to target the 950 million . . . But there is another way. The client feels great pain in getting the same level of service in the markets where US\$50 million (as opposed to where US\$950 million) is being spent. If you want to be relevant, you have to service these markets. And then you can become close to the client.'[10] Pursuing a 'global network delivery model' strategy, TCS soon opened new development centres in Brazil, France, Germany, Mexico, Japan, South Africa, Canada and China. Chandrasekaran says, 'We said, in each of these markets, how do we scale—(how do we work) with the big (global) clients, and at the same time leverage the local delivery capability to service local clients.'[11]

Towards the end of the 2000s, several large Indian and even global IT companies like Oracle, Cisco and Microsoft were not just servicing global clients from India but also forayed into servicing the Indian market, with a special focus on big government projects. Commenting on the government's Digital India initiative launched in 2014–15, Bhaskar Pramanik, then chairperson of Microsoft India, says, 'We took Digital India and made it core to our (Microsoft) national plan. It's focused on education, governance of skills, digital economy and cyber security.'[12]

Key Metrics for the IT Services and Consulting Business

Kris Gopalakrishnan suggests that the primary axis of the growth model of the Indian IT services industry is the 'client' in different industries, and the secondary axis of growth is defined by marketing, geography, services, technology and partnerships.

These factors translated into the key metrics that the company leaders tracked—company financials, sales and employee-related (such as revenue, repeat business, net margins, utilization), client-relationship-health-related (such as size and depth of relationship) and corporate-branding-related (such as corporate governance, thought-leadership).

Key Financial and Sales Metrics	Client Relationship Health Indicators	Factors Contributing to Branding

• Revenues
  • Revenues by business segment
  • Revenues by geography
  • Revenues from new services
• Operating and net margin
• EPS (Earnings per share)
• Total number of clients
  • New clients
  • Million-dollar clients (1M+, 10M+, 50M+, 100M+)
• Repeat business
• Large deals
• Employee headcount and attrition
• Employee utilization
	• Size in revenue terms and number of people
	• Growth
	• Years of relationship
	• Date of next renewal
	• Number of services
	• Number of departments (coverage)
	• Profitability
	• Client senior management visibility
	• Joint R&D and innovation
	• Reference client
		• Quality systems
		• Financial strength
		• Size
		• Longevity
		• Corporate governance
		• Thought leadership
		• Campus
		• Education and training
		• Financial markets
		• Awards and recognition
		• Events
		• CSR
		• Senior leadership visibility

Extracted from a lecture by Kris Gopalakrishnan on 'Services Marketing'.

Continuing this narrative on the new markets and services of the Indian IT industry, let us turn our attention to business process outsourcing (BPO), also known as IT-enabled services (ITeS)—a domain in which India achieved spectacular success and earned itself the moniker of 'back office of the world'.

—————

Business Process Outsourcing in India—From Back-Offices of American Express and GE to Start-ups like Genpact and Spectramind

The genesis of BPO in India lies in the tales of corporate 'intrapreneurship' at companies like American Express and GE. And this industry was nurtured by the extraordinary zeal and belief in India demonstrated by business leaders like Raman Roy and Pramod Bhasin.

In 1983, Raman Roy launched the American Express credit card in India and consequently set up a small credit-card processing team. It was in 1991, when the India team handled the bank reconciliation for the Korean won (for American Express), that the proverbial floodgates opened for India BPO. Roy says, 'That is the germ that started the potential of doing international work out of India. And downstream, Amex decided to invest and set up a separate centre (in India). As a by-product, the industry was born. At one point, we were closing books for thirty-two different countries out of this facility.'[13]

By 1996–97, GE had taken notice of this interesting trend out of India. Pramod Bhasin, a GE veteran who had set up GE Capital in the country, recalls with much mirth pitching the idea to his boss, Gary Wendt, for GE's 'India BPO' at a car park in Chennai. The irony was that even as he made the pitch his call was continually dropping![14] Bhasin was not deterred. He soon hired Raman Roy to manage GE's BPO operations. 'We knew we had to convince a lot of people in the US who had probably never travelled (to India), to come here and trust us with their business processes. We had some things going for us. I was a GE officer, and my team had credibility. Also, I had the backing of my bosses and that was invaluable. Roy figured out about the telecom licence and T1 bandwidth to do the work from India. GE was entrepreneurial and they were willing to let us try.'[15]

Soon, a twenty-member pilot project ran GE Capital's back-office services operations in Gurgaon, India. It then transformed, within a few years, into a large-scale captive company, GE Capital International Services (GECIS), with operations in Dalian, China to service Japan; in Budapest, Hungary to service Europe; and in Juarez, Mexico to service the US.

Bhasin recalls how GECIS caught the attention of Jack Welch, CEO of GE: 'We began experimenting with mortgage applications and car-loan processing. We could save 30 to 40 per cent of our money. Our productivity was great, thanks to the subject matter and operations expertise. We were delivering as a Six Sigma beta site.'[16] Jack Welch, when he visited India in 2000, received an enthusiastic welcome from the GECIS employees, and he fell in love with them and with the country. He said, 'In America, I am running around every fast-food restaurant to find somebody who can work for me in the back office. And in India, we have qualified graduates standing here, ambitious, energized, and loving to do this work.'[17] Bhasin recalls Welch's address to GE's corporate executive council comprising the top 120 officers of the company: 'In his own inimitable style, he said, "Anybody who hasn't been to India is an idiot." And he sat down . . . At the end (of that meeting), I took applications for visas from everybody in the room. In two–three years, we were doing very complex work—treasury management, doing the trades at the end of the day, sweeping the cash, moving money around GE Capital, closing the books.'[18]

In the mid-2000s, GECIS reached an inflection point. Bhasin says, 'We were then about 350 million dollars in revenues. By then, WNS and EXL (Indian BPO start-ups) had come up. McKinsey was setting up its knowledge centre (in India). GE would not allow us to do third-party business. If it had, we would have been ten times our size then. So, on 1 January 2005, GECIS was spun off from GE. Atlantic and Oak Hill came in and bought 60 per cent of the businesses. GE retained 40 per cent.'[19] That was how Genpact (derived from 'generating global impact') was formed. And in 2007, Genpact had a successful listing on the NYSE.

Raman Roy walked down a different entrepreneurial road when he started Spectramind in 2000: 'With Amex, we proved India could work (for BPO). In GE we showed it was scalable. But at the end of the day we were all a cost centre, a captive. We dreamed even bigger and came up with the proposal to go third-party.'

In 2002, like the other Indian IT service providers, Wipro was looking to expand its portfolio to include BPO. It made such an attractive offer that the VC firm Chrys Capital, which had invested in Spectramind, exercised its drag-along rights to accept the acquisition offer. Roy stayed on as CEO of Wipro–Spectramind. Commenting on the advantages of the merger with Wipro, he says, 'I guess that ability to have the funding, the ability to have the branding, the ability to leverage the salesforce, played a role in us becoming the single largest BPO provider at that time.' Life came a full circle for Roy when the company won American Express as a customer.

The Indian Business Process Outsourcing Industry— Anecdotes and Innovations

Frugal Innovations from India Save the Day[20, 21]

American Express implemented a US$10-million software solution for its time-sensitive bank reconciliations processing, but it failed spectacularly during its global roll-out. Fortunately, Raman Roy had developed in India, for US$5000, an alternative 'recon step' solution, which ultimately became the global standard for reconciliation at Amex!

At GE Capital, the India BPO centre processed data that went into creating an earthquake certificate required for mortgage loans in the US. The finely tuned two-to-three-day process of printing and couriering the certificates abroad fell apart when the high-end Xerox printer in India, a machine whose servicing was done from Singapore, broke down. One computer whiz-kid on the team figured out that they could capture a digital image from the printer and send the image as an attachment over email on the same day. Raman says, 'Thanks to an accident, we became heroes within GE, because from a paper process we were able to convert to a digital process.'

Attracting Women into the BPO Industry[22, 23]

Pramod Bhasin recounts the significant impact that GECIS had on women in the BPO industry: 'We did a brilliant recording for Public Broadcasting Service (PBS) in the US on the lives of three women who were working for us. One from a middle-class family, one from a lower middle-class family but very independent, and one whose father was a cook. The sociological impact was enormous—the empowerment of women, giving them careers. We were very strong on (prevention and tackling of) sexual harassment and women protection.'

In 2013, TCS tied up with Saudi Aramco and GE to establish the world's first 'all-women' business process services centre in Riyadh, Saudi Arabia. N. Chandrasekaran says, 'When I got a call about this concept from Jeff Imelt (from GE) and Khalid Al-Falih (from Aramco), I went ahead and committed. I must compliment the TCS women—we got twenty women leaders who went there and stayed for one to three years, hired and trained the first hundred local hires and set it up. It is a very large centre now.'

Thus, Indian IT successfully brought new services into their fold in this decade. But, what about their presence in software products? Let us discover the story of a hidden gem, the global dominance of Indian IT in the core banking product segment.

Indian Core Banking Systems are World Leaders

In this decade, Indian IT commenced its journey towards global leadership in the product category of core banking, which was essentially a system that processed daily banking transactions and offered deposit, loan and credit-processing capabilities. Almost all large multibranch banks in most countries in the world run on core banking systems. By 2019, three out of four core retail banking products in the 'Leaders' Magic Quadrant of Gartner, an independent market analyst company, were Indian or had an Indian lineage.[24] These products were from Infosys, TCS and Oracle (through the acquisition of the Indian core banking specialist company, i-flex Solutions).

Nandan Nilekani provides a bird's eye view of the journey of Infosys' core banking product—Bancs 2000, which evolved into Finacle and is now EdgeVerve Finacle: 'In the mid-80s, the Indian Banks' Association actually had a few projects where they tied up software vendors with banks to build a branch banking solution. And we built Bancs 2000 and rolled it out with Canara Bank. Then I think the big push happened in the early 1990s as part of liberalization . . . In 1994, the government allowed new private banks, like ICICI Bank, UTI Bank and IDBI Bank to come up. Those banks wanted to use the latest technology for their bank-wide computerization. This led to our product, Finacle, becoming the dominant product in the Indian market. And, today, it is a global product. I think that played a very important role in demonstrating that Indian companies could build world-class enterprise products for the global market.'[25]

TCS too had built a lot of experience in the banking sector. Ramadorai says, 'Historically, if you look at TCS, interbranch reconciliation, banking and financial services were very strong competencies. We consciously built on projects like Western Trust and Savings, Savings and Loan Association in the US, and SegaInterSettle in Switzerland.'[26] TCS built on these competencies to enter the banking product space. It first partnered with TKS-Teknosoft in Switzerland to develop SEGA (SegaInterSettle), a real-time security settlement system for the Swiss National Bank. TCS continued this relationship further and, in the early 1990s developed Quartz, a banking platform for small banks in

Switzerland. In 2002, TCS partnered with the Australian Financial Network Services (FNS) to win the world's largest centralized core banking system implementation for State Bank of India.[27] By the mid-2000s, TCS acquired TKS-Teknosoft as well as FNS to create BaNCS, a banking solution that now services more than 25 per cent of the global population.[28]

i-flex Solutions had its origins in the Indian IT subsidiary of Citibank. In the mid-1980s, Jerry Rao, who headed Citi's retail banking in India, helped set up Citicorp Overseas Software Limited (COSL) for developing software for the bank's internal requirements globally. Rajesh Hukku of COSL led the development of MicroBanker, a basic banking system targeted at developing countries. COSL spun off Citicorp Information Technology Industries Limited (CITIL) in 1992. CITIL, which was later renamed i-flex Solutions, created a newer banking product. i-flex Solutions was eventually acquired for US$592 million by Oracle in 2005 to create Oracle Financial Services.[29]

Given India's legacy and strength in the enterprise IT domain, it appears that the Indian success in core banking systems will be carried on by the emerging Indian start-ups in the enterprise SaaS domain, a story that we will visit soon. The success of American Express, GE and Citibank with their IT and BPO subsidiaries in India inspired other MNCs to follow suit. We have seen how TI was among the first MNCs to set up a subsidiary in India for its R&D and engineering. Let us now look at the growth of R&D, IT and BPO subsidiaries of MNCs in India, also known as global capability centres (GCCs).

India-based Global Capability Centres Become an Integral Part of the IT Industry

India has the largest concentration of GCCs in world today. By the end of FY 2018–19, it was estimated that over 1250 MNCs set up about 1750 GCCs in India and directly employed about 1 million people.[30] The wave of R&D services at GCCs began with the IT product MNCs getting intrigued by the success of early movers like TI, Lucent and Motorola. The 1990s saw the advent of companies like IBM, Cisco and SAP. By the 2000s, the numbers exploded with the likes of Google, Dell and Amazon setting up their R&D centres in India. India witnessed a similar growth in IT services and BPO GCCs with the arrival of MNCs like Standard Chartered and J.P. Morgan (in financial services), Target and Walmart (in retail) and Microsoft and Intel (in technology). The GCCs were concentrated in the Deccan plateau cities of Bengaluru, Pune and Hyderabad, mimicking the geographical spread of Indian software services companies.

It is interesting to understand the path taken by the Indian R&D GCCs to achieve their pre-eminent scale and scope of operations. Srini Rajam, who headed TI India, says, 'TI was very welcoming of the companies coming into India and helping them to realize the potential here. They needed a proof of concept, because it was a very big decision in the 1980s and early 1990s to locate a strategic R&D centre in India, away from the headquarters.'[31]

Most of these GCCs, which were controlled by the leaders in their headquarters, started with the objective of augmenting their product development teams for completing R&D projects. After a few years, and based on successful project execution, the GCCs took on more end-to-end and independent ownership of R&D and engineering projects. This was a phase when the Indian R&D GCCs got staffed with professionals with many years of domain expertise. The reporting of the Indian GCC teams shifted to the business and product executives in headquarters rather than the engineering leadership there.

Some R&D GCCs soon stepped up to take entire ownership of products and product lines. For example, Advanced Services Router (ASR) 901, which was Cisco's first commercial product developed end-to-end in India in 2011, marked a key milestone in its R&D services GCC.[32] A decade into their GCC in India, Veritas engineers from Pune were instrumental in developing hugely successful global products, such as the cluster server and the continuous data replication server for large companies, especially in financial services and telecommunications. Some of these GCCs also produced leadership talent for several Indian start-ups. 'In 2006–07, one of the principal engineers of Veritas, Milind Borate, stepped away with two other people (Jaspreet Singh and Ramani Kothandaraman) to democratize continuous data replication for Indian assemblies and small companies. That company is Druva (which is now a unicorn SaaS provider),'[33] says Sharad Sharma, former head of Yahoo India R&D.

The rapid growth of GCCs focusing on IT services was exemplified by the growth of IBM in India. The first decade of the twenty-first century saw IBM India increase its intake of employees to over 1 lakh, largely from IT services and BPO businesses, probably making India house the largest headcount for IBM.[34] The IT services GCCs typically started with Level 3 (basic) IT support and software development resulting from a work overflow from existing onsite teams. The GCC usually interacted with and mirrored the IT organization at its headquarters and focused on the supply side or back-end of the IT function, like programming. The GCCs ran operations with cost arbitrage as the major benefit. A 'follow the sun' model, with staff in both India and the US or Europe, also increased the number of hours in a workday available for a project.

After a few years of operation, and having won the confidence of headquarters based on their capabilities, the India IT services GCCs were then given independent assignments consisting of a portfolio of IT projects focused on value creation and innovation. The GCCs directly interacted with the business units in the MNC and were responsible for the entire IT life cycle of planning, building, implementing and maintaining IT systems for the business unit. Some IT services GCCs today are also the innovation engines for their parent MNCs. Walmart Labs India is one example of how the India GCC model is leveraged for cutting-edge projects, working in partnership with Walmart Labs in the Silicon Valley.[35]

Many MNCs developed a hybrid model and created sophisticated frameworks to decide what part of their IT portfolio was kept in-house in their Indian GCCs and what was outsourced to their IT services partners. Over the years, some MNCs have unlocked value by selling their GCCs to Indian IT services partners. For example, Citibank sold its IT services GCC to Wipro and its BPO GCC to TCS in the late 2000s.[36, 37] Chandrasekaran, who was then COO of TCS, narrates the fascinating story behind the acquisition of Citigroup Global Services: 'In 2002–03, TCS had a BPO joint venture with HDFC. We divested it before we went public. In line with our strategy of offering a full range of services to our clients, BPO capability was important for us. We signed the preliminary term sheet for the Citi BPO deal in June (2008). And in September, the Citi stock collapsed. The bankers involved in the deal suggested invoking force majeure and getting out of the deal. The risk was that the Citi contract could go bad. However, this was a deal which put us in a business relationship with the CEO and CFO of Citi at that time. We decided to go ahead with the deal for US$510 million. Not many would know . . . in five years we generated US$500 million in free cash flow from the deal, and it was the platform on which we built our financial services BPO and analytics business.'[38]

The rapid of growth of GCCs in India can be attributed to factors similar to those that nurtured the growth of the Indian IT industry. India's IT talent pool is among the largest in the world and stands at over 4 million in 2020–21. Indian engineering colleges see an enrolment of more than 1 million students a year, which provides a healthy supply to the IT workforce. The R&D GCCs are also reasonably well connected with the R&D ecosystem in India. They fund research projects in the top technology and engineering universities and also provide sabbatical opportunities for faculty members. Many MNCs that have GCCs also do business in India, and there is an increasingly symbiotic relationship between the India business and the India GCCs. Last but not least, these organizations, such as Netapp R&D services and Target IT GCCs, are also increasingly tapping into the vibrant Indian start-up ecosystem by setting up incubators, nurturing the start-ups and then providing access to their parent company and their customers with the objective of spurring innovation.

Now, we turn to the 2008 financial crisis and the Satyam scandal, two events that shook the Indian IT industry and catalysed a reset to a new normal.

Indian IT Navigates the 2008 Financial Crisis to Emerge Resilient

The trigger for the 2008 financial crisis was speculative activity fuelled by availability of cheap credit in the global financial markets, especially in mortgage transactions, in the US and western Europe. The financial crisis culminated in the collapse of the investment banking giant Lehman Brothers in September 2008, and resulted in a situation which required the US government to bail out banks there.

Almost all the large Indian IT services companies had a significant number of clients from the financial services industry in the US and Europe and got a first-hand shock from their mortgage clients. Kris Gopalakrishnan, who took over as CEO of Infosys in 2007, recalls navigating these difficult times: 'Everything was going fine, we grew by about 35 per cent, and suddenly the world around us collapsed. The financial crisis happened overnight. We were looking at decreasing revenues . . . The (next) four years were probably the most traumatic for the company (Infosys), but we came out stronger . . . We made 25,000 (job) offers on campuses, honoured all offers and let these people join in staggered periods. We extended our training programme to six months and trained people on two technologies (instead of one) . . . We introduced new services like consulting and focused on IP creation.'[39]

Around this time, Cognizant had built a strong position in the financial services industry domain, with many of the top ten global investment banks and retail banks as their clients. Around 2007, Cognizant, during its discussions with the executives of IndyMac, a new-age US mortgage company that sold mortgages electronically using the Internet, sensed that something was amiss. And later, when

IndyMac and Bear Sterns, another financial services client with an exposure to mortgages, collapsed, Cognizant realized that there would be serious trouble ahead. Lakshmi Narayanan vividly recalls the crisis and the plans put in place to mitigate the impact: 'When the financial meltdown happened, close to about 45 per cent of our business was from the financial services sector. And no bank was left untouched. So, we were staring at a very bleak future at that point in time. And that's when we decided that this was an opportunity . . . The top fifty or sixty people in the company were actively engaged in rebuilding the business, thinking of new solutions and coming up with ideas for reducing the pain of our customers. We would meet in Frankfurt. It was easy for people from Europe, India and the US to meet there over a weekend at an airport hotel. We did it every month, and then switched to quarterly meetings . . . We had to necessarily do it because it was almost a question of survival. Once we got through the 2008–09 period, we started winning more (business) because our clients like JP Morgan and Wells Fargo would acquire a company and we had to work on the integration. We participated in the transformation of the financial services industry.'[40]

The financial crisis of 2008 made Indian software companies increasingly focus on differentiation and adding value to clients in the emerging global economic context where businesses became more competitive. Narayana Murthy puts this in perspective: 'I created a project called "Business Value Addition". When a customer makes a choice, they look at what price they are going to pay for the project and what value they get from it. The "business-value leverage" is value over price. Suppose I say, "You give me a dollar and I will give you back a value of two dollars" and somebody else says, "Give me US$1.6 and I will give you a value of US$4." His business-value leverage is 4 over 1.6, which is 2.5, whereas my business value leverage is 2 over 1, which is 2. Therefore, you will automatically go with him. And the beauty of that is that he gets a 60 per cent higher price than I do but at the same time he is giving 25 per cent higher business-value leverage. We have to create mathematical models that convert our technical effort into impact of what we do, and convert the impact into the financial benefit that the customer gets. That's the business value addition.'[41]

While the 2008 financial crisis was a macroeconomic event that affected the global markets, the second crisis to hit the Indian IT industry was company specific and involved one of its own, Satyam.

The Satyam Scandal is Resolved in Quick Time by NASSCOM, the Government of India and the Indian IT Industry

In 1987, a serial entrepreneur, Ramalinga Raju, founded Satyam Computer Services, an export-oriented software services company in Secunderabad. As we saw earlier, Satyam partnered with Dun & Bradstreet Corporation for IT services and held a minority stake in the latter's subsidiary in India, a company that later became Cognizant Technology Solutions. Satyam moved on from this investment, got on to the Y2K bandwagon at the end of the 1990s, and witnessed a period of rapid growth. By the beginning of the 2000s, Satyam was one of the top five Indian IT services companies, with a strong capability in the hot and emerging domain of ERP implementation.

One of the most dramatic events in the history of the Indian IT industry occurred in January 2009 when Raju sent a bombshell of a letter to Satyam's board of directors with a copy to the stock exchanges and the Securities and Exchange Board of India (SEBI). The letter was a confession that Satyam's cash and bank balances were inflated, and that it had an understated liability and an overstated debtor position. That was not all—the company's revenue and profit margins were inflated for the September quarter of that financial year. It was a governance failure and corporate fraud of the gravest order. The line in the letter—'It was like riding a tiger, not knowing how to get off without getting eaten'—has now passed into Indian IT folklore.

This letter sent shockwaves across the government, IT industry and NASSCOM. In fact, Raju had been an active member of NASSCOM and had been its chairperson during 2006–07. Kiran Karnik, who was NASSCOM's president in those years, puts the scandal in context: 'This was a very shocking case because Satyam was very highly regarded and had received all the possible awards for governance . . . they were audited by not just some auditor but by one of the global top-four companies. The concerns were threefold. First, people would lose their jobs if the company just wound up; 50,000 jobs gone . . . The second concern was (that) a big company among the top five going under was not a very good signal. Third was what it did for (the reputation of) the Indian IT industry in terms of customers abroad suddenly getting concerned and asking the question, "What about other vendors in India, should we be looking elsewhere?" So, India as a favoured destination for IT might take a hit. At a broader level, India was seen as a great investment destination. Would this (incident) indicate poor governance standards in India and put off investors?'[42]

The way the government assessed the context of the scandal with the IT industry and NASSCOM was proactive and supportive.

Karnik remembers the decision-making process and says, 'One strong view was—"It is terrible and sad, but this is part of the corporate world. Companies suddenly go under and shareholders will lose. We are very concerned about people who (might) lose their jobs. But frankly, what do we do?" There was a view at the other extreme—"This is terrible. It is a disaster for the country. A loss of 50,000 jobs, and (a situation) with political implications. Let us nationalize the company."

'Finally, after a lot of discussions, which some of us were involved in, the government took a sensible approach. It did not take over the company, but the government superseded the existing board and put its own nominees there; initially the three of us—Deepak Parikh, C. Achuthan and I—and three others were added later.'[43]

The primary focus of the government-appointed board was on Satyam's clients and employees. The board assured the clients that they would ensure uninterrupted service and even do a smooth transition to a different vendor if the client needed that. This assuaged the immediate concerns of the clients who had chosen Satyam because of its competence. The board boosted the morale of the employees by reiterating that the entire company was not at fault and that this scam was committed only by a few individuals; and that the board was doing all it could to ensure that the business remained ticking.

NASSCOM played a crucial role in resolving the crisis. Som Mittal, who was its president then, recalls the happenings in the first few days that followed Raju's letter: 'We called for a meeting of past chairpersons of NASSCOM and the executive council . . . there was a need for us to show our best face. First, it was to tell the stock market that we (Indian IT service companies) would re-verify our cash and give a statement that we have audited the cash (to assuage investors and clients that their financials were healthy) . . . Collectively, we all agreed to issue a statement that we would not wilfully poach either customers or employees (from Satyam). That statement was extremely important to build confidence . . . And we made many calls as NASSCOM to Satyam's customers stating just the facts and saying, "This is what the government is doing, we would have a board coming in . . . this was a fraud committed by a few people, the law would take its course and we will support you." And when I look back on my long career, I would look at those seventy-two hours as probably the most defining ones because NASSCOM could step in, get the support of everyone and make a difference at that point in time.'[44]

The resolution of the Satyam scandal is still used as a case study of how India quickly solved this issue with minimal disruption. Karnik sums it up: 'Keep in mind that these frauds, though rare, have happened around the world. I have ten examples, including from Europe and the US . . . Satyam is the only company which came back on its feet.'[45] Tech Mahindra subsequently bought a majority stake in Satyam.

Kris Gopalakrishnan succinctly describes the challenges that beset the Indian IT industry in the 2000s: 'It was not just sunshine throughout. We also witnessed some dark moments and a few events of concern in the Indian IT industry. Eventually we rallied and came out stronger . . . The Satyam scandal could have had an adverse impact on the Indian IT industry. It was creditable for the industry, NASSCOM and the government to work in sync to resolve the crisis in quick time.'[46]

It is to the important role that NASSCOM played in shaping the Indian IT industry that we will turn our focus next, in a decade when the industry association contended with issues such as the fallout of the global financial crisis and the Satyam scam, the US visa-related imbroglio, the sundowning of the tax holiday in India and more.

―――――

NASSCOM Becomes an Exemplar Industry Association

We covered the humble origins of NASSCOM earlier. It found its feet in the 1990s, and by the 2000s was a dominant force and the visible face of the Indian IT industry. True to its inclusive spirit, NASSCOM invited BPO companies, R&D/IT/BPO India GCCs and Indian start-ups too, to become its members. This diversity of membership and their global scale resulted in many important NASSCOM initiatives that fostered all segments of the Indian IT industry.

By 2001, the Y2K problem was over, and the technology landscape went from one of Internet-boom to Internet-bust. And then 9/11 happened. The US was the biggest market for India and accounted for about 75 per cent to 80 per cent of Indian software services exports. Kiran Karnik, president of NASSCOM in the early 2000s, recollects those testing times: 'NASSCOM and the IT industry were a bit shaken with all these things (happening) together. It was a time of great uncertainty and doubt. The resilience of the industry was tested very strongly, and we proved ourselves by bouncing back. And hats off to all the industry leaders who had the vision and capability (to put together the right bouquet of services).'[47]

One of the assumptions of the GDM model has been that there would be free movement of software professionals from India to client locations on project-related work, like requirements gathering and user-acceptance testing. The availability of US work visas, influenced by the domestic politics there, became more challenging from the mid-2000s. Phrases like 'US jobs were moving from Buffalo to Bangalore' started to enter the public debate. Karnik weighs in on this subject: 'On the matter of Mexican immigrants and of Indian H1B visa holders in the US—you get into a discussion on a bill on immigration which ties up these two topics sometimes. And there are concerns that they're (immigrants and H1B visa holders) displacing jobs or lowering wages in the US . . . We (NASSCOM) go every time with data and make presentations, talk to senators, congressmen and their staff, to emphasize that US companies are benefiting from this (US work visas for Indians) . . . When the gap between supply and demand of high-skilled IT workers is very high, it not always filled. It is not as if low-wage labour is just rushing in there.'[48]

While NASSCOM managed the US visa-related aspects on the international front, it adroitly handled matters related to tax holidays and campus recruitment on the domestic front. Som Mittal, who became president of NASSCOM in 2007, says, 'This was the first time, after ten years, that we were seeing a change in the quarter-over-quarter growth rates because we did have real headwinds. This was also the year that our ten years of tax holiday was ending. So, when the downturn happened, people needed support and the cash that we used to save through the tax holiday was important. The first three months went away in trying to convince the government of India that the industry needs support, and they gave us (extension of the holiday) for one year at a time, for two years. It was a good relief.'[49]

Among the most unique roles of NASSCOM in the aftermath of the financial crisis was its help in resetting the campus recruitment process across the IT industry. During the heady days of growth post the dotcom collapse, the Indian IT industry used to make offers to engineering undergraduates as early as during the sixth semester of their BE programme—about one year before the students graduated. This was meant to ensure a steady stream of engineering graduates fresh out of college ready to join the IT companies. The slowdown for IT services companies post the 2008 financial crisis meant that the IT industry was not able to honour all the job offers they had made. Som describes how a consensus was reached: 'NASSCOM not only worked with the industry in developing a staggered plan for entry of these freshers, but also went a step further in streamlining campus recruitments. It required enormous lobbying, collectively and individually. Finally, the industry agreed that they would hire only in the eighth semester. The biggest resistance we got was not from industry; it was from academia, who were used to their students getting placed two years in advance of their graduating.'[50]

When R. Chandrashekhar took over as NASSCOM president in 2013, he believed he had his job cut out. He had to stabilize an even bigger NASSCOM with representation from multiple industry segments—from software services to BPO to start-ups—and focus on the big challenges: 'My job was to create separate councils for each of these (industry) segments. Seven such councils were created. Start-ups, for example, required one kind of support—a start-up policy was being framed by the government and we provided policy inputs for that. The large global service delivery model of the IT services companies had other issues relating to transfer pricing or taxation, and how these were administered. If you look at engineering and R&D GCCs, it would be issues relating to IP and royalties. NASSCOM also had to provide holistic policy inputs to the government for the sector as a whole.'[51]

In 2018, Debjani Ghosh became the fifth president of NASSCOM and the first woman at its helm. She was instrumental in developing its 'Think Digital, Think India' strategy, aimed at establishing India as a hub for digital talent and innovation. Ghosh says, 'I have three priorities—talent development and re-skilling, which have become imperatives for the industry to keep pace with global digital transformation; augmentation of the innovation culture in the country; and working with governments across the world to open up new opportunities for the Indian IT industry.'[52]

When the Covid-19 pandemic disrupted the world, NASSCOM worked with the government to facilitate for the Indian IT industry a smooth transition to work-from-home and hybrid models of work. Ghosh says, 'We are moving to a hyper-digital world, everything is going to be touched by technology. This is an opportunity for Indian IT to completely rewrite its playbook.'[53]

In this decade, there was yet another area that witnessed a dramatic rewriting of its playbook—the fascinating world of the IT-enabled start-up ecosystem in India.

The Next Wave of IT Start-ups Across Multiple Domains

We have already taken a deep-dive into the first two waves—the first consisting of hardware and software 'start-ups' like HCL, Wipro and Infosys in the period 1975 to 1995, and the second consisting of IT and BPO services companies like Mindtree and Spectramind, between 1995 and 2005. In the 2000s, start-ups like Ittiam Systems and Pico Peta Simputers took Indian IT down the software products and licencing path, while those like Strand Genomics and Mu Sigma created the space for the data analytics-based services business. The third wave, in the period between 2005 and 2015, produced B2C or consumer-facing start-ups like Flipkart, Ola and Paytm, and B2B product and SaaS companies like InMobi, Druva and Zoho. Post-2016, the Indian start-up ecosystem witnessed the advent of more seasoned and second-time founders, and start-ups with a focus on deep-tech and solutions for India-specific challenges.

Start-ups Open New Vistas for Indian IT in Product Licencing and Data Analytics

Srini Rajam, who led TI India, founded Ittiam Systems in 2001, with a focus on creating intellectual property out of India. He says, 'Usually, you think of technology coming into India. Here we were licensing our technology to the leader in video technology, Sony. We also licensed our communication technology to Silicon Laboratories in the US.'[54] The Ittiam IP (intellectual property), in terms of video streaming, video playback and video recording, touched the lives of 20–30 million smartphone or tablet users annually. Ittiam garnered over 80 per cent of the market in software powering on-demand entertainment systems in aircraft.[55] Those who visited India's first Wi-Fi enabled café that opened shop in the early 2000s, the Coffee Day at Brigade Road, Bengaluru, might not have realized that they experienced Ittiam's 802.11b wireless technology in action there.[56]

Another hardware start-up from this era was Pico Peta Simputers, which, along with Strand Genomics, accounted for the first few instances of academic entrepreneurship in India. It was co-founded by professors Vijay Chandru, Ramesh Hariharan, Swami Manohar and V. Vinay, and was spun off from the Indian Institute of Science in 2000. The low-cost handheld computing device designed by them—the 'Simple Inexpensive and Multilingual People's Computer' or Simputer—was truly ahead of its time. Vinay says, 'We began experimenting with the accelerometer and even created a game called *Goli* using it. Another innovation we had was that you could annotate every screen or application, whether it was a web page or image. This idea, amazingly, became mainstream only ten–twelve years later.'[57] The team even built a software for converting text to speech in multiple Indian languages.

Despite its advanced capabilities, the Simputer did not taste commercial success. Swami Manohar says, 'The environment in the late 1990s–2000s was not conducive to risk-taking in product or hardware ventures. We had angel investors, but we did not get VC funding at all.'[58] Even after partnering with a large public sector entity, BEL (Bharat Electronics), Simputer floundered in getting its hardware boxes manufactured locally. The lack of a vibrant venture capital network and the absence of a strong hardware ecosystem with mass contract manufacturing in India proved to be big stumbling blocks.

Strand Genomics, on the other hand, fared better in securing funding as its focus was entirely on software. And its initial customers, like the start-up GCI, were from the US and provided export income. Strand became India's first start-up in bioinformatics and successfully provided software services, such as speeding up algorithms for drug discovery, for pharmaceutical companies.

Mu Sigma was founded by Dhiraj Rajaram in 2004 and was one of the pioneers in offering pure-play data analytics services. Rajaram says, 'Unlike traditional IT services companies which combined business and technology, Mu Sigma combined business, technology and maths to help with decision-making in client organizations.'[59] And, like the IT services companies that placed emphasis on training and processes, Mu Sigma soon developed an in-house training programme called MuSigma University to train freshers in Bengaluru in high-end data analytics skills and a process platform to support the journey from data to decisions.

IT-led Consumer-Facing Start-ups

Sachin Bansal and Binny Bansal had studied at IIT Delhi, worked together on their BTech project in the field-programmable gate array hardware lab there, and later became colleagues in the payments group of Amazon Web Services in Bengaluru. The Flipkart story began in 2007, when the two young men launched an online bookstore. In 2009, they got their first round of institutional funding with Accel Partners investing US$1 million, and they set about defining the building blocks for a successful e-commerce venture in India. Features like 24/7 customer service, cash-on-delivery (COD), a thirty-day return policy, next-day shipping guarantee[60]—all provided a unique retail experience to Indian consumers, who were used to the more constrained processes of the brick-and-mortar world. The COD model, in particular, was an innovation tailored for India, where consumers were wary of making online payments. COD orders accounted for 80 per cent of overall orders for Flipkart.[61]

Flipkart set the template and benchmark for others when it came to funding, acquisitions and exits. It became India's second unicorn, after InMobi, in 2012 and successfully attracted some of the storied global investors like Tiger Global Management, Naspers, DST

Global and Softbank. Flipkart acquired a number of companies, including Myntra and PhonePe, to rapidly expand its offerings. In 2018, a decade after it began in a two-bedroom apartment in the leafy suburbs of Koramangala in Bengaluru, Flipkart was acquired by Walmart for US$18 billion in the world's largest e-commerce deal. Flipkart became the poster child of Indian start-ups, and Sachin and Binny an inspiration for a new generation of entrepreneurs.

The story of Paytm is equally inspiring, not only because of its extraordinary success in touching the lives of millions of Indians but also in the stirring triumph-against-all-odds of its founder, Vijay Shekhar Sharma—a small-town lad who overcame his lack of proficiency in English, found comfort in the computer room of the Delhi College of Engineering, and realized his dream of working in Silicon Valley through a start-up of his own in India. The initial days of One97 Communications, which he started in 2001, were tough and Sharma had to take up even petty jobs to make ends meet.[62] But he persevered, found success in the mobile value added services market, and soon raised funding from Intel Capital.[63] 2010 marked a watershed year for the company—Sharma proposed entering the world of digital payments and mobile recharge, but found his board resisting the idea. Once again, he persisted, put US$2 million of his equity at stake, and launched Paytm.

Paytm fashioned itself on the Chinese 'super-app' model. It provided the services of a digital wallet, mobile payments, online shopping and banking through a single app. In 2015, the Ant Group, China's largest payment platform, recognized the potential of Paytm from its own vantage point—Paytm had 23 million users whereas Ant had 190 million—and paid US$550 million for a 25 per cent stake in Paytm to replicate its playbook in India.[64] Sharma, viewing Paytm's growth in three phases, says, 'The first three-year phase went into finding the right product-market fit, the next phase was about revenue and monetization, and the last phase would be about profitability and free cash flows. We are in the second phase of that journey.'[65] Paytm went public in late 2021.

Another Indian consumer-facing start-up, and one among the few of its ilk, which not only stormed the domestic markets but also successfully went global, is Ola Cabs. Bhavish Aggarwal got the idea for Ola in 2010 after he was left stranded by his taxi driver on a trip from Bengaluru to Bandipur. Ola is today one of the world's largest ride-hailing companies, serving 250+ cities across India, Australia, New Zealand and the UK. In 2019, Ola spun off its electric vehicle business into a separate entity called Ola Electric Mobility and announced plans to create the world's largest electric two-wheeler factory in Tamil Nadu.

Start-ups Riding the Cloud and SaaS Wave

Sridhar Vembu founded, with five others, AdventNet Inc. in 1996. This was a software start-up that sold primarily to networking companies like Cisco. By 2002, in the aftermath of the dotcom bust, its customers dried up and AdventNet faced an existential crisis. Sridhar pivoted to selling its network management software to all enterprises rather than to only networking OEMs and also started developing business applications. By 2005, the company released its first cloud-based business application, Writer, and Zoho CRM, which became one of its bestselling apps. In 2009 the company's name was changed to Zoho Corporation. By 2019, Zoho had over forty-five business and productivity apps servicing 50 million business users worldwide.[66] Zoho inspired Chennai, where it is headquartered, to become the 'SaaS capital of India'. The city's Saas industry now employs over 10,000 people and generates over US$1 billion in revenue.[67]

Vembu shaped Zoho with his radically different ideas. Sramana Mitra, founder of One Million by One Million, a Silicon Valley virtual accelerator, says, 'His thought process is completely contrarian to the Silicon Valley philosophy of "entrepreneurship = financing". He believes that "entrepreneur = customers + revenues + profits".'[68] Unlike other start-ups that chased venture capital, Zoho remained completely bootstrapped and profitable throughout its journey. Vembu says, 'There is no Series A, B funding, I call it Series QE, quantitative easing. It is possible to bootstrap a company if you give yourself enough time and room. You are building the capital required for the next stage of growth.'[69]

Vembu took some counter-intuitive decisions on sourcing talent too. In 2011, Zoho set up a small office in Tenkasi, a village in Tamil Nadu. By 2019, Vembu relocated there with the idea of creating the next innovations of Zoho for the world from rural India. Vembu says, 'This is the new normal at Zoho—most of the jobs will be created from rural centres in India. Even if 1–2 per cent of jobs are high-paying, globally competitive jobs, the rural economy will come into balance.'[70]

Another start-up that emerged in India and became successful globally was InMobi. It started in 2007 as MKhoj, an SMS-based search engine, and pivoted to a mobile-advertising network business model. While Google developed its ad-network business on the back of Internet penetration in the US, InMobi took advantage of the mobile-first world in India and other Asian markets. Naveen Tewari, CEO and founder of InMobi, says, 'We realized that the mobile ecosystem was on the verge of a mighty explosion and we wanted to be a part of it. We used the reverse market strategy, where the emerging markets formed the development and test base for the product which then enters the global markets.'[71]

InMobi's global ambitions were fuelled by the funding it received, first from Kleiner Perkins Caufield and Byers, and later US$200 million from Softbank, which catapulted it to become the first unicorn start-up in India. InMobi built the largest ad network in Asia, including China and Japan, and expanded in global markets like the UK and Europe. On being named as one of the fifty most disruptive companies in the world by *MIT Technology Review*, Tewari says, 'People expect great products and innovations coming out of Silicon Valley and probably didn't expect that innovation to come from an Indian company.'[72]

Start-ups in Deep-Tech and Catering to the Next Billion Indians

Start-ups that used advanced technologies such as artificial intelligence, machine learning, robotics, big data, augmented reality and virtual reality, and blockchain technologies received only about 1.5 per cent of the total start-up funding in India during 2014–18.[73] Consequently, deep-tech became an important rallying cry for the Indian start-up ecosystem.

The ecosystem welcomed the advent of more experienced founders in deep-tech start-ups. Geetha Manjunath, founder of Niramai, brought to the table her rich experience of working in high-tech environments at CDAC, where she was part of the team that developed the PARAM supercomputer, and at Xerox India, where she headed the data analytics team developing camera applications for medical diagnosis. She says, 'In 2017, we started Niramai (Non-invasive Risk Assessment with Machine Learning and Artificial Intelligence) by leveraging thermal imaging, AI and ML to offer a radiation-free method of identifying breast cancer.'[74]

The incubators run by the leading academic institutions in India also provided a nurturing environment for deep-tech start-ups. Organizations like the Society for Innovation and Development at IISc, which incubated Pico Peta and Strand, and the IIT Madras Incubation Cell, which produced companies like Ather Energy, an electric scooter start-up, and Plansys, a submersible robotics start-up, have catalysed the emergence of academic-incubator programmes in India. Plansys brings together multiple disciplines like ocean engineering, mechanical engineering, electronics and computer science to develop solutions for inspection of marine structures, and for underwater assessment of dam gates for agriculture. Often, reservoirs are too turbid for effective human diver inspection. Many a time, such an exercise is dangerous since the reservoirs are home to crocodiles! A deep-tech solution, like an inspection by submersible robots, is a life-saver, literally. Deep-tech start-ups have steadily grown in the country over the last decade, and a NASSCOM study in 2020 found that they constituted 19 per cent of the start-up ecosystem in India.[75]

Another rallying cry for the Indian start-up ecosystem was to solve India-specific challenges. Two years after Reliance Jio, a telecom start-up, was founded in 2016, the dramatic 'Jio-fication' effect[76] was visible in India—215 million subscribers were added to Jio's mobile network; the cost of data plummeted more than tenfold; and India became no. 1 in data consumption in the world, from its earlier lowly rank of 155 prior to Jio's launch.[77] New consumers from rural India, and from tier 2 and tier 3 towns, came online.

That online consumer world presented a picture of sharp contrast between the relatively affluent, westernized, largely English-speaking users on the one hand, and the much larger lot of budget-conscious users on the other. A new online India emerged, one that was seeking access to blue-collar jobs and agriculture-related information and was hungry for infotainment in Indian languages.[78] And the Indian entrepreneurial ecosystem needed to create more start-ups that catered to the next billion Indians and solved India-specific challenges.

Uniphore, founded by Umesh Sachdev and Ravi Saraogi and incubated at IIT Madras's Rural Technology and Business Incubator, developed a software solution using vernacular speech recognition and voice biometrics. In its initial years, Uniphore focused on providing access to content, banking and farming services to the rural and non-English speaking population in India. John Chambers, former CEO of Cisco and an investor in Uniphore, says, 'They first built their products for India, which is one of the hardest markets to build specific solutions for, given the different languages and dialects that exist. After successfully rolling out in India, they were able to scale and bring their products to the world. Uniphore's solutions can now recognize and respond to more than 100 global languages and multiple dialects.'[79]

A number of interesting start-ups—like Swasth Alliance in healthcare and telemedicine, CropIn in agriculture and crop advisory services, EkStep Foundation and ShikshaLokam in K–12 education for both students and teachers, and Dailyhunt in vernacular news content—have emerged, focusing on affordable access and adoption of digital-powered services by the next-billion Indians in India. A number of government initiatives, such as the Atal Community Innovation Centres, have been undertaken to nurture social and micro-entrepreneurship in the unserved/ underserved areas of India.

They say it takes a village to raise a child. The proliferation and success of these start-ups were intertwined with the growth of the Indian start-up ecosystem. Let us turn our attention to the 'ecosystem village' that raised the 'start-up child'.

The Start-up Ecosystem—VCs, Angel Investors, Incubators and Associations

India has had a rich tradition of lending and risk capital for business, but mainly in terms of loan financing and not in terms of equity financing. Venture Capital (VC) probably started in India in 1986, when ICICI (that was called Industrial Credit and Investment Corporation of India in that era) set up a division to invest in small and medium-sized businesses. The first Indian VC fund started in 1988, when ICICI along with Unit Trust of India established Technology Development and Information Company of India (TDICI).

TDICI, set up with an initial capital of Rs 20 crore, targeted financing of technology for small and medium enterprises, with 30 per cent of their focus on electronics and computers-related start-ups.[80] One successful company that TDICI backed was Mastek. Ashank Desai, its founder, says, 'We decided to do ERP products and needed Rs 60–70 lakh, which was big money then. TDICI funded us. The profit from sale of Mastek shares doubled their venture fund! They got twenty-times' appreciation in two years, when Mastek went public (in 1992).'[81]

IT veteran Saurabh Srivastava recounts the genesis of the Infinity Venture Fund: 'We launched it in 2000. And it was great fun, although it was a terrible time to do venture capital funding because everything fell off the cliff post the dotcom bust. But we ended up creating nineteen companies, including marquee ones like Indiabulls, Avendus and India Games which later became part of Disney. And the angel investing kind of followed.'[82] Saurabh and his friends soon founded the Indian Angel Network.

Gopal Srinivasan, founder and chairperson of TVS Electronics, also got into venture funding and angel investing in this decade. Gopal says, 'In 2006–07, with C.K. Prahalad, we decided to get into investing as a business and raised Rs 600 crore for the TVS Capital Funds only from India and in Indian rupees. We had R. Thyagarajan of Shriram Group, and some wonderful IT mentors like Kris (Gopalakrishnan) and Lakshmi Narayanan of Cognizant. At the same time, angel investing was picking up. So, R. Ramaraj and I put together this group of people who form the Chennai Angels.'[83]

Venture capital funding in India was characterized by smaller deal sizes and consequently, smaller returns in its initial years. One marquee deal was the Warburg Pincus investment of US$300 million and the subsequent fourfold returns from the Bharti Airtel IPO in 2002.[84] VC funding increased over the years and experienced rapid growth between 2011 and 2015 with hedge funds like Tiger Global taking quick and audacious bets on Indian start-ups.[85] Despite a period of funding moderation between 2015 and 2017, the Indian VC industry bounced back, buoyed by big exits of companies such as Flipkart and MakeMyTrip, and witnessed US$10 billion of capital being deployed in 2019, the highest-ever until then.[86]

While VCs and angels provided the financial support, a few organizations provided a sort of entrepreneurial safety net and nurtured a culture of contribution and 'paying forward', and of creating public goods in the Indian start-up ecosystem. In 1993, the successful Indian NRI tech community in Silicon Valley, led by entrepreneurs like Kanwal Rekhi, came together to form The Indus Entrepreneurs (TiE). Sridhar Mitta, who became president of the TiE Bengaluru chapter in 2002, says, 'I spearheaded the Entrepreneurship Acceleration Programme, where TiE would support young entrepreneurs until they got institutional funding through various activities by different chartered members . . . one such start-up from the first batch of entrepreneurs was Redbus (an online bus ticketing platform which was later acquired by the Ibibo Group).'[87]

NASSCOM started its 10000 Start-ups initiative in 2013 to scale up the start-up ecosystem in India. That same year, Sharad Sharma founded iSPIRT (Indian Software Products Industry Round Table). He says, 'iSPIRT is a manifestation of four elements coming together right for the idea of making India a product nation—one, we have a group of activists who have this self-belief that they can change the future; two, we have people who are able to turn intentions into implementations; third, public goods got created and, finally, thanks to social media communication, we were able to suddenly grow this movement.'[88]

On the dimension of entrepreneurship development in the country, India took its first steps in 1983 with the establishment of the Entrepreneurship Development Institute of India in Ahmedabad, Gujarat. By 2000, the needle moved when Raghavan, co-founder of Infosys, started the N.S. Raghavan Centre for Entrepreneurial Learning at IIM Bangalore. He says, 'There are three areas we addressed. At IIMB, research on entrepreneurship was one area. The second was various kinds of educational and training courses for entrepreneurship. The third was provision of basic facilities for start-ups. Some are doing well, like the management programme for entrepreneurs and family businesses, and the women entrepreneurship programme.'[89]

By 2019, the Indian start-up ecosystem comprised 20,000 start-ups, 270 incubators and accelerators, 200 venture capital firms, 231 angel investors and eight angel networks, making India one of the top three start-up ecosystems in the world along with the US and China.[90]

Like this ecosystem, India's trailblazing mission-mode IT projects like Aadhaar too were making global headlines. How did India manage to provide a digital identity to well over 1 billion citizens, and make it the backbone for other digital services?

Government Catalyses IT Policies, E-Governance Initiatives and Mission-Mode Projects—Aadhaar and UPI become Central to Digital India

By the late 1990s, there was healthy competition brewing between the cities of Bengaluru in Karnataka and Hyderabad in Telangana, in attracting IT companies and talent to their shores.

The Karnataka government pressed home its advantage of having a thriving IT industry in Bengaluru with some forward-looking measures. It was the first state in India to articulate an IT policy and to have a dedicated secretary for information technology, with enterprising IAS officers like Sanjay Dasgupta and Vivek Kulkarni at the helm in the initial years. In 2000, Kulkarni put together the Karnataka Millennium IT Policy, titled *Mahiti* and positioned as 'IT for the Common Man'. Recalling the impact that the policy had through the Karnataka IT and Biotechnology task forces it created, Kulkarni says, 'Usually, all committees (appointed by the government) are recommendatory in nature. But the IT task force headed by Narayana Murthy had the powers of the cabinet. Once (anything was) approved by the IT task force, we went ahead, and that way we could implement every single para in the policy.'[91]

From a talent development and research perspective, the IT policy led to the creation of several institutions like the International Institute of Information Technology Bangalore (IIITB). The policy also led to the creation of an important IT industry event called 'BangaloreIT.com'. Sadagopan, founder-director of IIITB, recalls how impactful the event became over the years. 'We had global people coming for the IT.com, people like Kenneth Keniston (founder of the MIT Programme in Science, Technology and Society) and AnnaLee Saxenian (professor in the School of Information at the University of California, Berkeley). The prime minister came to inaugurate the event. In 2002–03, we conducted the 'Internet festival'—we had a 100 Mbps pipe in one of the stadiums where 3000 students were connecting to the Internet, an unheard-of scale in those days.'[92]

Hyderabad played catch-up, being the hungry and enterprising IT competitor to Bengaluru. R. Chandrashekhar, then IT Secretary of unified Andhra Pradesh and Telangana (AP), says, 'We worked out plans to make Hyderabad the IT destination and looked at three components—one was infrastructure for the industry, which had to be at a global level; the second was in terms of skills availability; and the third was adoption of technology by the local government itself as a driver of demand.'[93] They went into a public–private partnership (PPP) with the construction company L&T, developed the 'HITEC City (Hyderabad Information Technology and Engineering Consultancy)' in record time and attracted companies like IBM, Microsoft and Oracle to set up their offices there. Similarly, the

International Institute of Information Technology, Hyderabad was established in 1998 in a PPP mode to nurture IT talent locally. The AP government initiated the eSeva Project, a portal to provide integrated citizen services. And the government also spearheaded the first two e-governance summits in India in 1997–98.

In 2001, after five years with the AP state government, Chandrashekhar moved to the Centre. He made a surprising choice of accepting a transfer from 'the Ministry of Defence, with a budget of Rs 8000 crore, to create a national plan for e-governance in the Department of IT with a budget of Rs 5 crore'.[94] Chandrashekhar, based on his learnings in AP, pushed for the PPP model for delivering e-governance initiatives nationally, especially where there was a citizen interface and where there were high volumes of transactions. The National Institute of Smart Government (NISG) was created in a PPP mode between the Department of Personnel (Government of India), NASSCOM and some state governments.[95]

NISG's first undertaking was the iconic 'MCA21 Project', which involved the end-to-end computerization of the ministry of corporate affairs. TCS and, after several years, Infosys, implemented the different phases of the MCA21 project. Chandrashekhar, who was acting as the de facto CEO of NISG at the time, says, 'People could verify online every piece of information about companies. And that took not just computerization but also a lot of revisiting of processes, of the entire administrative structure. It was a big culture shock. It created a new paradigm in the central government, where other projects like the Passport Seva Project took shape. The idea of public–private partnerships and the private sector implementing projects on a turnkey basis and looking after citizen services became acceptable.'[96]

This period also witnessed the passing of the Information Technology Act 2000, an act that provided legal recognition for electronic commerce. The IT Act came into the public consciousness first in 2015, when the Supreme Court of India struck down Section 66A upholding the right of free speech online.[97] Section 69A of the IT Act made headlines in 2020–21, when the Indian central government banned several Chinese apps and issued a notice to Twitter.[98]

India's most ambitious mission-mode programmes that built the foundation for a digital India soon followed.

Aadhaar and UPI

The most important mission-mode IT project in India is an incredible IT product as well. In 2016, this product raced from zero to 1 billion users in only 5.5 years,[99] the fastest for any product in the world until then. To reach 1 billion users, Microsoft Windows took 25.8 years,[100] Apple iPhone took fourteen years,[101] Google Search took twelve years, Facebook 8.7 years, and Tencent Wechat seven years.[102] The product is Aadhaar, India's biometric identity system, and the 'start-up' is the Unique Identification Authority of India (UIDAI), originally set up under the Planning Commission of India before it became a statutory authority.

The story of Aadhaar began in 2009, when Nandan Nilekani, co-founder of Infosys, was invited by Manmohan Singh, then prime minister of India, to become the founding chair of UIDAI. Nilekani says, 'The government was increasing its public spending on individuals, in the form of NREGA (National Rural Employment Guarantee Act) wages or PDS (Public Distribution System). And they realized that unless there was a sound way of identifying beneficiaries, there would be a lot of wastages, which were estimated to be 30–40 per cent.'[103]

Aadhaar, which in Sanskrit means 'foundation', 'base' or 'basis', was to provide a unique identity to every resident of India. Nilekani put together a stellar team comprising bureaucrats and technologists to navigate the complex waters of the government-led project. Indeed, they faced several hurdles—from political opposition to turf wars with other government projects, to being accused of creating a surveillance infrastructure and infringing on the privacy of citizens. There were some technological questions too that were asked. The Aadhaar team successfully addressed these challenges and secured a legal stamp of approval in 2018 from the Supreme Court of India, which upheld the constitutional validity of the Aadhaar Act.

The Aadhaar number, which is a twelve-digit random number issued by the UIDAI, was not conceived to act like any other identity proof, like the driver's licence card or the voter ID card. Nilekani says, 'We built a very sophisticated platform using biometric de-duplication, online authentication, online know-your-customer (KYC). And we built it like a platform, just like GPS is a platform or the Internet is a platform. An ID platform on which you can build innovations.'[104] Thus, the Aadhaar identity platform, with its inherent features of uniqueness, authentication and e-KYC (electronic Know Your Customer), enabled the government to directly reach residents of India for delivery of various subsidies and benefits.

In 2014, as part of a national mission for financial inclusion, Prime Minister Narendra Modi announced the Jan Dhan programme. This is India's national mission for financial inclusion to ensure all Indians have access to financial services, namely, basic savings and deposit accounts, remittance, credit, insurance, pension in an affordable manner. The World Bank estimated that Aadhaar e-KYC brought down the customer onboarding cost for an Indian bank from Rs 1500 to Rs 10.[105] Consequently, it made economic sense for these banks to reach the unbanked at the bottom of the pyramid. By 2018, thanks to Aadhaar and Jan Dhan, the number of adult Indians who had bank accounts more than doubled in seven years and stood at 80 per cent of India's population.[106] Along with banks, telecom companies also benefited massively from Aadhaar e-KYC, where the customer verification process, which typically took days or weeks, could be completed in just five minutes! Reliance Jio, the Indian telecom major, onboarded over 100 million customers using Aadhaar, in the first six months of its operations.[107]

Nilekani, commenting on how transformational Aadhaar had been (by 2016–17), says, '200 million bank accounts have been linked to Aadhaar. The LPG programme (cooking gas subsidies programme) has been very successful, and 114 million people are getting direct benefits transfer. The prime minister talked about savings of Rs 15,000 crore on LPG subsidies. You can think about the progression from the basic requirements of life like "*roti, kapada, makaan*" (food, clothing, housing) to infrastructure like "*bijli, sadak, pani*" (electricity, roads, water) and to "JAM—Jan Dhan (bank account), Aadhaar, mobile", the three digital numbers that are the basis for your future.'[108] By 2021, Aadhaar had provided digital identities to 1280 million people that is about 93 per cent of India's population and had completed 8960 million eKYC transactions.[109]

Another area where the government catalysed remarkable digital transformation was in financial services, where the narrative behind the innovations was 'financial inclusion'. The term was used for the first time in April 2005 in the annual policy statement of the Reserve Bank of India; and by 2008, the National Payments Corporation of India (NPCI) had been created.

NPCI went on to have a tremendous impact on the retail payment world in India. Its RuPay system is India's domestic card scheme that competes with Visa and MasterCard. RuPay helped bring down transaction costs; for instance, ATM transaction charges came down from Rs 4 to 5 to Rs 0.50 per transaction,[110] and enabled banks to issue more cards in rural areas. As the government leveraged the JAM trinity and experimented with Direct Benefits Transfer to citizen's accounts, it introduced a nuance to its financial inclusion narrative—a move towards a cashless society. The cashless narrative reached its crescendo in the aftermath of India's demonetization initiative. The emphasis was on ease of conducting a financial transaction, and the mobile phone, and not cash or the credit or debit card, became the all-important financial instrument.

In 2016, NPCI introduced the Unified Payments Interface (UPI) technology, which established a real-time payment system. By 2021, 207 of the top Indian banks had connected to the UPI system and 20 companies provided apps for consumers to make payments.[111] UPI proved to be wildly successful, and in just four years since its launch, it grew to become the world's fifth largest payment network by volume, behind only Visa, Alipay, WeChat Pay and MasterCard.[112] An NPCI study showed that by 2021, one-third of Indian households used digital payments, and this included one out of four households in the poorest 40 per cent of India.[113] The financial inclusion needle had truly moved.

Besides Aadhaar and UPI, India witnessed the development of several other digital platforms, which have collectively and informally been referred to as the 'India stack'. The stack was figuratively the technical 'Lego' pieces, using which entrepreneurs or the government could develop interesting products. Nandan

Nilekani explains how this evolved in the Indian context and says, 'We actually thought, how do we layer API (which allows two applications to talk to each other) on Aadhaar. The initial API was for authentication, and then we built an API for KYC. We also designed it to be an electronic signature; you can sign a document using the Aadhaar, and on top of that the government is launching something called a Digital Locker. So, all the financial companies will add financial documents to the Digital Locker, and so on. We also built the Unified Payments Interface, and on top of that, the government launched the BHIM application (an Indian mobile payments app developed by NPCI based on UPI to facilitate e-payments).'[114]

The 2000s saw the Indian IT services industry solidify its position as the No. 1 choice for outsourced work in the world. Over six decades, Indian IT had proven to be a prime driver of India's economy and its digital aspirations, and had generated significant impact across different vectors—as of 2021, it contributed to 8 per cent of India's GDP, around 52 per cent of total Indian services exports, was the largest private employer in India employing around 4.5 million IT professionals, and housed 1000-plus IT and R&D services subsidiaries of MNCs.[115] Indian IT is expected to grow at a brisk pace in the 'techade' of the 2020s, as it wins in the digital battlegrounds.

7

Quō Vādis: Where Are We Heading?

ndia's tryst with computing for over six decades has placed us in a unique position of strength and at the start of the next phase in the evolution of Indian IT. We are all curious to know what comes next. Predicting the future, however, especially the future of technology, can be a tricky affair. Just ask these industry experts.[1]

'Almost all of the many predictions now being made about 1996 hinge on the Internet's continuing exponential growth. But I predict the Internet will soon go spectacularly supernova and in 1996 catastrophically collapse.'—Robert Metcalfe, founder of 3Com, 1995.

'There's just not that many videos I want to watch.'—Steve Chen, CTO and co-founder of YouTube, 2005.

'There's no chance that the iPhone is going to get any significant market share.'—Steve Ballmer, Microsoft CEO, 2007.

In the comfort of hindsight, we can wonder how they did not see something that was so obvious, but such is the power of technology to blindside and disrupt. On a lighter note, we may be closer to our mark in technology forecasts perhaps by revisiting what science fiction writers envisaged—predictions by A.C. Clarke about geosynchronous satellites for communication, by Douglas Adams about real-time audio language translation, and by George Orwell about a world of surveillance have all come true.

In this chapter, we will gaze into the future of Indian IT by analysing a few important visible trends. We will explore the trends in the following areas: 1) emerging technologies and emergent business opportunities—worldwide and in India, 2) the Indian IT services industry, 3) Indian GCCs, 4) deep-tech start-ups, 5) the government's IT-led mission-mode programmes, 6) digital learning and skilling, 7) Indian research in domains like IT, AI/ML, brain sciences, and 8) the future of Indian governance and regulations, especially around data and algorithms.

Emerging Technologies and Emergent Business Opportunities—Worldwide and in India

We are in the middle of the fourth industrial revolution.[2] After the world first utilized steam power to mechanize, then used electric power to mass-produce, and next harnessed electronics and IT to automate, it is now leveraging a mix of technologies like AI, Internet of Things (IoT), robotics and genomics to reimagine businesses and unlock human productivity. According to Barclays' analysts, if human productivity was 100 units in 1765, when the steam engine was invented, it increased to 1500 in the 1960s, and doubled to 3000 in just five decades thereafter.[3]

Examples of Some Emerging Technologies and Innovative Applications

1. Cloud computing that is increasing in processing power and storage capacity and decreasing in costs

2. Mobile phones that place amazing computing power at very low costs in the hands of every human being

3. Social networks that provide collaboration and communication platforms to connect people

4. 5G-powered ultra-high-speed Internet and ubiquitous connectivity facilitating remote surgery

5. Robotics and drones that can completely automate manufacturing and logistics

6. IoT and sensors, which provide real-time data and hence provision of control to machines as diverse as airplanes, electric utility meters, personal blood sugar monitors, etc.

7. 3D printing, which can allow production of individual parts or personalized products commercially viable

8. Augmented reality and virtual reality that can revolutionize diverse fields like education and industrial maintenance

9. Blockchain and distributed ledger technologies to improve integrity and trust in transactions manyfold

10. Computational biology and gene editing that can potentially provide treatment and cure to diseases like AIDS and cancer

11. Quantum computing with applications in cybersecurity and drug development

12. AI, along with ML, which is becoming one of the most important technologies of all time

Commenting on computing in the future, Kris Gopalakrishnan says, 'Computing is becoming more ubiquitous—in the next ten–twenty years, we will have 50–60 billion connected devices in the world. Imagine a world where every one of the 7 billion people has a smart personal device. We are generating massive amounts of data. With new tools for pattern recognition using AI/ML we can get new information and insights from this data. Imagine a world where you can recognize anyone in the world using your smart phone, even if you have not met that person ever before. And with automated language translation, you can converse with that person in your language and she can reply in her language.'[4]

We are seeing the confluence of at least three technologies (mechanical automation, computing and communications, and biology) that are likely to lead to an explosion of innovations in the future. Let us consider a few scenarios. In the Industry 4.0 context of an automobile factory, the workers may use augmented-reality goggles that will guide them to fix doors on the car chassis. Once fixed, the inventory system is automatically updated. AI computer vision technologies will assist the workers in conducting quality inspection of the car. The consumers of the vehicle will experience technology in a more intuitive way. The navigation route will be overlaid on their windscreen as they view the road. The pin on the map for a building disappears from view as they drive past it.

Some of these use cases will be accelerated by the heady mix of IT and telecommunications technologies. India is already contributing to the creation and development of emerging telecommunications technologies like 5G. For instance, the 5G radio interface technology developed by India makes 5G technology work well in rural areas with low-speed mobility and doubles the range of large cell towers, thereby increasing coverage.[5] There will be even bigger opportunities for Indian IT to become an integrator of these technologies, both globally and for domestic usage.

Biology and IT are combining to power a new generation of medical breakthroughs. mRNA (messenger RNA) technology, which became popular with the Covid-19 vaccines from Pfizer–BioNTech and Moderna, is described as an 'operating system' designed to programme human beings to produce a specific protein[6] or as the 'software of life'.[7] In the future, it may create new treatments for other diseases like cancer. CRISPR, a revolutionary new technology for gene editing, is used for potential therapies for diseases like sickle-cell anaemia and β-thalassaemia,[8] as well as for developing medical diagnostic solutions that can be used for testing at home. Some are even comparing this 'point of care' CRISPR-diagnostics moment, which is a democratization of biotechnology, to the PC revolution in the IT journey.

Researchers are working on IT tools to make CRISPR gene editing as efficient and mistake-free as possible.[9] When it works perfectly, gene editing should behave like the autocorrect feature of many word processors, replacing problematic genes with healthy ones in the way typos are automatically corrected. However, this binding process is highly complex and oftentimes imperfect. Finding binding sites is mostly guesswork, where researchers try each binding site experimentally in the lab, one at a time. Emerging hardware and software tools directly measure the genomes and DNA segments with which CRISPR will interact and develop a way to understand the kind of errors that CRISPR might make. Soon, with the power of AI/ML, these tools may become predictive.

From among all the technologies shaping IT today, AI/ML, just like the fundamental technologies of the steam engine and electricity, will have the most profound impact on humankind. Consider some AI-enabled innovations from the automotive and healthcare industries. Autonomous vehicles use AI/ML techniques to offer various levels of driving automation—from automatic detection of obstacles in the path and avoiding collisions, to assisting humans to drive, to completely taking over the navigation. Stanford University researchers developed an ML algorithm that offers diagnoses based on chest X-ray images.[10] It can, in a restricted context, diagnose up to fourteen types of medical conditions and is able to diagnose pneumonia better than expert radiologists working alone.

While AI/ML is showing promise in many contexts, we may need to tread with caution. AI/ML models are not entirely without some inherent bias. Till recently, the general reason for the bias was attributed to fact that the IT research and industry community is predominantly male and socio-culturally homogeneous. However, a recent multidisciplinary study from Stanford reveals something more fundamental—ML algorithms may be learning from society's deep-rooted biases that are ingrained in the data used to train them. For instance, adjectives such as 'intelligent, logical and thoughtful' are found to be associated more with men than women in general writing, a bias that has improved only since the 1960s.[11] Thus, an AI system fed on earlier writing as training data is more likely to picture a man when describing an intelligent person. Similarly, studies have shown that popular social media apps using facial recognition ML algorithms to detect emotions (such as happy, sad, or angry) of a subject in a photo[12] consistently scored African-American faces as angrier than Caucasian-American faces. The AI systems showed this bias because they were not adequately trained on faces with darker skin colour.

It is our responsibility to ensure that the emerging technologies are used appropriately. We need to ensure greater diversity while selecting AI and ML professionals. We also need to work on methods that can caution us about the inherent biases in the data used to train AI/ML systems. Despite these challenges, we remain hopeful about these technologies and that they will ultimately be used for the greater benefit of humanity.

What does the march of emerging technologies mean for India? We should harness technologies to meet the needs and aspirations of Indians, especially the underserved and those at the bottom of the pyramid. We believe it is unwise to supplant external solutions directly, and we need to develop uniquely Indian solutions that carry forward both urban and rural India. For instance, India should develop robust machine translation solutions to seamlessly translate between its official languages. Such a solution may be used as a real-time personal digital language assistant or to translate existing documents. In the Indian agricultural context of small landholdings of 0.5 to 1 acre per farmer, applying sensors to fields to obtain crop and soil data becomes cost-prohibitive. AI solutions which combine weather data and earth-sensing satellite data with mobile photos and other data input by the farmers themselves are being developed. Such solutions produce fine-grained insights for the Indian farmer, including crop-yield forecasts, pest and disease prediction, and crop advisories in their vernacular languages.

At the same time, aspects like digital divide, connectivity, affordability and fairness need to be addressed. Azim Premji articulates his aspirations for Indian IT in the future: 'Owing to large-scale urbanization, digitization, skill development and automation, I hope India paves its way into the coveted club of advanced nations of the world. The Indian IT industry is bound to play the role of a growth engine. Concepts like digital, cloud, automation, artificial intelligence, smart systems and green IT will witness their peak utilization in 2040, and I see an affordable version of these solutions absorbed into the market.'[13]

Overall, there is immense opportunity for India and Indian industry in this context. We believe that both IT services and product companies as well as deep-tech start-ups from India will benefit by aiding the digital transformation of businesses and societies worldwide.

Indian IT Services Companies are Preferred Partners for Digital Transformation

We discussed the resilience and robustness of the Indian IT services industry during the Covid-19 pandemic in the first chapter. We believe that the Indian IT services are poised to enter their next orbit and become partners in the digital transformation of their clients. This headline sums up the trend well: 'IT Cos Win Record Large Deals as Demand for Digital Spikes'.[14] The total contract value of new deals was the highest ever in the financial quarter that ended on 31 March 2021. New deals worth more than US$1 billion in contract value are now a consistent feature across most large Indian IT services players. TCS announced a large deal from Prudential Financial and bought Postbank Systems AG from Deutsche Bank during the period of the Covid-19 pandemic. Infosys signed large deals from automotive major Daimler AG and from US investment management firm Vanguard, while Wipro signed large deals from retailer Metro AG and telco Telefónica Germany. TCS, Infosys, HCL and Wipro had a combined revenue of over US$54 billion in FY 2020–21, more than double their combined revenue of about US$23 billion in FY 2010–11, an increase of about 135 per cent in a decade.[15] A good chunk of their revenue today is generated from digital services that power digital transformation for their clients.

N. Chandrasekaran, chairperson of TCS, looks at the current global digital transformation as the start of a new technology cycle, much like the previous cycles involving the transition from mainframe technology and the adoption of the Internet. He writes in a letter to the shareholders of TCS in the Annual Report for FY 2020–21, 'Technological change is far more perceptible when it comes to consumer technology, and less so in the enterprise world. Enterprise adoption of new technologies tends to be very measured, and it is only much later, with the benefit of hindsight, that the scale of change and the key inflection points become more evident. To my mind, the year gone by saw an important inflection point that has huge ramifications on enterprise consumption of technology in the coming years, and on demand for your company's services.'[16]

How are Indian IT services players preparing for becoming partners to their clients in their digital transformation? Nandan Nilekani, the current chairperson of Infosys, provides the answer to this in his letter to the shareholders in the Annual Report for FY 2020–21, 'The company is investing in designing and developing the right solutions required for accelerating digital transformation . . . cloud solutions, modernization without disruption, big data and analytics, applied AI and automation, cybersecurity, consumerization of user experience, or a robust innovation ecosystem—these have struck the right chord with our clients who are keen to assimilate new ideas to reinvent themselves and become more like digital natives.'[17]

Narayana Murthy provides a pathway for Indian IT companies to enhance their value in the future: 'There is going to be a huge opportunity for the Indian industry as long as we become the leaders in observing new technology and deploying it for the benefit of our customers, even before our customers are comfortable with the technology. So, our job is cut out. Our job is to attract the best and the brightest; our job is to make sure that we invest adequately in research and development, much more (in) development I would say. And that we improve our work productivity and enhance our innovation capabilities. If we do all of these, I have no doubt at all that the Indian software industry will become even more valuable to India and the world.'[18]

Indian Global Capability Centres Are In-House Engines of Innovation and Digital Capabilities

Apart from the Indian IT services companies, the global capability centres (GCCs) of multinational companies (MNCs) are also upping their game to become the digital transformation engines for their companies. There are about 1700 GCCs in India, with about 25 new GCCs set up in 2020 during the pandemic.[19] Today, Indian GCCs are becoming strategic to the digital transformation of their parent companies.

Mercedes-Benz's engineering R&D GCC works on important domains like connected cars, which are critical to Mercedes-Benz's digital transformation. Thomas Weber, a former member of the board of management of Daimler AG, the parent company of Mercedes-Benz, makes an important observation that we think sets the stage for the evolution of Indian GCCs. In reply to a question on whether the preferred model is for the R&D team in Silicon Valley to conceptualize and for the engineering R&D team in India to build, Thomas says, 'That's the process we started with, but it's totally changed now. The India teams are competitors of those in Silicon Valley.'[20]

Indian GCCs are rightfully taking their seat at the table in other industry domains too. The Indian GCC of global investment bank Goldman Sachs played an important role in the launch of the Goldman Sachs Apple Card.[21] They followed it up by powering the new-age IT required for the company's digital consumer bank, Marcus. Goldman Sachs believes that their India GCC is central to the success of Marcus and is on par with any of their global offices thanks to the quality of Indian talent across the spectrum of consumer banking domains, including product design, risk management, data analytics, engineering and operations. Many more MNCs are likely to architect, engineer and operate their digital platforms from their India GCCs in the future. India GCCs are getting very deeply intertwined with their parent companies' business.

S. Ramani, founding director of NCST, makes an interesting and bold estimation of the value that Indian IT professionals can bring in the future: 'Michael Dertouzos, professor at MIT, in his book *The Unfinished Revolution* imagines a future when 50 million Indians are working on software. Let's consider this—it's not just software, it's not just the network-based industries like outsourcing, call centres, BPO; it's the whole range of technological services like engineering, management of technology (including GCCs). It is entirely possible to have 50 million Indians doing that in the future. What do you think will be the economic value of that? At US$50,000 per person (per annum) for 50 million people, it is a pretty big number (US$2500 billion).'[22]

While Indian IT services providers and GCCs are upping the ante when it comes to digital technologies, the Indian start-up ecosystem is also going digital.

The Rise of Deep-Tech Start-ups from India

One of the important positive spillovers of the success of Indian IT is that it has inspired and accelerated entrepreneurial activity in India over the past couple of decades. In the last chapter, we read about Indian deep-tech start-ups, like Niramai and Plansys, that are applying technologies like AI and ML, virtual reality/augmented reality, drones, robotics and blockchain in multiple industry domains. But, why should India care about creating and sustaining more deep-tech start-ups?

Some of the most valuable companies today started as deep-tech start-ups. Take the S&P 500 market capitalization-weighted index as an illustration. In 1970, the top five American companies were IBM, AT&T, General Motors, Standard Oil and Eastman Kodak. In 2020, this list includes Microsoft, Apple, Amazon, Alphabet (parent company of Google) and Facebook[23]—all IT companies, and all at the forefront of creating new technologies and knowledge in fields like AI/ML. And none of these companies even existed in 1970.

Kris captures the importance of deep-tech start-ups for India when he says, 'If India needs to become a developed economy, it has to focus on deep-tech. In the US, the most amount of wealth is being generated in companies with deep-tech as their starting point. Today, with our deep-engineering capabilities, when India does something in deep-tech, the entire world benefits. India has the potential to create products for 100 per cent of the world, not just the top 10 per cent.'[24] S. Ramadorai believes that India will become the innovation capital of the world: 'I think innovation, and innovation across domains, whether it is in healthcare, affordable or frugal innovation, which translates into global products, will become a way of life.'[25]

Deep-tech start-ups are also important for boosting human productivity in a resource-constrained economy like India's. N. Chandrasekaran, chairperson of Tata Sons, explains the importance of integrating technology and people in building a 'bridgital nation': 'India suffers from a lack of access—we don't have enough hospitals, enough doctors, enough judges, enough teachers, enough infrastructure. In everything there is shortage. And on the other side we have a jobs problem. There is plenty of talent but we don't seem to do a good job of matching demand and supply. It is that way because we are attacking both problems differently. The two have to meet each other—an integration of technology with people. We have to remove the halo or the aura around technology. I think AI/machine learning should be in the hands of every citizen. How do you build tools based on technology so that they will empower the people who have low or no skills so they operate at a higher level? This also ensures that the productivity of an expert doubles or triples.'[26]

We can witness this idea in action in how Indian deep-tech start-ups are addressing some of the wicked problems in Indian healthcare. For instance, Forus Health has developed an innovative AI/ML-based image recognition system—a portable device that can screen common eye problems leading to blindness, such as the early onset of diabetic retinopathy. During mass eyecare check-ups conducted in remote locations, the AI system checks the eye image as soon as it is clicked and prompts the local technician to click another image in case it is not good enough. Once usable images are captured, the system grades the images, again in real time, and ascertains whether the patient has diabetic retinopathy. If that is the case, then the patient is advised to consult an ophthalmologist to determine the next course of action. Deep-tech solutions enhance the productivity of both the low-skilled technician in Indian villages as well as the expert ophthalmologist in Indian cities.

Deep-tech start-ups need a nurturing environment, rich in scientific research and engineering capabilities, to thrive. As we noted in the last chapter, they are discovering it in incubators in Indian universities. The IIT Madras Research Park, established in 2006, is modelled on the famous Stanford Research Institute. It offers an interesting model of nurturing the academia-start-up ecosystem for deep-technology start-ups. Its main objectives are to develop innovation capabilities and to transfer basic research to applications that can be commercialized. The research park creates a collaborative environment between industry and academia through joint research projects and consulting assignments. It nurtures a self-sustaining and technologically fertile environment that aligns R&D to the potential needs of the industry. It also facilitates the development of a high-quality and technology-competent workforce. It does this by providing opportunities for students to work in the companies in the park and by encouraging employees of the companies in the park to enrol in part-time master's and PhD programmes at the institute. India needs more of such research parks. In 2017–18, the government approved the setting up of eight more such parks, one each at IIT Kharagpur, IIT Bombay, IIT Gandhinagar, IIT Delhi, IIT Guwahati, IIT Kanpur, IIT Hyderabad and IISc Bangalore.[27]

Other structured mechanisms are required to promote deep-tech start-ups. Initiatives like the NASSCOM DeepTech Club and the India Deep Tech, a pan-industry alliance of deep-tech start-ups, deep-tech-focused incubators and venture capital funds, promote start-ups in India focused on scientific research and engineering innovation. Another programme is the Gopalakrishnan Deshpande

Centre for Innovation and Entrepreneurship, which was established in 2017 in IIT Madras. Through a structured training programme, this centre works with STEM colleges and scientific research institutions across India to implement a 'Lab to Market' mission by helping faculty, researchers and students commercialize their research ideas by creating deep-tech start-ups. We are beginning to see some green shoots of the positive impact of such efforts—by 2018–19, about 35 per cent of the total portfolio of 170 deep-tech start-ups established at the IIT Madras Incubation Cell had faculty members as founders or minority shareholders.[28]

It is not just industry that is riding the new IT wave, the Indian government too is looking at IT to power some of its largest programmes to ensure that every one of its people benefits from public services. IT enhances the effectiveness and efficiency of government's engagement with citizens.

Next-Generation IT-led Government Mission-Mode Programmes

We have come a long way from the days when the Indian government was suspicious about computers and IT. In the last chapter, we delved into the stories of Aadhaar and UPI, successful government mission-mode programmes that have touched the lives of millions of Indians.

The National e-Governance Division (NeGD) carries forward the tradition of mission-mode projects with the national programme on AI that focuses on nine priority areas, including healthcare, agriculture and smart cities. The National Centre of Geo-Informatics (NCoG), a GIS-based decision-support system platform, is another key mission project that supports critical applications, like a surveillance system to detect illegal mining, and a monitoring system for Indian roadways and water-stressed districts. The office of the principal scientific adviser to the government of India runs large technology missions in India, in areas such as waste-to-wealth, deep-sea exploration, quantum frontiers and translation technologies for Indian languages, all of which necessitate strong IT intervention.

The Indian government has also created some significant digital learning platforms—the National Programme on Technology Enhanced Learning (NPTEL) is probably the largest online repository in the world of courses in engineering, basic sciences and in select humanities and social sciences. With over 1 billion views on YouTube, it is probably the most subscribed/viewed education channel in the world.[29] The SWAYAM MOOCs platform is the world's largest online free e-learning platform portal covering school/vocational, undergraduate, postgraduate, engineering and other professional courses;[30] and Diksha is a digital infrastructure for school education with over 3 billion learning sessions.[31] The National Education Policy 2020 is expected to provide further impetus to adoption of technology in education.

The Ayushman Bharat Digital Mission (ABDM), which was earlier called the National Digital Health Mission (NDHM), is an ambitious project launched in 2020. In the same way that creation of digital infrastructure like UPI transformed the payments space, this mission is expected to catalyse digitization of the Indian healthcare ecosystem. As part of its first phase, it is being piloted in six union territories in India. The key building blocks of the digital National Health Stack include standardized registries of doctors and healthcare facilities like hospitals and diagnostic centres, a unique patient health ID and electronic health/medical records. Its Unified

Health Interface will be leveraged by both public and private enterprises to build and provide innovative healthcare solutions. We are already seeing a few not-for-profit organizations, such as Swasth Alliance, developing telemedicine apps and other healthcare pilots that will plug into the National Health Stack.

Kris, commenting on the paradoxical nature of the Indian healthcare system and how technology and the mission-mode projects play a crucial role in it, says, 'On the one hand, it (India) boasts of "best in class" healthcare delivery, attracting medical tourists from across the world, while on the other, it is characterized by a near absence of accessible, affordable quality health services for a large part of the population. Some of these challenges have been made visible during the current pandemic. A robust public digital infrastructure, to be implemented by ABDM, can help bridge these gaps and lays out the imperatives for the healthcare industry, leveraging digital technologies, IT talent in the country and emerging technologies like AI/ML.'[32]

A mission-mode programme around cyber security is also becoming a national priority. With the increasing digitization of industry and society, there is an enhanced threat of cybercrimes. But this topic goes beyond business. Cyber security is a matter of national security too. We are increasingly seeing hackers and some nation-states indulging in cyber warfare and targeting critical national infrastructure like utilities or banking.

In the future, we can expect some of these Indian technology platforms to go global. The Reserve Bank of India is actively considering export of its low-cost payment solutions like UPI.[33] India is sharing the development story of the Co-WIN platform with more than twenty countries looking at adopting the portal to run their own vaccination drives.[34] While Aadhaar is a proprietary system designed specifically for India and not available for use by another country, the open-source platform for national foundational identity anchored by IIITB, Modular Open Source Identity Platform (MOSIP), is being implemented in countries like Morocco and the Republic of the Philippines.[35]

The bedrock of IT, whether in industry or government, is the capability of Indian IT professionals and entrepreneurs. Keeping oneself updated with the latest technologies, and from the comfort of one's mobile phone, is becoming easier with the explosion in digital education.

Digital Learning and Skilling Come of Age

Consider the recent anecdote involving David Malan, a computer science faculty member at Harvard University, and Anirudh Konduru, a young engineer at Walmart Labs in Bengaluru.[36] Malan posted a photo on social media after receiving his first Covid-19 vaccine at a Walmart centre in the US. He was elated to receive a reply to his post from Konduru, who was part of the team in India that developed Walmart's vaccination reservation system. Six years earlier, while still in school, Konduru had learnt programming from Malan's popular online course, 'Introduction to computer science and the art of programming'. What a wonderful illustration of online education empowering Indian IT talent.

As always, the employees are at the core of Indian IT industry's aspiration to become the world's partners in digital transformation. It is estimated that about 2 lakh IT professionals were skilled on digital technologies in 2019–20.[37] And it is expected that more than 40 lakh will be trained in digital skills between 2020 and 2025. Indian IT companies are leveraging their in-house or third-party digital learning platforms like EdX, Coursera and Upgrad to educate and certify their employees in disciplines like AI/ML, data science and other programming and industry-domain skills. Indian universities too are embracing online education to offer certifications and even degrees—IIT Madras launched its entirely-online BSc programming and data science programme in June 2020—the first by any IIT.[38] Such programmes will supply the Indian IT industry with quality talent.

Kiran Karnik visualizes what skills would be required in the future: 'I think twenty-five years from now it is going to be a completely different world. There may be no drivers because it's safer to have a driverless car; there may be no programmers because everything is automated, some system design and architecture may exist. The only way we can cope with that is not by trying to foresee what it might be, but by preparing people who can live in a world of uncertainty. The half-life of knowledge now is probably five years, and so, you've got to be able to learn how to learn. Our country will need a lot of very competent, sharp engineers, but we also need a lot of poets and writers, because there's going to be a creative, different world.'[39]

Skilling and education go hand in hand with research. India has been steadily increasing its focus on IT, AI/ML research. Not only that, India is also focusing on research in emerging related multi-disciplinary domains like brain science.

Future of Research in India—IT, AI/ML and Brain Sciences

Science, technology, research and innovation are the key drivers of economic growth, societal impact and human development for a nation. However, India's R&D spend of 0.7 per cent of GDP and its human resource capacity of 156 researchers per million inhabitants do not compare well with the equivalent numbers for other countries, such as the US (2.7 per cent and 4205), China (2 per cent and 1089) and South Korea (4.3 per cent and 6826).[40]

In December 2020, the Indian government announced a new national Science Technology and Innovation Policy (STIP 2020), whose broad vision was for India to achieve technological self-reliance, be positioned among the top three scientific superpowers in the next decade, and to nurture and strengthen critical human capital. It aims to double the number of researchers, gross domestic expenditure on R&D (GERD) and private sector contribution to the GERD every five years.[41] Let us look at the emerging research landscape in India in two domains—IT and AI/ML, and brain sciences.

Among the most ambitious research programmes in IT and related domains in India today is the Rs 3660-crore National Mission on Interdisciplinary Cyber–Physical Systems (NM-ICPS).[42] Cyber–physical systems are emerging from the integration of embedded computing devices, IoT, people and physical environments powered by a high-speed data communication network. Twenty-five premier technology universities in India, including many of the IITs, form the research hubs of NM-ICPS. The research programme also plans to identify application areas in domains like smart cities, agriculture, healthcare, infrastructure and public transport.

AI and ML are among the most foundational of technologies in which India has to acquire a national capability. NITI Aayog reiterated the importance of AI and ML in its report 'National Strategy for Artificial Intelligence' and provided a road map for India.[43] At itihaasa Research and Digital, we identified the building blocks that will propel the country in its journey to becoming world-class in AI/ML research and application:[44]

1) We need to increase the number of PhD students in India. This can be done by creating a special fund to attract world-class faculty to India, by instituting research fellowships for PhD and post-doc students and by developing programmes to inculcate interest in AI/ML among undergraduate students.

2) We need to augment computing infrastructure for AI/ML research by setting up world-class national high-performance computing centres with specialized hardware for AI research, and at the same time encourage the domestic capability to design and make such computing systems in India.

3) We need to create India-specific AI challenges, tools and data sets by focusing on India-specific problems that affect large numbers of citizens and by creating resource repositories and data sets for research in India.

4) We need to set up Centres of Excellence for AI/ML research. These centres should be multidisciplinary and include a range of engineering and humanities disciplines. The centres should also facilitate close interaction among researchers and industry. It is imperative to align AI/ML and ethics so that the benefits of Indian AI/ML research, by design, is inclusive of all Indians.

5) And, finally, we need to adopt an 'AI Grand Challenges' approach so that the efforts of the many researchers from multiple disciplines are channelled towards a common purpose. This would entail linking of institutional mechanisms to the start-up ecosystem and strengthening of the academic incubators to help translate AI/ML research into market applications.

As the new science and technology policy points out, Indian IT can help with the development and deployment of frontier disruptive technologies, such as quantum computing. AI/ML and quantum computing can become a potent combination. For instance, they can be applied in biology to significantly improve our ability to make structural predictions of complex structures like proteins much faster than it takes the most powerful conventional supercomputers.

Indian IT can play an enabling, funding and collaborative role in each of these dimensions. It can align its corporate social responsibility investments with research and innovation. Private funding has played an important role in the transformation of emerging nations. For example, in the mid-2000s, about 65 per cent of Taiwan's R&D was from private sector funding, up from about 30 per cent in the past.[45] India is at a point in history where private funding can supplement government funding in research, and this includes philanthropic funding.

Kris Gopalakrishnan has directed significant philanthropic investments towards Indian science and research, especially in brain sciences, one of the most promising interdisciplinary domains of the future.

Brain science is a grand challenge of the current era. When US President Barack Obama unveiled the BRAIN initiative—a collaborative, public–private research initiative focused on brain science—in 2013, he said, 'As humans, we can identify galaxies light years away, we can study particles smaller than an atom. But we still haven't unlocked the mystery of the three pounds of matter that sits between our ears. So as a result, we're still unable to cure diseases like Alzheimer's or autism, or fully reverse the effects of a stroke. And the most powerful computer in the world isn't nearly as intuitive as the one we're born with. There is this enormous mystery waiting to be unlocked.'[46]

Other international brain programmes, such as the European Human Brain Project and the Chinese Brain Project, have also emerged. It is important for India too to build strong competence in this area.

Commenting on how he zoned in on funding brain research in India after stepping down from Infosys, Kris says, 'Research, innovation and entrepreneurship—that is the complete chain I decided to support. I chose brain sciences and decided to explore two areas: brain-inspired computing and understanding how the brain ages and disorders that arise due to ageing, such as Alzheimer's, dementia, Parkinson's and other neurological disorders.'[47]

He has set up two research centres supporting six distinguished visiting chairs in brain science in India—the Centre for Computation Brain Research (CCBR) at IIT Madras focuses on how knowledge of the brain's functioning can be applied to enhance computer architecture and develop next-generation algorithms to extend AI/ML; and the Centre for Brain Research (CBR) at IISc Bangalore focuses on clinical research to understand age-related brain disorders, and to model how the brain works.

Neuroscience studies how the brain works at different levels— the cellular level, the level of a network of cells and at the level of a system. There is a lot of IT used in brain research, and vice versa. Already, some interesting industry/scientific collaborations are underway at the brain research centres.[48] A global chip major is collaborating on designing a neuroscience inspired chip, and an Indian IT services company is using a neuroscience computational model to identify treatment for brain strokes. India cannot afford to miss the boat in brain research and to develop its own neuroscience models and systems. We believe that brain science's potential in wide areas like IT and medicine can become as big as AI/ML's.

Industrial activity and government programmes collect data and generate information about all of us. They also use newer and more powerful algorithms to develop more accurate and innovative IT models. Thus, we need the right governance safeguards that will both protect our rights and also foster innovation.

Future of IT Governance and Regulations in India, Especially around Data and Algorithms

Emerging technologies create and facilitate new businesses, social connections and government-citizen interactions. As we move to a paperless, cashless and borderless world, and as IT permeates every aspect of our lives, whether it is commerce, education or entertainment, governments around the world, including India, have to devise new regulations to govern these technologies. Through these rules, governments aim to provide more control in the hands of the citizen, protect his or her privacy, enable business innovations, and promote economic and social value addition.

India has created or is in the middle of enacting myriad new regulations that will have huge implications for Indian IT and how technology-enabled businesses and start-ups will operate in the country. These regulations include: the Aadhaar Act 2016, the Personal Data Protection (PDP) Bill 2019/Data Protection Bill 2021, the E-Commerce Bill 2019, the Digital Information Security in Healthcare Act and the Information Technology Rules 2021 on intermediary guidelines.

What is the future of IT governance regulations in India from a data and algorithms perspective? These perspectives are important, as India is becoming data-rich, thanks to the explosion of smart phones, availability of cheap bandwidth, and the ubiquity of planet-scale digital platforms in the hands of its citizens.

The PDP Bill, which is similar to the European Union's General Data Protection Regulation (GDPR), aims to protect the privacy of individuals with respect to their personal data and governs the relationship between individuals and entities processing their personal data. Once enacted, the law will have implications for how Internet businesses in India operate and there will be significant IT opportunities in making the businesses compliant with the law. India is already experimenting with a unique consent-based personal data-sharing framework, called 'Data Empowerment and Protection Architecture',[49] in areas like financial inclusion and healthcare. This will mean that a shopkeeper's financial data or a patient's electronic healthcare record will be protected from unauthorized access, unless the owner-individual approves sharing of the data.

The Indian government has formed a committee headed by Kris Gopalakrishnan to develop a governance framework for non-personal data, a first of its kind in the world.[50] What is envisaged by the committee is a new model where non-personal data sets that are of high value from a public-interest perspective, and currently with data collectors—typically private companies or government departments—are shared with Indian communities. For example, residents' welfare associations and waste management firms share data on solid waste disposal in the Whitefield locality in Bengaluru with a non-profit citizens' group. This group can then make available the data to those interested in further analysis. BBMP, the Bengaluru city corporation, can use the data, along with similar data from other localities to benchmark, compare and contrast solid waste management operations in different parts of the city. A start-up that is creating a new technology for processing biodegradable solid waste can use this data to help assess demand; or the public policy department of a university can use this data for their research on management of urban waste in India. This has led to the release of the draft India Data Accessibility & Use Policy 2022.

Kris Gopalakrishnan, commenting on the importance of data, says, 'Data should be treated as a strategic asset at the national level. It is important for policymaking, improving public service and for supporting a wide range of societal objectives, including in science, healthcare and so on. Take the case of gene mapping. Although India has 20 per cent of the world's population, the DNA sequences of its people make up less than 1 per cent of global genetic databases. Such data is required to create healthcare solutions specific for India.'[51]

Data becomes extremely valuable when insights are derived from it. More often than not, data analysis today involves big data and AI/ML algorithms. But AI systems present certain challenges, of which policymakers must be aware. Some facial recognition AI systems have biases against dark skin. How such AI systems work in a diverse setting like India is anybody's guess. Other AI applications, such as for loans or résumé processing, may have biases around gender, geographic location and other factors. For example, the AI system may inappropriately reject an application because the applicant is a woman. An AI system is often a black box; its ML algorithms cannot be easily and entirely interpreted. Thus, there arise ethical questions around a disease diagnosis done by an AI system analysing medical scans and images. As AI systems become more prevalent in all walks of life in India, the government will explore laws to regulate this domain.

We need to work on standards to ensure that ML models and training data are robust, do not discriminate and are explainable. Already, there are interdisciplinary research centres in India, like the Robert Bosch Centre for Data Science and Artificial Intelligence at IIT Madras and the School of Artificial Intelligence at IIT Delhi, which are working on different aspects of ML for social good.[52]

We believe that regulations in India around the Internet and emerging technologies will play out in three ways. First, they will aim to enhance access and reduce the digital divide in online platforms and create a prosperous and equitable future for its citizens; second, regulations will focus on democratizing data availability and spurring Indian innovation and entrepreneurship; and third, the Internet, 5G, security and allied technologies will be the turf of economic wars of the twenty-first century, and regulations will be important strategic elements in the nation's armoury.

A Final Word

India's current GDP is about US$2.9 trillion dollars, which will increase at a healthy pace in the coming years.[53] A significant portion of this growth is likely to come from different sectors of the economy leveraging new information technologies and new entrepreneurial activity driven by these technologies. In his book *Critical Path*, futurist and inventor Buckminster Fuller estimated that if we took all the knowledge that mankind had accumulated and transmitted by the year 1 CE as equal to one unit of information, it probably took about 1500 years until the sixteenth century for that amount of knowledge to double.[54] The next doubling of knowledge from two to four units was completed in 250 years by the mid-eighteenth century. By the turn of the twentieth century, 150 years later, human knowledge had doubled again, to eight units. The speed at which information doubled was getting faster and faster. The doubling speed is now estimated at between one and two years.

India needs to be at the forefront of this new knowledge creation to reap the economic and social benefits it will bring. This is a golden era for research, innovation and entrepreneurship. We have built a rock-solid foundation in IT over the past six decades. It is our collective responsibility to carry forward this legacy and ensure that India remains a leader in IT and related technology domains.

Acknowledgements

We thank all our teachers who have influenced our lives.

Infosys provided us with fantastic opportunities to be part of Indian IT. We have incredible experiences and memories as Infoscions.

We thank the leaders of Indian IT who were extremely generous with their time and shared their recollections with us—Ajai Chowdhry, Ashank Desai, Ashok Soota, Azim H. Premji, B.V. Naidu, Bharat Goenka, Bhaskar Pramanik, Debjani Ghosh, Dhiraj Rajaram, Diju Raha, Diwakar Nigam, F.C. Kohli, Geetha Manjunath, Gopal Srinivasan, Harish Mehta, Jaithirth Rao, K. Dinesh, K.V. Ramani, Kiran Karnik, Krishnakumar Natarajan, Lakshmi Narayanan, Lalit Kanodia, N. Chandrasekaran, N.R. Narayana Murthy, N.S. Raghavan, N. Vittal, Nandan Nilekani, Pradeep Gupta, Pradeep Kar, Pramod Bhasin, Prof. C.R. Muthukrishnan, Prof. Deepak Phatak, Prof. Gio Wiederhold, Prof. H.N. Mahabala, Prof. Kamala Krithivasan, Prof. Kesav Nori, Prof.

M.G.K. Menon, Prof. N. Balakrishnan, Prof. P.V.S. Rao, Prof. Pankaj Jalote, Prof. R.K. Shyamsundar, Prof. S. Sadagopan, Prof. T.P. Rama Rao, Prof. V. Rajaraman, R. Chandrashekhar, Rajendra Pawar, Raman Roy, S.D. Shibulal, S. Mahalingam, S. Ramadorai, S. Ramani, S.S. Oberoi, S. Srinivasan, Sandeep Dadlani, Saurabh Srivastava, Sharad Sharma, Som Mittal, Sridhar Mitta, Srini Rajam, Subroto Bagchi, Swami Manohar, V. Vinay, V.K. Harindran, Vinay L. Deshpande, Vivek Kulkarni, and others.

Our thanks to the IISc archives, IIT Madras archives, Infosys archives, TIFR archives, Wipro archives, and leaders who shared historically significant material.

Penguin Random House India has made this book a reality. Manish Kumar, our editor. Vineet Gill and Radhika Agarwal, our copy editors. Prateek Agarwal, the marketing expert. Milee Ashwarya got us started on the book. Amol Agarwal of Ahmedabad University made the initial introductions to Penguin. We thank Gurcharan Das for the introduction.

Also, thanks to our partners. Srikanth Shroff, S.H. Suman and team at Grasshopper. Pranab Sen, Anirudh Parvatikar and team at ResearchFox. Dr. C.S. Yogananda and D. Shivashankar at Sriranga Digital. Pallavi Kanakagiri and team at Induslaw. They have ably supported us in the history of Indian IT project.

Finally, we thank all our colleagues in Indian IT from whom we have learnt about different aspects of this fascinating domain.

This book is for everyone who is curious about Indian IT.

Notes

CHAPTER 1: AB INITIO: THE INDIAN IT INDUSTRY DISCOVERS A NEW NORMAL

1   https://timesofindia.indiatimes.com/2020/1/30/archivelist/year-2020,month-1,starttime-43860.cms, accessed on 20 April 2021.

2   https://epaper.hindustantimes.com/delhi?eddate=30/01/2020&Pageview=list, accessed on 20 April 2021.

3   https://pib.gov.in/PressReleaseIframePage.aspx?PRID=1601095, accessed on 20 April 2021.

4   https://www.who.int/emergencies/diseases/novel-coronavirus-2019/technical-guidance/naming-the-coronavirus-disease-(covid-2019)-and-the-virus-that-causes-it, accessed on 20 April 2021.

5   https://www.livemint.com/news/india/india-s-it-industry-braces-for-coronavirus-impact-11582267149734.html, accessed on 20 April 2021.

6   Ibid.

7   https://www.ndma.gov.in/sites/default/files/PDF/covid/COVID-19-Indian-Experience.pdf, accessed on 20 April 2021.

8   https://www.infosys.com/newsroom/features/2020/face-to-face-with-covid-19.html, accessed on 20 April 2021.

9 https://www.infosys.com/newsroom/features/2020/resilient-prepared-navigate-covid19.html, accessed on 20 April 2021.

10 https://www.tcs.com/company-overview/tcs-response-covid-19, accessed on 20 April 2021.

11 https://www.businessinsider.in/business/corporates/news/tcs-ceo-says-the-business-model-is-20-years-old-and-its-time-to-go-employee-lite/articleshow/75243124.cms, accessed on 20 April 2021.

12 https://www.thenewsminute.com/article/tech-industry-will-be-impacted-demand-side-nasscom-s-debjani-ghosh-tnm-122557, accessed on 20 April 2021.

13 Sandeep Dadlani in conversation with the authors, May 2020.

14 https://www.tcs.com/content/dam/tcs/investor-relations/financial-statements/2019-20/ar/annual-report-2019-2020.pdf, accessed on 20 April 2021.

15 https://www.infosys.com/investors/reports-filings/annual-report/annual/documents/infosys-ar-20.pdf, accessed on 20 April 2021.

16 https://www.linkedin.com/pulse/atoms-become-more-local-bits-global-times-after-covid-19-ravi-kumar-s/, accessed on 20 April 2021.

17 https://www.aarogyasetu.gov.in/wp-content/uploads/2020/11/mygov-9999999991925749197.pdf, accessed on 23 April 2021.

18 https://twitter.com/amitabhk87/status/1250132730899238912, accessed on 23 April 2021.

19 https://www.aarogyasetu.gov.in/, accessed on 23 April 2021.

20 https://actu.epfl.ch/news/epfl-researchers-put-proximity-tracing-app-to-the-/, accessed on 23 April 2021.

21 https://timesofindia.indiatimes.com/india/icmrs-2nd-sero-survey-results-here-are-the-key-findings/articleshow/78385542.cms, accessed on 23 April 2021.

22 https://www.aarogyasetu.gov.in/wp-content/uploads/2020/11/mygov-999999999120976654.pdf, accessed on 23 April 2021.

23 https://www.business-standard.com/article/current-affairs/india-s-digital-backbone-for-vaccination-is-remarkable-nandan-nilekani-121042001111_1.html, accessed on 23 April 2021.

24 'The Digital Journey in the New Normal—How Are Organizations Leveraging Emerging Technologies in Response to COVID-19?', CII—itihaasa Research and Digital study, August 2020.

25 Ibid.

26 https://indianexpress.com/article/books-and-literature/book-on-how-world-class-ventilator-was-designed-and-built-in-iit-kanpur-during-lockdown-released-7232010/, accessed on 24 April 2021.

27 https://www.business-standard.com/article/finance/digital-transactions-could-reach-rs-15-trillion-a-day-by-2025-rbi-120072201431_1.html, accessed on 23 April 2021.

28 https://yourstory.com/2020/11/sameer-nigam-phonepe-entrepreneur-advice-prime-knowledge-series, accessed on 23 April 2021.

29 'Ed-Tech in India', An Omdiyar Network India—RedSeer Report 2019-20.

30 https://www.forbesindia.com/article/take-one-big-story-of-the-day/can-edtech-keep-up-its-momentum-after-covid19/63895/1, accessed on 23 April 2021.

31 https://www.businessinsider.in/business/startups/news/ronnie-screwvala-explains-why-covid-edtech-boom-is-unlike-demonetisation-boost-for-digital-payments/articleshow/78119790.cms, accessed on 23 April 2021.

32 V. Rajaraman, 'History of Computing in India (1955–2010)', IEEE Computer Society.

33 itihaasa, History of Indian IT, H.N. Mahabala, Video 'Faith in computing', https://itihaasa.com/describe/sartefact/001_001_0224?term=Faith+in+computing&sf=1

34 itihaasa, History of Indian IT, S. Gopalakrishnan, Video 'Evolution of Global Delivery Model (GDM)', https://itihaasa.com/describe/sartefact/001_001_0731?term=Evolution+of+Global+Delivery+Model+%28GDM%29&sf=1

35 itihaasa, History of Indian IT, Kiran Karnik, Video 'Camaraderie in the Indian IT Industry', https://itihaasa.com/describe/sartefact/001_001_0340?term=Camaraderie+in+the+Indian+IT+Industry&sf=1

36 itihaasa, History of Indian IT, S. Gopalakrishnan, Video 'Evolution of IT Entrepreneurship in India', https://itihaasa.com/describe/sartefact/001_001_0741?term=Evolution+of+IT+Entrepreneurship+in+India&sf=1

37 Peter Cappelli et al., 'Leadership Lessons from India', *Harvard Business Review*, March 2010.

38 https://www.pbs.org/wgbh/commandingheights/shared/minitext/int_narayanamurthy.html#7, accessed on 6 May 2021.

39   N. Dayasindhu, 'itihaasa, History of Indian IT: Case Study of a Unique
     Digital Museum', *SIGMIS-CPR '17: Proceedings of the 2017 ACM
     SIGMIS Conference on Computers and People Research*, ACM, pp. 141–146,
     2017.
40   John T. Seaman Jr. and George David Smith, 'Your Company's History
     as a Leadership Tool', *Harvard Business Review*, December 2012.
41   Five-Year Plans (FYPs) are centralized and integrated national
     programmes providing plans for economic development of the country.

CHAPTER 2: EMERGENCE OF IT IN INDIA AND CAPABILITY-BUILDING

1   'Future of Technology Services—Winning in this Decade', NASSCOM,
     February 2021.
2   http://planningcommission.nic.in/plans/planrel/fiveyr/welcome.html,
     accessed on 9 December 2019.
3   http://planningcommission.nic.in/plans/planrel/fiveyr/2nd/2planch3.
     html, accessed on 9 December 2019.
4   http://planningcommission.nic.in/plans/planrel/fiveyr/3rd/3planch5.
     html, accessed on 9 December 2019.
5   'Prasantha Chandra Mahalanobis 1893-1972', Biographical Memoirs of
     Fellows of the Royal Society, C.R. Rao, 1973.
6   *Biometrika* is primarily a journal of statistics and published by Oxford
     University Press on behalf of the Biometrika Trust.
7   https://humansofdata.atlan.com/2019/08/historical-humans-of-data-
     mahalanobis/, accessed on 9 December 2019.
8   P.C. Mahalanobis, 'On Large-Scale Sample Surveys', Statistical
     Laboratory, Kolkata, 1943.
9   https://www.theatlantic.com/science/archive/2016/12/the-women-
     computers-who-measured-the-stars/509231/, accessed on 9 December
     2019.
10   The tabulating machine, invented by Herman Hollerith, was an
     electromechanical machine designed to assist in summarizing
     information stored on punched cards.
11   https://blogs.lse.ac.uk/impactofsocialsciences/2016/04/08/from-
     computing-clerks-to-androids-two-bits-on-material-lives-of-social-data-
     in-india/, accessed on 9 December 2019.
12   An Annotated Chronological History of Indian Statistical Institute,
     Available at https://www.isical.ac.in/~repro/history/public/, accessed on
     9 December 2019.

13 itihaasa, History of Indian IT, V. Rajaraman, 'Computing in IISc,
    ISI and TIFR in the Mid-1950s', https://itihaasa.com/describe/
    artefact/001_001_0272?interviewee=Prof.+V.+Rajaraman

14 http://www.bbk.ac.uk/about-us/obituaries/obituary-professor-andrew-
    booth, accessed on 9 December 2019.

15 http://www.computerconservationsociety.org/resurrection/res22.htm#c,
    accessed on 9 December 2019.

16 ALGOL is short for 'Algorithmic Language' and is a family of computer
    programming languages suited for scientific computations.

17 Ganesan Venkataraman, *Bhabha and His Magnificent Obsessions*,
    Universities Press (India) Limited, 1994. p. 8.

18 itihaasa, History of Indian IT, Prof. M.G.K. Menon,
    Video 'Prof. M.G.K. Menon on Prof. R. Narasimhan
    (Courtesy: Dr S. Ramani)', https://itihaasa.com/describe/
    artefact/001_001_1024?interviewee=Prof.+M+G+K+Menon

19 Narasimhan, R. oral history interviews conducted by Indira Chowdhury,
    Bengaluru, India, 4 May–17 May 2005, TIFR Archives.

20 itihaasa, History of Indian IT, Prof. P.V.S. Rao, Video 'TIFRAC – The
    first digital computer designed and built in India', https://itihaasa.com/
    describe/sartefact/001_001_1037?term=TIFRAC&sf=1

21 http://abdulkalam.nic.in/sp170206-3.html, accessed on 9 December
    2019.

22 'Extract from Report of the Narasimhan Computer Committee Choice
    Between 3600 and IBM 7090 Systems', by M.G.K. Menon dated
    22/1/63, TIFR Archives.

23 Letter from J. Schemy to Homi Bhabha, dated 16 November 1965,
    TIFR archives.

24 itihaasa, History of Indian IT, F. C. Kohli, Video 'Modern
    computers come to India', https://itihaasa.com/describe/
    sartefact/001_001_0459?term=Modern+computers+come+to+India&sf=1

25 Proceedings of National Conference on Electronics Organized by
    Electronics Committee (Mumbai 24-28 March, 1970), Electronics
    Commission, 1971.

26 Ibid.

27 Ibid.

28 Ibid.

29 Ibid.

30 C.R. Subramanian, *India and the Computer–A Study of Planned
    Development*, Oxford University Press, New Delhi, 1992.

31 itihaasa, History of Indian IT, N. R. Narayana Murthy, Video 'Computer center in IIM Ahmedabad', https://itihaasa.com/describe/sartefact/001_001_0177?term=Computer+center+in+IIM+Ahmedabad&sf=1

32 Key-punches were machines that would make holes in a card that would hold the data. A card-reader read the data and then transferred it to a computer or storage device like a magnetic tape or disc.

33 itihaasa, History of Indian IT, Subroto Bagchi, Video 'Early history of IT adoption in India, starting with the jute mills', https://itihaasa.com/describe/sartefact/001_001_0443?term=Early+history+of+IT+adoption+in+India%2C+starting+with+the+jute+mills&sf=1

34 C.R. Subramanian, *India and the Computer – A Study of Planned Development*, Oxford University Press, New Delhi, 1992.

35 itihaasa, History of Indian IT, S. Srinivasan, Video 'Working at IBM India in the 1960s and 1970s', https://itihaasa.com/describe/sartefact/001_001_0137?term=Working+at+IBM+India+in+the+1960s+and+1970s&sf=1

36 itihaasa, History of Indian IT, Dr Lalit Kanodia, Video 'Tata Computer Centre in the mid-1960s', https://itihaasa.com/describe/sartefact/001_001_0980?term=Tata+Computer+Centre+in+the+mid-1960s&sf=1

37 itihaasa, History of Indian IT, Prof. Deepak Phatak, Video 'Computer culture in IIT Bombay in the late 1960s', https://itihaasa.com/describe/sartefact/001_001_0375?term=Computer+culture+in+IIT+Bombay+in+the+late+1960s&sf=1

38 The Public Law (PL) 480 or Agricultural Trade Development and Assistance Act created the Food for Peace programme of the United States that has provided food assistance around the world.

39 Education Development Centre, Kanpur Indo-American Program Final Report, 1962–1972, Appendix A.

40 Madhura Gopinath, 'Dr. P. K. Kelkar 1909–1990', https://www.iitk.ac.in/doaa/convocation/data/PK_Kelkar.pdf, accessed on 9 December 2019.

41 itihaasa, History of Indian IT, H.N. Mahabala, 'Joining IIT Kanpur', https://itihaasa.com/describe/sartefact/001_001_0221?term=Joining+IIT+Kanpur&sf=1

42 itihaasa, History of Indian IT, V. Rajaraman, 'Setting up the IBM 1620 at IIT Kanpur in the 1960s', https://itihaasa.com/describe/sartefact/001_001_0267?term=Setting+up+the+IBM+1620+at+IIT+Kanpur+in+the+1960s&sf=1

43 Kanpur Indo-American Programme, Monthly Report to USAID, October 1965.

44 itihaasa, History of Indian IT, V. Rajaraman, 'Setting up the IBM 1620 at IIT Kanpur in the 1960s', https://itihaasa.com/describe/sartefact/001_001_0267?term=Setting+up+the+IBM+1620+at+IIT+Kanpur+in+the+1960s&sf=1

45 Computer History Museum, 'Oral History of Harry Huskey', February 2006, CHM, reference number: X3455.2006.

46 Authors in conversation with Prof. Gio Wiederhold, December 2019.

47 V. Rajaraman, 'John McCarthy—Father of Artificial Intelligence', *Resonance*, March 2014.

48 itihaasa, History of Indian IT, V. Rajaraman, 'Setting up the IBM 1620 at IIT Kanpur in the 1960s', https://itihaasa.com/describe/sartefact/001_001_0267?term=Setting+up+the+IBM+1620+at+IIT+Kanpur+in+the+1960s&sf=1

49 itihaasa, History of Indian IT, H.N. Mahabala, 'The First High Level Programming Course at IIT Kanpur and in India', https://itihaasa.com/describe/sartefact/001_001_0223?term=The+First+High+Level+Programming+Course+at+IIT+Kanpur+and+in+India&sf=1

50 itihaasa, History of Indian IT, V. Rajaraman, 'IIT Kanpur's M.Tech Program with CS Specialization and its illustrious students', https://itihaasa.com/describe/artefact/001_001_0270?interviewee=Prof.+V.+Rajaraman

51 itihaasa, History of Indian IT, V. Rajaraman, 'Prof. Rajaraman's seminal text books on programming and computers', https://itihaasa.com/describe/artefact/001_001_0273?interviewee=Prof.+V.+Rajaraman

52 itihaasa, History of Indian IT, V. Rajaraman, 'IIT Kanpur's M.Tech Program with CS Specialization and its illustrious students', https://itihaasa.com/describe/artefact/001_001_0270?interviewee=Prof.+V.+Rajaraman

53 itihaasa, History of Indian IT, Saurabh Srivastava, 'Computer culture in IIT Kanpur', https://itihaasa.com/describe/sartefact/001_001_0142?term=Computer+culture+in+IIT+Kanpur&sf=1

54 itihaasa, History of Indian IT, N.R. Narayana Murthy, 'Computer culture in IIT Kanpur in the late 1960s', https://itihaasa.com/describe/sartefact/001_001_0172?term=Computer+culture+in+IIT+Kanpur&sf=1

55   itihaasa, History of Indian IT, N.R. Narayana Murthy, 'Seeing a computer for the first time', https://itihaasa.com/describe/sartefact/001_001_0171?term=Seeing+a+computer+for+the+first+time&sf=1

56   itihaasa, History of Indian IT, H.N. Mahabala, 'Matchmaker make me a match', https://itihaasa.com/describe/artefact/001_001_0231?interviewee=Prof.+H.+N.+Mahabala

57   itihaasa, History of Indian IT, N.R. Narayana Murthy, 'Life in IIT Kanpur: Training Anecdote', https://itihaasa.com/describe/sartefact/001_001_0173?term=Life+in+IIT+Kanpur%3A+Training+Anecdote&sf=1

58   Education Development Centre, Kanpur Indo-American Programme Final Report, 1962-1972, p. 105.

59   The differential analyser was a computer which solved differential equations and not algebraic equations.

60   itihaasa, History of Indian IT, V. Rajaraman, 'Computing in IISc, ISI and TIFR in the Mid-1950s', https://itihaasa.com/describe/artefact/001_001_0272?interviewee=Prof.+V.+Rajaraman

61   http://www.ourcomputerheritage.org/ccs-f3x1.pdf, accessed on 9 December 2019.

62   V. Rajaraman, 'History of Computing in India (1955-2010)', IEEE Computer Society.

63   N. Dayasindhu, 'Creating an Entrepreneurship Milieu for Electronics and Information Technology Industries', *International Journal of Entrepreneurship and Innovation Management*, Vol. 3, Nos. 5/6, 2003.

64   Tamil Nadu Administration Report 1965–66, http://14.139.60.153/handle/123456789/11824, accessed on 9 December 2019.

65   Reports on Computer Society of India, Fifth Annual Meeting published in *The Hindu*, 8 January 1970, available via the Stanford Infolab Website, http://infolab.stanford.edu/pub/gio/personal/1965India, accessed on 9 December 2019.

66   Roland Wittje, 'Indo-German Entanglements in Science and Technology: The Indian Institute of Technology Madras', MIDA Archival Reflexicon, 2019.

67   itihaasa, History of Indian IT, C.R. Muthukrishnan, 'Computer culture in IIT Madras in the 1960s', https://itihaasa.com/describe/sartefact/001_001_0095?term=Computer+culture+in+IIT+Madras+in+the+1960s&sf=1

68   Dr Prahalada Ramarao, *Build Up to Blast Off—DRDL 1962 to 1982*, Frontier India, 2016.

69   CSI Communications, Volume 38, Issue 6, September 2014.

70   Faculty and staff of KIAP, via the Stanford Infolab Website http://
     infolab.stanford.edu/pub/gio/personal/1965India, accessed on 9
     December 2019.

71   itihaasa, History of Indian IT, S. Kris Gopalakrishnan, Video 'Role
     of Computer Society of India (CSI)', https://itihaasa.com/describe/
     sartefact/001_001_0728?term=Role+of+Computer+Society+of+India+
     %28CSI%29&sf=1

72   V. Rajaraman, 'History of Computing in India (1955–2010)', IEEE
     Computer Society.

CHAPTER 3: EMPHASIS ON SELF-RELIANCE AND THE DOMESTIC HARDWARE INDUSTRY

1   itihaasa, History of Indian IT, Prof. P.V.S. Rao, Video
    'Genesis of the ADGES project', https://itihaasa.com/describe/
    sartefact/001_001_1045?term=ADGES+project&sf=1

2   itihaasa, History of Indian IT, Prof. P.V.S. Rao, Video
    'ADGES project', https://itihaasa.com/describe/
    sartefact/001_001_1046?term=ADGES+project&sf=1

3   itihaasa, History of Indian IT, Saurabh Srivastava, Video 'Manufacture
    only 50 computers per license in the 1970s', https://itihaasa.com/
    describe/sartefact/001_001_0144?term=Manufacture+only+50+
    computers+per+license+in+the+1970s&sf=1

4   itihaasa, History of Indian IT, Prof. V. Rajaraman, Video 'The genesis of
    the Masters of Computer Applications (MCA) program in India', https://
    itihaasa.com/describe/sartefact/001_001_0275?term=The+genesis+of+
    the+Masters+of+Computer+Applications+%28MCA%29+program+
    in+India&sf=1

5   itihaasa, History of Indian IT, S. Sadagopan, Video 'Conceptualizing
    the Masters in Computer Applications program', https://itihaasa.com/
    describe/sartefact/001_001_0258?term=Conceptualizing+the+
    Masters+in+Computer+Applications+program&sf=1

6   itihaasa, History of Indian IT, F.C. Kohli, Video 'Genesis of the Tata
    Burroughs Joint Venture', https://itihaasa.com/describe/sartefact/001_
    001_0463?term=Genesis+of+the+Tata+Burroughs+Joint+Venture&sf=1

7   Ibid.

8   itihaasa, History of Indian IT, S. Ramadorai, Video 'Genesis of the
    TCS and Burroughs collaboration', https://itihaasa.com/describe/

sartefact/001_001_0419?term=Genesis+of+the+TCS+and+Burroughs+collaboration&sf=1

9   itihaasa, History of Indian IT, S. Mahalingam, Video 'Tata Burroughs Joint Venture and Its impact on TCS', https://itihaasa.com/describe/sartefact/001_001_0396?term=Tata+Burroughs+Joint+Venture+and+Its+impact+on+TCS&sf=1

10 itihaasa, History of Indian IT, S. Mahalingam, Video 'Tata Burroughs Joint Venture and Its impact on TCS', https://itihaasa.com/describe/sartefact/001_001_0396?term=Tata+Burroughs+Joint+Venture+and+Its+impact+on+TCS&sf=1

11 itihaasa, History of Indian IT, S. Mahalingam, Video 'Import of IBM 3090 by TCS', https://itihaasa.com/describe/sartefact/001_001_0394?term=Import+of+IBM+3090+by+TCS&sf=1

12 itihaasa, History of Indian IT, N. Chandrasekaran, 'MCA Internship at TCS', https://itihaasa.com/describe/sartefact/001_001_1136?term=MCA+Internship+at+TCS&sf=1

13 Ibid.

14 American Standard Code for Information Interchange is a character encoding standard for electronic communication.

15 Extended Binary Coded Decimal Interchange Code is character encoding used mainly on IBM mainframe and IBM midrange computer operating systems.

16 itihaasa, History of Indian IT, Kesav Nori, Video 'First software project in TRDDC – Citibank UK project', https://itihaasa.com/describe/sartefact/001_001_1111?term=First+software&sf=1

17 itihaasa, History of Indian IT, F.C. Kohli, 'Getting into Tata Consultancy Services', https://itihaasa.com/describe/sartefact/001_001_0458?term=Getting+into+Tata+Consultancy+Services&sf=1

18 itihaasa, History of Indian IT, F.C. Kohli, 'First Impression of Tata Consultancy Services', https://itihaasa.com/describe/sartefact/001_001_0461?term=First+Impression+of+Tata+Consultancy+Services&sf=1

19 itihaasa, History of Indian IT, S. Mahalingam, 'Rule at TCS: Getting syntax right in 3 attempts', https://itihaasa.com/describe/sartefact/001_001_0389?term=Rule+at+TCS&sf=1

20 itihaasa, History of Indian IT, S. Ramadorai, 'About Mr F.C. Kohli', https://itihaasa.com/describe/sartefact/001_001_0436?term=About+Mr.+F.+C.+Kohli&sf=1

21 C.R. Subramanian, *India and the Computer: A Study of Planned Development*, Oxford University Press, New Delhi, 1992.

22 Ibid.

23 itihaasa, History of Indian IT, Ajai Chowdhry, Video 'Working in DCM Data Products', https://itihaasa.com/describe/sartefact/001_001_1090?term=Working+in+DCM+Data+Products&sf=1

24 itihaasa, History of Indian IT, Ajai Chowdhry, Video 'Genesis of HCL', https://itihaasa.com/describe/sartefact/001_001_1091?term=Genesis+of+HCL&sf=1

25 PPS-4 or 'Parallel Processing System - 4-bit word' was a family of 4-bit microprocessor chips.

26 itihaasa, History of Indian IT, Ajai Chowdhry, Video 'First computer from HCL', https://itihaasa.com/describe/sartefact/001_001_1093?term=First+computer+from+HCL&sf=1

27 itihaasa, History of Indian IT, Rajendra Pawar, Video 'Minicomputers in the late 1970s – 1', https://itihaasa.com/describe/sartefact/001_001_0474?term=Minicomputers+in+the+late+1970s+-+1&sf=1

28 itihaasa, History of Indian IT, Rajendra Pawar, Video 'Minicomputers in the late 1970s – 2', https://itihaasa.com/describe/sartefact/001_001_0474?term=Minicomputers+in+the+late+1970s+-+2&sf=1

29 itihaasa, History of Indian IT, Ajai Chowdhry, Video 'HCL's entry in the US market: Pivot from hardware to software', https://itihaasa.com/describe/sartefact/001_001_1097?term=HCL%27s+entry+in+the+US+market%3A+Pivot+from+hardware+to+software&sf=1

30 itihaasa, History of Indian IT, Dr Sridhar Mitta, Video 'Using Microprocessors in Electronics Corporation of India Ltd.', https://itihaasa.com/describe/sartefact/001_001_0320?term=Using+Microprocessors+in+Electronics+Corporation+of+India+Ltd&sf=1

31 itihaasa, History of Indian IT, Azim Premji, Video 'Early Days of Wipro in the Computer Business', https://itihaasa.com/describe/sartefact/001_001_0037?term=Early+Days+of+Wipro+in+the+Computer+Business&sf=1

32 itihaasa, History of Indian IT, Dr Sridhar Mitta, Video 'Building an Ecosystem Around Wipro', https://itihaasa.com/describe/sartefact/001_001_0327?term=Building+an+Ecosystem+Around+Wipro&sf=1

33 itihaasa, History of Indian IT, Ashok Soota, Video 'Minicomputers Based on Intel Microprocessors from Wipro- Among the first in the world', https://itihaasa.com/describe/artefact/001_001_0021?interviewee=Ashok+Soota

34 itihaasa, History of Indian IT, Azim Premji, Video 'Software Products of Wipro Systems in the Early 1980s', https://itihaasa.com/describe/sartefact/001_001_0039?term=Software+Products+of+Wipro+Systems+in+the+Early+1980s&sf=1

35 itihaasa, History of Indian IT, Dr Sridhar Mitta, Video 'Genesis of R&D Services', https://itihaasa.com/describe/sartefact/001_001_0322?term=Genesis+of+R%26D+Services&sf=1

36 itihaasa, History of Indian IT, Subroto Bagchi, Video 'Opening the Sun Microsystems Account, with a world map', https://itihaasa.com/describe/sartefact/001_001_0452?term=Opening+the+Sun+Microsystems+Account%2C+with+a+world+map&sf=1

37 itihaasa, History of Indian IT, Gopal Srinivasan, Video 'TVS Electronics' strategy in the early 1990s', https://itihaasa.com/describe/artefact/001_001_1084?interviewee=Gopal+Srinivasan

38 itihaasa, History of Indian IT, Diwakar Nigam, Video 'Computer Culture in IIT Madras in the Early 1970s', https://itihaasa.com/describe/sartefact/001_001_0635?term=Computer+Culture+in+IIT+Madras+in+the+Early+1970s&sf=1

39 itihaasa, History of Indian IT, Diwakar Nigam, Video 'Application Software Products at Softek Limited', https://itihaasa.com/describe/sartefact/001_001_0645?term=Application+Software+Products+at+Softek+Limited&sf=1

40 itihaasa, History of Indian IT, M.G.K. Menon, Video 'Prof. MGK Menon on Prof. Narasimhan', https://itihaasa.com/describe/sartefact/001_001_1024?term=Menon&sf=1

41 itihaasa, History of Indian IT, R.K. Shyamsundar, Video 'Genesis of NCSDCT', https://itihaasa.com/describe/sartefact/001_001_0249?term=Genesis+of+NCSDCT&sf=1

42 itihaasa, History of Indian IT, S. Ramani, Video 'Genesis of computer networking in India', https://itihaasa.com/describe/sartefact/001_001_0071?term=Genesis+of+computer+networking+in+India&sf=1

43 itihaasa, History of Indian IT, S.D. Shibulal, Video 'Training Programs in Tata Institute of Fundamental Research (TIFR)', https://itihaasa.com/describe/sartefact/001_001_0127?term=Training+Programs+in+Tata+Institute+of+Fundamental+Research+%28TIFR%29&sf=1

44 itihaasa, History of Indian IT, S. Ramani, Video 'Focus of National Centre for Software Technology', https://itihaasa.com/describe/sartefact/001_001_0073?term=Focus+of+National+Centre+for+Software+Technology&sf=1

45   itihaasa, History of Indian IT, S. Ramani, Video 'Genesis of Computer
      Networking in India', https://itihaasa.com/describe/sartefact/001_
      001_0071?term=Genesis+of+Computer+Networking+in+India&sf=1

46   itihaasa, History of Indian IT, S. Sadagopan, Video 'National Mission
      Mode IT Driven Programs – ERNET', https://itihaasa.com/describe/
      sartefact/001_001_0257?term=National+Mission&sf=1

47   itihaasa, History of Indian IT, Deepak B. Phatak, Video, 'ERNET
      Project and the first email sent in India', https://itihaasa.com/
      describe/sartefact/001_001_0378?term=ERNET+Project+and+the+first
      +email+sent+in+India&sf=1

48   itihaasa, History of Indian IT, S. Sadagopan, Video, 'National Mission
      Mode IT Driven Programs – ERNET', https://itihaasa.com/
      describe/sartefact/001_001_0257?term=National+Mission+Mode+IT+
      Driven+Programs&sf=1

49   Utpal Kumar Banerjee, *Information Management in Government*, Concept
      Publishing Company, 1984.

50   Interview with Dr N. Seshagiri, available at https://www.rediff.com/
      computer/2000/mar/13ses.htm, accessed on 15 March 2020.

51   Seshagiri et al., 'NICNET - a Hierarchic distributed computer-
      communication network for decision support in the Indian
      Government', NIC, http://repository.ias.ac.in/85175/

52   N. Seshagiri, 'Evolution of NICNET as an incrementally intelligent
      network', *International Conference on Globalization of Computer and
      Communication (INFOCOM)*, 1993.

53   Informatics Quarterly Newsletter, Vol. 5, No. 4, April 1997, National
      Informatics Centre.

54   Interview with Dr N. Seshagiri, available at https://www.rediff.com/
      computer/2000/mar/13ses.htm, accessed on 15 March 2020.

55   itihaasa, History of Indian IT, Bhaskar Pramanik, Video 'Computer
      Culture in IIT Kanpur in the Late 1960s and Early 1970s',
      https://itihaasa.com/describe/sartefact/001_001_0625?term=Computer+
      Culture+in+IIT+Kanpur+in+the+Late+1960s+and+Early+1970s&sf=1

56   itihaasa, History of Indian IT, Prof. V. Rajaraman, 'IIT Kanpur
      launches a B.Tech. Program in computer science in 1978',
      https://itihaasa.com/describe/sartefact/001_001_0283?term=IIT+
      Kanpur+launches&sf=1

57   itihaasa, History of Indian IT, S. Mahalingam, Video 'Industrializing the
      TCS training programme', https://itihaasa.com/describe/sartefact/
      001_001_0390?term=Industrializing+the&sf=1

58   itihaasa, History of Indian IT, S. Sadagopan, Video 'IIT Kanpur and
     computer science in India', https://itihaasa.com/describe/sartefact/001_
     001_0255?term=IIT+Kanpur+and+computer+science+in+India&sf=1

59   itihaasa, History of Indian IT, Prof. C.R. Muthukrishnan, 'History of
     computers at IIT Madras', https://itihaasa.com/describe/sartefact/001_
     001_0100?term=History+of+computers+at+IIT+Madras&sf=1

60   itihaasa, History of Indian IT, Prof. H.N. Mahabala, 'Prof. Mahabala and
     the IBM 370 come to IIT Madras', https://itihaasa.com/describe/
     sartefact/001_001_0225?term=Prof.+Mahabala+and+the+IBM+370+
     come+to+IIT+Madras&sf=1

61   itihaasa, History of Indian IT, Prof. C.R. Muthukrishnan, 'History of
     computers at IIT Madras', https://itihaasa.com/describe/sartefact/001_
     001_0100?term=History+of+computers+at+IIT+Madras&sf=1

62   itihaasa, History of Indian IT, S. Srinivasan, 'Days at the IIT Madras
     computer center', https://itihaasa.com/describe/sartefact/001_001_
     0138?term=Days+at+the+IIT+Madras+computer+center&sf=1

63   itihaasa, History of Indian IT, Prof. H.N. Mahabala, 'The computer
     culture at IIT madras – bridging industry and academia', https://itihaasa.
     com/describe/sartefact/001_001_0226?term=The+computer+culture+
     at&sf=1

64   itihaasa, History of Indian IT, Prof. H.N. Mahabala, 'The computer
     culture at IIT madras – bridging industry and academia', https://itihaasa.
     com/describe/sartefact/001_001_0226?term=The+computer+
     culture&sf=1

65   itihaasa, History of Indian IT, Prof. C.R. Muthukrishnan, 'IIT Madras
     computer center helping industry and scientists', https://itihaasa
     .com/describe/sartefact/001_001_0102?term=IIT+Madras+computer+
     center+helping+industry+and+scientists&sf=1

66   itihaasa, History of Indian IT, Prof. C.R. Muthukrishnan, 'IIT Madras
     allows MSC students to do MTech in computer science', https://
     itihaasa.com/describe/sartefact/001_001_0103?term=IIT+Madras+
     allows&sf=1

67   itihaasa, History of Indian IT, S. Gopalakrishnan, 'Computer culture in
     IIT Madras in the Late 1970s', https://itihaasa.com/describe/sartefact/
     001_001_0724?term=Computer+culture+in+IIT+Madras+in+the+Late+
     1970s&sf=1

68   itihaasa, History of Indian IT, S. Kris Gopalakrishnan, 'First tryst with
     computers and programming', https://itihaasa.com/describe/sartefact/
     001_001_0722?term=First+tryst+with+computers+and+programming&sf=1

69 itihaasa, History of Indian IT, S. Kris Gopalakrishnan, 'Interesting projects in IIT Madras', https://itihaasa.com/describe/sartefact/001_001_0725?term=Interesting+projects+in+IIT+Madras&sf=1

70 itihaasa, History of Indian IT, Kamala Krithivasan, 'Theoretical Computer Science in 1960s', https://itihaasa.com/describe/sartefact/001_001_0232?term=Theoretical+Computer+Science+in+1960s&sf=1

71 IIM Ahmedabad, Tenth Annual Report 1971-72, available at http://hdl.handle.net/11718/10877, accessed on 9 December 2019.

72 itihaasa, History of Indian IT, N. R. Narayana Murthy, Video 'Joining the computer center in IIM Ahmedabad', https://itihaasa.com/describe/sartefact/001_001_0175?term=Joining+the+computer&sf=1

73 itihaasa, History of Indian IT, N.R. Narayana Murthy, Video 'Computer center in IIM Ahmedabad', https://itihaasa.com/describe/sartefact/001_001_0177?term=Computer+center+in+IIM+Ahmedabad&sf=1

74 itihaasa, History of Indian IT, Ashank Desai, Video 'Computer culture in IIM Ahmedabad in the late 1970s', https://itihaasa.com/describe/sartefact/001_001_0003?term=Computer+culture+in+IIM+Ahmedabad+in+the+late+1970s&sf=1

75 V. Rajaraman, 'History of Computing in India (1955–2010)', IEEE Computer Society.

CHAPTER 4: GROWTH OF SOFTWARE SERVICES AND MISSION-MODE GOVERNMENT IT PROJECTS

1   S.S. Oberoi, 'Software Export Development and Export Case Study—India', May 1996, Department of Electronics.

2   V. Rajaraman, 'History of Computing in India (1955–2010)', IEEE Computer Society.

3   itihaasa, History of Indian IT, N.R. Narayana Murthy, Video 'Genesis of Infosys', https://itihaasa.com/describe/sartefact/001_001_0179?term=Genesis+of+Infosys&sf=1

4   itihaasa, History of Indian IT, N.R. Narayana Murthy, Video 'Genesis of Infosys', https://itihaasa.com/describe/sartefact/001_001_0179?term=Genesis+of+Infosys&sf=1

5   E.F. Codd, 'A Relational Model of Data for Large Shared Data Banks', *Communications of the ACM*, vol. available at https://dl.acm.org/doi/10.1145/362384.362685, accessed on 4 August 2020.

6   itihaasa, History of Indian IT, Kris Gopalakrishnan, Video 'Genesis of Infosys', https://itihaasa.com/describe/sartefact/001_001_0729?term=Genesis+of+Infosys&sf=1

7 itihaasa, History of Indian IT, S.D. Shibulal, Video 'Genesis of Infosys', https://itihaasa.com/describe/sartefact/001_001_0128?term=Genesis+of+Infosys&sf=1

8 itihaasa, History of Indian IT, N.R. Narayana Murthy, Video 'Genesis of Infosys', https://itihaasa.com/describe/sartefact/001_001_0179?term=Genesis+of+Infosys&sf=1

9 itihaasa, History of Indian IT, N. S. Raghavan, Video 'Opening a Client Account', https://itihaasa.com/describe/sartefact/001_001_0085?term=Opening+a+Client+Account&sf=1

10 itihaasa, History of Indian IT, N.R. Narayana Murthy, Video 'Global delivery model', https://itihaasa.com/describe/sartefact/001_001_0182?term=Global+delivery+model&sf=1

11 itihaasa, History of Indian IT, Kris Gopalakrishnan, Video 'Genesis of Infosys', https://itihaasa.com/describe/sartefact/001_001_0729?term=Genesis+of+Infosys&sf=1

12 itihaasa, History of Indian IT, Kris Gopalakrishnan, Video 'Evolution of Global Delivery Model (GDM)', https://itihaasa.com/describe/sartefact/001_001_0731?term=Evolution+of+Global+Delivery+Model+%28GDM%29&sf=1

13 itihaasa, History of Indian IT, Nandan Nilekani, Video 'Infosys building a scalable and employee friendly business', https://itihaasa.com/describe/sartefact/001_001_0367?term=Infosys+building+a+scalable+and+employee+friendly+business&sf=1

14 itihaasa, History of Indian IT, N.S. Raghavan, Video 'Genesis of ESOPs in Infosys', https://itihaasa.com/describe/sartefact/001_001_0088?term=Genesis+of+ESOPs+in+Infosys&sf=1

15 itihaasa, History of Indian IT, N.R. Narayana Murthy, 'A project manager needs to be a techno-manager', https://itihaasa.com/describe/sartefact/001_001_0181?term=A+project+manager+needs+to+be+a+techno-manager&sf=1

16 itihaasa, History of Indian IT, Nandan Nilekani, 'Infosys in the Early 1980s', https://itihaasa.com/describe/sartefact/001_001_0361?term=Infosys+in+the+Early+1980s&sf=1

17 itihaasa, History of Indian IT, Kris Gopalakrishnan, 'Hardware ideas at Infosys', https://itihaasa.com/describe/sartefact/001_001_0730?term=Hardware+ideas+at+Infosys&sf=1

18 itihaasa, History of Indian IT, S.D. Shibulal, 'Interesting Anecdotes while at Infosys', https://itihaasa.com/describe/sartefact/001_001_0135?term=Interesting+Anecdotes+while+at+Infosys&sf=1

19 itihaasa, History of Indian IT, K. Dinesh, 'Early days at Infosys', https://itihaasa.com/describe/sartefact/001_001_0673?term=Early+days+at+Infosys&sf=1

20 itihaasa, History of Indian IT, N.S. Raghavan, 'Becoming a Chef in France', https://itihaasa.com/describe/sartefact/001_001_0094?term=Becoming+a+Chef+in+France&sf=1

21 itihaasa, History of Indian IT, Ashank Desai, Video 'Genesis of Mastek', https://itihaasa.com/describe/sartefact/001_001_0002?term=Genesis+of+Mastek&sf=1

22 itihaasa, History of Indian IT, Ashank Desai, Video 'Software Exports in the 1980s', https://itihaasa.com/describe/sartefact/001_001_0005?term=Software+Exports+in+the+1980s&sf=1

23 itihaasa, History of Indian IT, K.V. Ramani, Video 'Origin story of Future Software', https://itihaasa.com/describe/sartefact/001_001_1123?term=Origin+story+of+Future+Software&sf=1

24 itihaasa, History of Indian IT, K.V. Ramani, Video 'Saga of the difficult first project of Future Software - Part 1', https://itihaasa.com/describe/sartefact/001_001_1124?term=Saga+of+the+difficult+first+project+of+Future+Software+-+Part+1&sf=1

25 itihaasa, History of Indian IT, K.V. Ramani, Video 'Product business at future soft and building one of the world largest protocol stacks company', https://itihaasa.com/describe/sartefact/001_001_1126?term=Product+business+at+future+soft&sf=1

26 itihaasa, History of Indian IT, Saurabh Srivastava, Video 'A defining project for IIS Infotech with an UK Client', https://itihaasa.com/describe/sartefact/001_001_0157?term=A+defining+project+for+IIS+Infotech+with+an+UK+Client&sf=1

27 ISO/IEC/IEEE 90003:2018 Software Engineering—Guidelines for the Application of ISO 9001:2015 to Computer Software, https://www.iso.org/standard/74348.html, accessed on 15 August 2020.

28 Evolution of TickITplus, https://www.tickitplus.org/en/evolution-of-tickitplus.html, accessed on 15 August 2020.

29 itihaasa, History of Indian IT, Bharat Goenka, Video 'Genesis of Noiseless & Codeless Software', https://itihaasa.com/describe/sartefact/001_001_0614?term=Genesis+of+Noiseless+%26+Codeless+Software&sf=1

30 itihaasa, History of Indian IT, Bharat Goenka, Video 'The Evolution of the Software Product Industry in India', https://itihaasa.com/describe/sartefact/001_001_0619?term=The+Evolution+of+the+Software+Product+Industry+in+India&sf=1

31   itihaasa, History of Indian IT, Rajendra Pawar, Video 'Genesis of NIIT',
     https://itihaasa.com/describe/sartefact/001_001_0480?term=Genesis+of
     +NIIT&sf=1

32   itihaasa, History of Indian IT, Rajendra Pawar, Video 'Launching NIIT',
     https://itihaasa.com/describe/sartefact/001_001_0481?term=Launching+
     NIIT&sf=1

33   itihaasa, History of Indian IT, Rajendra Pawar, Video 'NIIT's role in
     capability development', https://itihaasa.com/describe/sartefact/001_
     001_0483?term=NIIT%27s+role+in+capability+development&sf=1

34   itihaasa, History of Indian IT, Srini Rajam, Video 'TI chooses Bangalore
     and India for its R&D GIC', https://itihaasa.com/describe/sartefact/
     001_001_0306?term=TI+chooses+Bangalore+and+India+for+its+R%
     26D+GIC&sf=1

35   itihaasa, History of Indian IT, Srini Rajam, Video 'TI Earth Station in
     Bangalore: The first dedicated data line in India', https://itihaasa.com/
     describe/sartefact/001_001_0307?term=TI+Earth+Station+in+Bangalore
     %3A+The+first+dedicated+data+line+in+India&sf=1

36   itihaasa, History of Indian IT, Srini Rajam, Video 'TI advises MNCs in
     setting up their R&D Global in-house centres in India', https://
     itihaasa.com/describe/sartefact/001_001_0308?term=TI+advises+
     MNCs&sf=1

37   itihaasa, History of Indian IT, Bhaskar Pramanik, Video 'Genesis of
     Manufacturers Association for Information Technology (MAIT)',
     https://itihaasa.com/describe/sartefact/001_001_0634?term=Genesis+of+
     Manufacturers+Association+for+Information+Technology+%28MAIT%
     29&sf=1

38   itihaasa, History of Indian IT, Saurabh Srivastava, Video 'The Software
     India Seminars', https://itihaasa.com/describe/sartefact/001_001_0149?
     term=The+Software+India+Seminars&sf=1

39   itihaasa, History of Indian IT, Harish Mehta, Video 'Genesis of
     NASSCOM', https://itihaasa.com/describe/sartefact/001_001_0649?
     term=Genesis+of+NASSCOM&sf=1

40   itihaasa, History of Indian IT, Ashank Desai, Video 'Genesis and Early
     Days of NASSCOM', https://itihaasa.com/describe/sartefact/001_001_
     0008?term=Genesis+and+Early+Days+of+NASSCOM&sf=1

41   itihaasa, History of Indian IT, K.V. Ramani, Video 'NASSCOM's
     Journey, Org Structure and Key People', https://itihaasa.com/describe/
     sartefact/001_001_1132?term=NASSCOM%27s+Journey%2C+Org+
     Structure+and+Key+People&sf=1

42 K.S. Raman and Swati Wig, 'Risk Management in Large Information Systems (IS) Projects: A Case Study of the Indian Railways Computerized Passenger Reservation System', *ASCI Journal of Management*, 2010.

43 http://www.indianrailways.gov.in/#, accessed on 9 August 2020.

44 itihaasa, History of Indian IT, Subroto Bagchi, Video 'Mission - Mode Government Computerization Programs: Railway', https://itihaasa.com/describe/sartefact/001_001_0449?term=Mission+-+Mode+Government+Computerization+Programs%3A+Railway&sf=1

45 Rekha Jain and G. Raghuram, 'Management of Large IT Projects: The Passenger Reservation System of Indian Railways', Working Paper No. 1085, IIM Ahmedabad, February 1993.

46 V. Rajaraman, 'History of Computing in India (1955-2010)', IEEE Computer Society.

47 itihaasa, History of Indian IT, S. Ramani, Video 'Genesis of the Passenger Reservation System for the Indian Railways', https://itihaasa.com/describe/sartefact/001_001_0078?term=Genesis+of+the+Passenger+Reservation+System+for+the+Indian+Railways&sf=1

48 itihaasa, History of Indian IT, Som Mittal, Video 'Passenger Reservation System of the Indian Railways', https://itihaasa.com/describe/sartefact/001_001_0439?term=Passenger+Reservation+System+of+the+Indian+Railways&sf=1

49 https://www.irctc.com/internet-ticketing.html, accessed on 15 August 2020.

50 itihaasa, History of Indian IT, Som Mittal, Video 'Passenger Reservation System of the Indian Railways', https://itihaasa.com/describe/sartefact/001_001_0439?term=Passenger+Reservation+System+of+the+Indian+Railways&sf=1

51 Rekha Jain and G. Raghuram, 'Management of Large IT Projects: The Passenger Reservation System of Indian Railways', Working Paper No. 1085, IIM Ahmedabad, February 1993.

52 K.S. Raman and Swati Wig, 'Risk Management in Large Information Systems (IS) Projects: A Case Study of the Indian Railways Computerized Passenger Reservation System', *ASCI Journal of Management*, 2010.

53 Rekha Jain and G. Raghuram, 'Management of Large IT Projects: The Passenger Reservation System of Indian Railways', Working Paper No. 1085, IIM Ahmedabad, February 1993.

54 itihaasa, History of Indian IT, S. Ramani, Video 'Genesis of the Passenger Reservation System for the Indian Railways', https://itihaasa.com/describe/

sartefact/001_001_0078?term=Genesis+of+the+Passenger+Reservation+System+for+the+Indian+Railways&sf=1

55 itihaasa, History of Indian IT, S. Sadagopan, Video 'National mission mode IT driven programs – computerized railway reservation', https://itihaasa.com/describe/sartefact/001_001_0266?term=National+mission&sf=1

56 itihaasa, History of Indian IT, Kiran Karnik, Video 'Importance of the Indian Railways Passenger Reservation System', https://itihaasa.com/describe/sartefact/001_001_0332?term=Importance+of+the+Indian+Railways+Passenger+Reservation+System&sf=1

57 https://www.foundingfuel.com/article/as-debate-rages-over-ai-displacing-jobs-history-offers-some-insights/, accessed on 15 August 2019.

58 itihaasa, History of Indian IT, Dataquest - Banks Computerisation, https://itihaasa.com/describe/sartefact/001_001_0528?term=Banks+dataquest&sf=1

59 C. Rangarajan, Speech at the inauguration of Andhra Bank Credit Card Transaction Automation Project, 30 August 1997.

60 itihaasa, History of Indian IT, Subroto Bagchi, Video 'Mission - Mode Government Computerization Programs: Banking', https://itihaasa.com/describe/sartefact/001_001_0449?term=Mission+-+Mode+Government+Computerization+Programs%3A+Railway&sf=1

61 itihaasa, History of Indian IT, Dataquest - Banks agreement, https://itihaasa.com/describe/sartefact/001_001_0542?term=Banks+dataquest&sf=1

62 Ibid.

63 Reserve Bank of India Publications, 'Committees on Computerisation', 1998, https://m.rbi.org.in/Scripts/PublicationsView.aspx?id=162, accessed on 15 August 2020.

64 itihaasa, History of Indian IT, N. Balakrishnan, Video 'Genesis of SERC', https://itihaasa.com/describe/sartefact/001_001_1029?term=Genesis+of+SERC&sf=1

65 itihaasa, History of Indian IT, N. Balakrishnan, Video 'Early years of SERC', https://itihaasa.com/describe/sartefact/001_001_1030?term=Early+years+of+SERC&sf=1

66 Ibid.

67 V. Rajaraman, 'History of the Establishment of the Centre for Development of Advanced Computing', *CSI Communications*, Volume No. 38, Issue No. 6, September 2014.

68 itihaasa, Research and Digital, 'Landscape of Artificial Intelligence / Machine Learning Research in India', 2018.

69   N. Seshagiri, 'Rangaswamy Narasimhan (1926-2007)', *Current Science*, Vol. 93, No. 7, October 2007, https://www.currentscience.ac.in/Downloads/article_id_093_07_1016_1017_0.pdf

70   Patrick Saint-Dizier, 'The Knowledge-Based Computer System Development Program of India: A Review', *AI Magazine*, Volume 12, Number 2 (1991), AAAI.

71   Utpal Kumar Banerjee, *Computer Education in India: Past, Present and Future*, Concept Publishing Company, 1996.

72   Krithi Ramamritham, 'A Detailed Report on R&D at Indian Computer-Science Establishments', Office of Naval Research Asian Office, 1995.

73   V. Rajaraman, 'History of Computing in India (1955–2010)', IEEE Computer Society.

74   itihaasa, History of Indian IT, Document, 'Times of India - Software Export Spurts 51%', https://itihaasa.com/describe/dartefact/001_001_0878?year=2000

CHAPTER 5: THE RAPID GROWTH OF INDIAN IT SERVICES

1   V. Rajaraman, 'History of Computing in India (1955–2010)', IEEE Computer Society.

2   Ibid.

3   Ibid.

4   itihaasa, History of Indian IT, Saurabh Srivastava, Video, 'Role of Dewang Mehta in NASSCOM', https://itihaasa.com/describe/sartefact/001_001_0152?term=Role+of+Dewang+Mehta+in+NASSCOM&sf=1

5   itihaasa, History of Indian IT, Harish Mehta, Video, 'N. Vittal's Contribution to the IT Industry', https://itihaasa.com/describe/sartefact/001_001_0651?term=N.+Vittal%27s+Contribution+to+the+IT+Industry&sf=1

6   itihaasa, History of Indian IT, N. Vittal, Video, 'The aspirational target of 400 M for IT Industry at the NASSCOM meeting', https://itihaasa.com/describe/sartefact/001_001_0191?term=The+aspirational+target+of+400+M+for+IT+Industry+at+the+NASSCOM+meeting&sf=1

7   itihaasa, History of Indian IT, N.R. Narayana Murthy, Video, 'Genesis of NASSCOM and STPI', https://itihaasa.com/describe/sartefact/001_001_0184?term=Genesis+of+NASSCOM+and+STPI&sf=1

8   itihaasa, History of Indian IT, S. Mahalingam, Video, 'Akbar and Birbal Story of the Indian IT Industry', https://itihaasa.com/describe/sartefact/

001_001_0400?term=Akbar+and+Birbal+Story+of+the+Indian+IT+
Industry&sf=1

9   itihaasa, History of Indian IT, Pradeep Gupta, 'World Bank Funded Report
    on India's Software and Services Export Potential and Strategies', https://
    itihaasa.com/describe/sartefact/001_001_0692?term=world+bank&sf=1

10 itihaasa, History of Indian IT, Pradeep Gupta, 'The 1992 World Bank
    Study on the Indian Software Industry', https://itihaasa.com/describe/
    artefact/001_001_0206?interviewee=Pradeep+Gupta

11 itihaasa, History of Indian IT, N. Vittal, Video, 'Genesis of STPI Policy:
    Learning from Kandla free trade Zone', https://itihaasa.com/describe/
    artefact/001_001_0198?interviewee=N.+Vittal

12 itihaasa, History of Indian IT, R. Chandrashekhar, Video, 'Light Touch
    Policy Interventions like STPI', https://itihaasa.com/describe/artefact/
    001_001_0113?interviewee=R.+Chandrashekhar

13 itihaasa, History of Indian IT, Saurabh Srivastava, Video, 'Role of
    N. Vittal', https://itihaasa.com/describe/artefact/001_001_0153?
    interviewee=Saurabh+Srivastava

14 itihaasa, History of Indian IT, B.V. Naidu, Video, 'STPI - Infrastructure
    and Training', https://itihaasa.com/describe/artefact/001_001_0052?
    interviewee=B.+V.+Naidu

15 itihaasa, History of Indian IT, Subroto Bagchi, Video, 'Key Government
    IT Policies in the 1980s and 1990s', https://itihaasa.com/describe/
    artefact/001_001_0450?interviewee=Subroto+Bagchi

16 https://www.thehindubusinessline.com/info-tech/Curtains-down-for-
    STPI/article20108890.ece#!, accessed on 10 September 2020.

17 itihaasa, History of Indian IT, B.V. Naidu, Video, 'STPI - Enabling
    GDM', https://itihaasa.com/describe/artefact/001_001_0051?
    interviewee=B.+V.+Naidu

18 itihaasa, History of Indian IT, Saurabh Srivastava, Video, 'Breaking
    the Videsh Sanchar Nigam limited monopoly and improving telecom
    infrastructure', https://itihaasa.com/describe/artefact/001_001_0154?
    interviewee=Saurabh+Srivastava

19 Ibid.

20 itihaasa, History of Indian IT, B.V. Naidu, Video, 'STPI breaking
    the VSNL monopoly', https://itihaasa.com/describe/artefact/001_001_
    0050?interviewee=B.+V.+Naidu

21 itihaasa, History of Indian IT, S. Mahalingam, Video, 'STPI and its
    impact on IT Services', https://itihaasa.com/describe/artefact/001_001_
    0406?interviewee=S.+Mahalingam

22 itihaasa, History of Indian IT, Ashok Soota, Video, 'Things that Impacted the IT Industry: Talent, Training and STPI Policy', https://itihaasa.com/describe/artefact/001_001_0026?interviewee=Ashok+Soota

23 itihaasa, History of Indian IT, Harish Mehta, Video, 'Dewang Mehta's Contribution to the IT Industry', https://itihaasa.com/describe/artefact/001_001_0662?interviewee=Harish+Mehta

24 itihaasa, History of Indian IT, N.R. Narayana Murthy, Video, 'Genesis of NASSCOM and STPI', https://itihaasa.com/describe/artefact/001_001_0184?interviewee=N.+R.+Narayana+Murthy

25 itihaasa, History of Indian IT, Azim Premji, Video, 'R&D Services at Wipro', https://itihaasa.com/describe/artefact/001_001_0042?interviewee=Azim+H.+Premji

26 itihaasa, History of Indian IT, Dr Sridhar Mitta, Video, 'Genesis of R&D Services', https://itihaasa.com/describe/artefact/001_001_0322?interviewee=Dr.+Sridhar+Mitta

27 https://www.wipro.com/content/dam/nexus/en/investor/annual-reports/2000-2001/11100-Wipro-Annual-Report-00-01-Corporate-Overview.pdf, accessed on 18 January 2021.

28 itihaasa, History of Indian IT, Dr Sridhar Mitta, Video, 'Genesis of R&D Services', https://itihaasa.com/describe/artefact/001_001_0322?interviewee=Dr.+Sridhar+Mitta

29 itihaasa, History of Indian IT, Diju Raha, Video, 'Discovering the Indian Software Industry', https://itihaasa.com/describe/artefact/001_001_0059?interviewee=Diju+Raha

30 itihaasa, History of Indian IT, Ashok Soota, Video, 'The Role of MNCs in Nurturing the IT and R&D Services Industry in India', https://itihaasa.com/describe/artefact/001_001_0028?interviewee=Ashok+Soota

31 itihaasa, History of Indian IT, Diju Raha, Video, 'Discovering the Indian Software Industry', https://itihaasa.com/describe/artefact/001_001_0059?interviewee=Diju+Raha

32 itihaasa, History of Indian IT, Sharad Sharma, Video, 'AT&T - an Early R&D Global In-house Center (GIC) in India', https://itihaasa.com/describe/artefact/001_001_0291?interviewee=Sharad+Sharma

33 itihaasa, History of Indian IT, Kris Gopalakrishnan, Video, 'History of MNCs in the Indian IT Industry', https://itihaasa.com/describe/artefact/001_001_0736?interviewee=S.+%27Kris%27+Gopalakrishnan

34 itihaasa, History of Indian IT, S. Mahalingam, Video, 'Import of IBM 3090 by TCS', https://itihaasa.com/describe/artefact/001_001_0394?interviewee=S.+Mahalingam

35   https://www.business-standard.com/article/pti-stories/ibm-s-deal-with-airtel-can-touch-1-bn-in-next-5-yrs-analyst-114040300811_1.html, accessed on 9 January 2021.

36   https://economictimes.indiatimes.com/tech/software/ibm-receives-9100-patents-in-2018-india-second-highest-contributor/articleshow/67440392.cms, accessed on 9 January 2021.

37   https://www.pbs.org/wgbh/commandingheights/shared/minitext/int_narayanamurthy.html#7, accessed on 9 January 2021.

38   itihaasa, History of Indian IT, N.S. Raghavan, Video, 'Recruitment and Training in Infosys', https://itihaasa.com/describe/artefact/001_001_0086?interviewee=N.+S.+Raghavan

39   Ibid.

40   itihaasa, History of Indian IT, S. Mahalingam, Video, 'Genesis of the TCS software engineering training program', https://itihaasa.com/describe/artefact/001_001_0399?interviewee=S.+Mahalingam

41   itihaasa, History of Indian IT, N.S. Raghavan, Video, 'You can disagree but you cannot be disagreeable', https://itihaasa.com/describe/artefact/001_001_0089?interviewee=N.+S.+Raghavan

42   https://www.hbs.edu/faculty/Pages/item.aspx?num=28128, accessed on 15 August 2020.

43   https://knowledge.wharton.upenn.edu/article/infosys-murthy-sharing-a-simple-yet-powerful-vision/, accessed on 15 August 2020.

44   itihaasa, History of Indian IT, S. Ramadorai, Video, 'Importance of a collaborative delivery organization', https://itihaasa.com/describe/artefact/001_001_0418?interviewee=S.+Ramadorai

45   itihaasa, History of Indian IT, N.R. Narayana Murthy, Video, 'Global delivery model', https://itihaasa.com/describe/sartefact/001_001_0182?term=Global+delivery+model&sf=1

46   itihaasa, History of Indian IT, Nandan Nilekani, Video, 'Global Delivery Model (GDM) and Critical Computerization Projects in India in the 1990s', https://itihaasa.com/describe/artefact/001_001_0368?interviewee=Nandan+Nilekani

47   itihaasa, History of Indian IT, Azim Premji, Video, 'Wipro's Focus on the Project Management and Quality', https://itihaasa.com/describe/artefact/001_001_0043?interviewee=Azim+H.+Premji

48   itihaasa, History of Indian IT, Pankaj Jalote, Video, 'A Sabbatical at Infosys: SEI, CMM Journey', https://itihaasa.com/describe/artefact/001_001_0238?interviewee=Prof.+Pankaj+Jalote

49 itihaasa, History of Indian IT, K. Dinesh, Video, 'Infosys' Quality and CMM Journey', https://itihaasa.com/describe/artefact/001_001_0668?interviewee=K.+Dinesh

50 itihaasa, History of Indian IT, K Dinesh, Video, 'Infosys adopts the Malcolm Baldrige National Quality Award Framework', https://itihaasa.com/describe/artefact/001_001_0678?interviewee=K.+Dinesh

51 V. Rajaraman, 'History of Computing in India (1955–2010)', IEEE Computer Society.

52 itihaasa, History of Indian IT, Nandan Nilekani, Video, 'Sales and Marketing initiatives at Infosys in the early 1990s', https://itihaasa.com/describe/artefact/001_001_0369?interviewee=Nandan+Nilekani

53 itihaasa, History of Indian IT, Ashank Desai, Video, 'Mastek IPO', https://itihaasa.com/describe/artefact/001_001_0007?interviewee=Ashank+Desai

54 itihaasa, History of Indian IT, N.R. Narayana Murthy, Video, 'Infosys listing on Indian Stock Exchanges and NASDAQ', https://itihaasa.com/describe/artefact/001_001_0183?interviewee=N.+R.+Narayana+Murthy

55 itihaasa, History of Indian IT, N.R. Narayana Murthy, Video, 'Infosys contract negotiation with GE', https://itihaasa.com/describe/artefact/001_001_0186?interviewee=N.+R.+Narayana+Murthy

56 Ibid.

57 itihaasa, History of Indian IT, N.S. Raghavan, Video, 'Genesis of ESOPs in Infosys', https://itihaasa.com/describe/artefact/001_001_0088?interviewee=N.+S.+Raghavan

58 itihaasa, History of Indian IT, Document, 'Times of India - Software Export Spurts 51%', https://itihaasa.com/describe/dartefact/001_001_0878?year=2000, accessed on 6 January 2021.

59 itihaasa, History of Indian IT, Lakshmi Narayanan, Video, 'Dun & Bradstreet and Satyam joint venture', https://itihaasa.com/describe/artefact/001_001_0352?interviewee=Lakshmi+Narayanan

60 itihaasa, History of Indian IT, Lakshmi Narayanan, Video, 'Evolution of Cognizant as Third Party Service Providers', https://itihaasa.com/describe/artefact/001_001_0354?interviewee=Lakshmi+Narayanan

61 itihaasa, History of Indian IT, Lakshmi Narayanan, Video, 'Cognizant's Strategic decisions during Y2K phase', https://itihaasa.com/describe/artefact/001_001_0355?interviewee=Lakshmi+Narayanan

62 itihaasa, History of Indian IT, Lakshmi Narayanan, Video, 'Genesis of Cognizant', https://itihaasa.com/describe/artefact/001_001_0353?interviewee=Lakshmi+Narayanan

63 itihaasa, History of Indian IT, Krishnakumar Natarajan, Video,
    'Introduction to ecommerce and the Mindtree Idea', https://itihaasa.
    com/describe/artefact/001_001_0997?interviewee=Krishnakumar+
    Natarajan

64 Ibid.

65 itihaasa, History of Indian IT, Subroto Bagchi, Video, 'Genesis of
    Mindtree', https://itihaasa.com/describe/artefact/001_001_0455?
    interviewee=Subroto+Bagchi

66 itihaasa, History of Indian IT, Ashok Soota, Video, 'Entrepreneurship
    in IT Services', https://itihaasa.com/listing/artefacts/Multimedia%20
    File?interviewee=Ashok+Soota

67 itihaasa, History of Indian IT, Krishnakumar Natarajan, Video,
    'Mindtree incorporated', https://itihaasa.com/describe/artefact/001_
    001_0999?interviewee=Krishnakumar+Natarajan

68 itihaasa, History of Indian IT, Krishnakumar Natarajan, Video, 'Early
    client wins in Mindtree', https://itihaasa.com/describe/artefact/001_
    001_1000?interviewee=Krishnakumar+Natarajan

69 itihaasa, History of Indian IT, Pradeep Kar, Video, 'Genesis of
    Microland in the late 1980s', https://itihaasa.com/describe/artefact/
    001_001_0210?interviewee=Pradeep+Kar

70 itihaasa, History of Indian IT, Pradeep Kar, Video, 'The Indian IT
    Market in the 1990s – Introduction of Laptops, Routers, and Browsers',
    https://itihaasa.com/describe/artefact/001_001_0212?interviewee=
    Pradeep+Kar

71 Ibid.

72 itihaasa, History of Indian IT, Pradeep Kar, Video, 'The First India visit
    of Bill Gates in 1997', https://itihaasa.com/describe/artefact/001_001_
    0213?interviewee=Pradeep+Kar

73 Available at https://www.si.edu/spotlight/y2k, accessed on 23 April 2020.

74 itihaasa, History of Indian IT, S. Mahalingam, Video, 'Y2K Factory',
    https://itihaasa.com/describe/artefact/001_001_0403?interviewee=S.+
    Mahalingam

75 itihaasa, History of Indian IT, S.D. Shibulal, Video, 'Genesis of
    Consulting in Infosys', https://itihaasa.com/describe/artefact/001_
    001_0131?interviewee=S.+D.+Shibulal

76 itihaasa, History of Indian IT, Kris Gopalakrishnan, Video, 'The Y2K
    opportunity', https://itihaasa.com/describe/artefact/001_001_0732?
    interviewee=S.+%27Kris%27+Gopalakrishnan

77   itihaasa, History of Indian IT, Lakshmi Narayanan, Video, 'Cognizant's strategic decisions during Y2K phase', https://itihaasa.com/describe/artefact/001_001_0355?interviewee=Lakshmi+Narayanan

78   itihaasa, History of Indian IT, Ashank Desai, Video, 'Y2K and Dotcom in the Late 1990s', https://itihaasa.com/describe/artefact/001_001_0010?interviewee=Ashank+Desai

79   itihaasa, History of Indian IT, *The Times of India*, Tackling Y2K: IT Proves Its Mettle, https://itihaasa.com/describe/sartefact/001_001_0876?term=y2k&sf=1"

80   V. Rajaraman, 'History of Computing in India (1955-2010)', IEEE Computer Society.

81   https://timesofindia.indiatimes.com/business/india-business/for-the-first-time-india-has-more-rural-net-users-than-urban/articleshow/75566025.cms, accessed on 12 January 2021.

82   https://www.livemint.com/news/india/how-the-internet-arrived-in-india-11581351034011.html, accessed on 12 January 2021.

83   https://www.timesnownews.com/technology-science/article/vsnl-1995-plan-indias-first-internet-connection-gave-40-minutes-per-day-usage-at-rs/636547, accessed on 12 January 2021.

84   itihaasa, History of Indian IT, S. Sadagopan, Video, 'National Mission Mode IT Driven programs - ERNET', https://itihaasa.com/describe/artefact/001_001_0257?interviewee=Prof.+S.+Sadagopan

85   itihaasa, History of Indian IT, S. Sadagopan, Video, 'Internet Era begins in Indian Management Institutions, with IIMB', https://itihaasa.com/describe/artefact/001_001_0259?interviewee=Prof.+S.+Sadagopan

86   itihaasa, History of Indian IT, Pradeep Kar, Video, 'The story of Indya.com', https://itihaasa.com/describe/artefact/001_001_0215?interviewee=Pradeep+Kar

87   https://www.nal.res.in/medias/content_image/other/1104/historyofnalfinal.pdf, accessed on 12 January 2021.

88   'The Little Known Story of How India's First Indigenous Supercomputer Amazed the World in 1991', https://www.thebetterindia.com/82076/india-first-supercomputer-param-cdac-vijay-bhatkar/, accessed on 12 January 2021.

89   'How US Sanctions Spurred India to Develop High-performance Computing', https://www.geospatialworld.net/blogs/isro-cdac-indian-supercomputer-param/, accessed on 12 January 2021.

90   itihaasa, History of Indian IT, N. Balakrishnan, Video, 'Dr. A.P.J. Abdul Kalam and Super Computing', https://itihaasa.com/describe/artefact/001_001_1034?interviewee=Prof.+N.+Balakrishnan

91   itihaasa, History of Indian IT, N. Balakrishnan, Video, 'Genesis of the National Super Computing Mission', https://itihaasa.com/describe/artefact/001_001_1032?interviewee=Prof.+N.+Balakrishnan

92   Ibid.

93   itihaasa, History of Indian IT, Prof. Deepak Phatak, Video, 'IIT Bombay attempts to design a computer', https://itihaasa.com/describe/artefact/001_001_0377?interviewee=Prof.+Deepak+B.+Phatak

94   itihaasa, History of Indian IT, Nandan Nilekani, Video, 'Computer culture in IIT Bombay in the late 1970s', https://itihaasa.com/describe/artefact/001_001_0359?interviewee=Nandan+Nilekani

95   Rohit Manchanda, *Monastery, Sanctuary, Laboratory: 50 Years of IIT-Bombay*, Macmillan India, 2008.

96   itihaasa, History of Indian IT, Prof. Deepak Phatak, Video, 'Genesis of Kanwal Rekhi School of Information Technology', https://itihaasa.com/describe/artefact/001_001_0382?interviewee=Prof.+Deepak+B.+Phatak https://itihaasa.com/describe/artefact/001_001_0382?interviewee=Prof.+Deepak+B.+Phatak

97   https://www.ibef.org/download/IT_ITeS_270111.pdf, accessed on 13 January 2021.

98   itihaasa, History of Indian IT, Document, 'Times of India - Software Export Spurts 51%' https://itihaasa.com/describe/dartefact/001_001_0878?year=2000

CHAPTER 6: INDIAN IT COMES OF AGE

1   itihaasa, History of Indian IT, Kris Gopalakrishnan, Video 'New Services Leveraging Global Delivery Model (GDM)', https://itihaasa.com/describe/artefact/001_001_0733?interviewee=S.+%27Kris%27+Gopalakrishnan

2   https://www.cbronline.com/news/erp_market_wont_slacken_after_year_2000/, accessed on 20 January 2021.

3   'Indian IT Services Industry in 2007' by Pankaj Ghemavat and Steven A. Altman, https://www.ghemawat.com/wordpress/wp-content/uploads/2016/10/Indian-IT-Industry.pdf, accessed on 20 January 2021.

4   itihaasa, History of Indian IT, Pradeep Kar, Video 'Y2K and Dotcom Era', https://itihaasa.com/describe/artefact/001_001_0219?interviewee=Pradeep+Kar

5   itihaasa, History of Indian IT, S.D. Shibulal, Video 'Genesis of Consulting in Infosys', https://itihaasa.com/describe/artefact/001_001_0131?interviewee=S.+D.+Shibulal

6   itihaasa, History of Indian IT, Lakshmi Narayanan, Video 'Focus on Future of work and SMAC', https://itihaasa.com/describe/artefact/001_001_0357?interviewee=Lakshmi+Narayanan

7   itihaasa, History of Indian IT, Ashok Soota, Video 'Entrepreneurship in IT Services', https://itihaasa.com/describe/artefact/001_001_0034?interviewee=Ashok+Soota

8   itihaasa, History of Indian IT, S.D. Shibulal, Video 'IP-led services', https://itihaasa.com/describe/artefact/001_001_0133?interviewee=S.+D.+Shibulal

9   itihaasa, History of Indian IT, N. Chandrasekaran, Video 'CEO challenges - Managing scale, regulations, IP-led revenues', https://itihaasa.com/describe/artefact/001_001_1147?interviewee=N.+Chandrasekaran

10 itihaasa, History of Indian IT, N. Chandrasekaran, Video 'Key strategies as CEO #3 - Global Network Delivery Model', https://itihaasa.com/describe/artefact/001_001_1145?interviewee=N.+Chandrasekaran

11 itihaasa, History of Indian IT, N. Chandrasekaran, Video 'CEO challenges - Managing scale, regulations, IP-led revenues', https://itihaasa.com/describe/artefact/001_001_1147?interviewee=N.+Chandrasekaran

12 itihaasa, History of Indian IT, Bhaskar Pramanik, Video 'Importance of Digital India', https://itihaasa.com/describe/artefact/001_001_0630?interviewee=Bhaskar+Pramanik

13 itihaasa, History of Indian IT, Raman Roy, Video 'Indian BPM industry is born with the Amex Center', https://itihaasa.com/describe/artefact/001_001_1056?interviewee=Raman+Roy

14 itihaasa, History of Indian IT, Pramod Bhasin, Video 'GE's BPO Idea', https://itihaasa.com/describe/artefact/001_001_1012?interviewee=Pramod+Bhasin

15 itihaasa, History of Indian IT, Pramod Bhasin, Video 'Genesis of GECIS', https://itihaasa.com/describe/artefact/001_001_1013?interviewee=Pramod+Bhasin

16 itihaasa, History of Indian IT, Pramod Bhasin, Video 'The success of GECIS', https://itihaasa.com/describe/artefact/001_001_1015?interviewee=Pramod+Bhasin

17 Ibid.

18 Ibid.

19 itihaasa, History of Indian IT, Pramod Bhasin, Video 'Genesis of Genpact', https://itihaasa.com/describe/artefact/001_001_1018? interviewee=Pramod+Bhasin

20 itihaasa, History of Indian IT, Raman Roy, Video, 'Local IT innovation power BPM', https://itihaasa.com/describe/artefact/001_001_1058? interviewee=Raman+Roy

21 itihaasa, History of Indian IT, Raman Roy, Video, 'Process innovations: Email replaces fax', https://itihaasa.com/describe/artefact/001_001_ 1061?interviewee=Raman+Roy

22 itihaasa, History of Indian IT, Pramod Bhasin, Video, 'Sociological impact of GECIS', https://itihaasa.com/describe/artefact/001_001_1016? interviewee=Pramod+Bhasin

23 itihaasa, History of Indian IT, N. Chandrasekaran, Video, 'Interesting anecdotes at TCS', https://itihaasa.com/describe/artefact/001_001_ 1152?interviewee=N.+Chandrasekaran

24 https://www.edgeverve.com/finacle/gartner-magic-quadrant-core-banking-2019/, accessed on 15 August 2020.

25 itihaasa, History of Indian IT, Nandan Nilekani, Video 'Banking Platforms from Infosys', https://itihaasa.com/describe/artefact/ 001_001_0363?interviewee=Nandan+Nilekani

26 itihaasa, History of Indian IT, S. Ramadorai, Video 'Building domain competence', https://itihaasa.com/describe/artefact/001_001_0417? interviewee=S.+Ramadorai

27 https://www.tcs.com/content/dam/tcs-bancs/pdf/bancsprotected/ TCSBaNCS_SBI_TowerGroup.pdf, accessed on 15 March 2021.

28 https://www.tcs.com/bancs/about-tcs-bancs, accessed on 15 March 2021.

29 https://knowledge.wharton.upenn.edu/article/i-flex-solutions-rajesh-hukku-no-one-dreamed-that-400000-would-become-almost-600-million-in-13-years/, accessed on 20 January 2021.

30 https://community.nasscom.in/communities/global-in-house-centers/ gcc-3.0-a-location-analysis.html#:~:text=As%20of%20FY2019%2C%20 over%201%2C250,have%20more%20than%20one%20centre, accessed on 20 January 2021.

31 itihaasa, History of Indian IT, Srini Rajam, Video 'TI advises MNCs in setting up their R&D Global in-house centres in India', https://itihaasa. com/describe/artefact/001_001_0308?interviewee=Srini+Rajam

32 https://www.dqindia.com/john-chambers-hints-manufacturing-india/, accessed on 20 January 2021.

33 itihaasa, History of Indian IT, Sharad Sharma, Video 'R&D GICs and Innovations from Pune and Bangalore', https://itihaasa.com/describe/artefact/001_001_0284?interviewee=Sharad+Sharma

34 https://www.nytimes.com/2017/09/28/technology/ibm-india.html, accessed on 20 January 2021.

35 https://timesofindia.indiatimes.com/business/india-business/walmart-labs-will-hire-2800-in-india-this-year/articleshow/75416495.cms, accessed on 20 January 2021.

36 https://www.tcs.com/tcs-to-acquire-citigroup-global-services#:~:text=Tata%20Consultancy%20Services%20To%20Acquire,Underscores%20Strong%20Long%2DStanding%20Relationship, accessed on 20 January 2021.

37 https://www.citigroup.com/citi/news/2008/081223a.htm, accessed on 20 January 2021.

38 itihaasa, History of Indian IT, N. Chandrasekaran, Video 'Acquiring the Citigroup Global Services business as COO of TCS', https://itihaasa.com/describe/artefact/001_001_1142?interviewee=N.+Chandrasekaran

39 itihaasa, History of Indian IT, Kris Gopalakrishnan, Video 'Impact on Infosys of the global economic crisis in 2008', https://itihaasa.com/describe/artefact/001_001_0738?interviewee=S.+%27Kris%27+Gopalakrishnan

40 itihaasa, History of Indian IT, Lakshmi Narayanan, Video 'Cognizant: Financial Melt Down and the Frankfurt meetings', https://itihaasa.com/describe/artefact/001_001_0356?interviewee=Lakshmi+Narayanan

41 itihaasa, History of Indian IT, N.R. Narayana Murthy, Video 'Importance of business value addition', https://itihaasa.com/describe/artefact/001_001_0180?interviewee=N.+R.+Narayana+Murthy

42 itihaasa, History of Indian IT, Kiran Karnik, Video 'Dealing with the Satyam episode', https://itihaasa.com/describe/artefact/001_001_0338?interviewee=Kiran+Karnik

43 Ibid.

44 itihaasa, History of Indian IT, Som Mittal, Video 'NASSCOM's role in the first 72 hours of the Satyam incident', https://itihaasa.com/describe/artefact/001_001_0437?interviewee=Som+Mittal

45 itihaasa, History of Indian IT, Kiran Karnik, Video 'Dealing with the Satyam episode', https://itihaasa.com/describe/artefact/001_001_0338?interviewee=Kiran+Karnik

46 itihaasa, History of Indian IT, Kris Gopalakrishnan, Video 'An overview of Indian IT in the 2000s and beyond', https://itihaasa.com/

describe/artefact/001_001_0977?interviewee=S.+%27Kris%27+
Gopalakrishnan

47 itihaasa, History of Indian IT, Kiran Karnik, Video 'NASSCOM in the
    Early 2000s', https://itihaasa.com/describe/artefact/001_001_0337?
    interviewee=Kiran+Karnik

48 itihaasa, History of Indian IT, Kiran Karnik, Video 'Work Visas', https://
    itihaasa.com/describe/artefact/001_001_0341?interviewee=Kiran+Karnik

49 itihaasa, History of Indian IT, Som Mittal, Video 'Tenure as
    NASSCOM President in Challenging Times', https://itihaasa.com/
    describe/artefact/001_001_0434?interviewee=Som+Mittal

50 itihaasa, History of Indian IT, Som Mittal, Video 'Changes in
    Fresher's Hiring in the Late 2000s', https://itihaasa.com/describe/
    artefact/001_001_0435?interviewee=Som+Mittal

51 itihaasa, History of Indian IT, R. Chandrashekhar, Video 'Focus
    Areas of NASSCOM from 2013', https://itihaasa.com/describe/
    artefact/001_001_0123?interviewee=R.+Chandrashekhar

52 Debjani Ghosh, president, NASSCOM, in conversation with the
    authors, January 2020.

53 https://www.thehindubusinessline.com/info-tech/Covid-19-has-
    forced-it-industry-to-rethink-its-core-strategies-nasscom-president/
    article31787511.ece, accessed on 7 April 2021.

54 itihaasa, History of Indian IT, Srini Rajam, Video 'The genesis of ittiam
    in 2001-Focus on intellectual property', https://itihaasa.com/describe/
    artefact/001_001_0305?interviewee=Srini+Rajam

55 itihaasa, History of Indian IT, Srini Rajam, Video 'Indian and ittiam
    intellectual property in popular electronics products', https://itihaasa.
    com/describe/artefact/001_001_0303?interviewee=Srini+Rajam

56 itihaasa, History of Indian IT, Srini Rajam, Video 'ittiam enables
    India's first Wi-Fi enabled internet café', https://itihaasa.com/describe/
    artefact/001_001_0302?interviewee=Srini+Rajam

57 itihaasa, History of Indian IT, V. Vinay, Video 'PicoPeta
    Simputers', https://itihaasa.com/listing/artefacts/Multimedia%20
    File?interviewee=Dr.+V.+Vinay

58 itihaasa, History of Indian IT, Swami Manohar, Video 'Lessons
    from Simputer Project – 2', https://itihaasa.com/describe/
    artefact/001_001_0169?interviewee=Dr.+Swami+Manohar

59 Dhiraj Rajaram in conversation with the authors, January 2018.

60 https://stories.flipkart.com/10-years-timeline-milestones/, accessed on
    18 February 2021.

61 https://www.businessinsider.com/cash-on-delivery-remains-the-preferred-method-of-payment-in-india-2016-6, accessed on 18 February 2021.

62 https://blog.paytm.com/the-inspiring-journey-of-paytm-founder-vijay-shekhar-sharma-2f9707c9e8c7, accessed on 24 February 2021.

63 https://one97.com/about-one97.php, accessed on 25 February 2021.

64 http://emerging.blog/, accessed on 25 February 2021.

65 https://asiatimes.com/2020/02/fintech-paytm-chief-sees-profits-in-two-years/, accessed on 25 February 2021.

66 https://www.zoho.com/news/zoho-charges-ahead-with-50-million-business-users.html, accessed on 18 February 2021.

67 https://www.deccanchronicle.com/nation/politics/111018/chennai-is-saas-capital-of-india-edappadi-k-palaniswami.html, accessed on 22 February 2021.

68 https://www.forbes.com/sites/anuraghunathan/2017/02/28/indian-cloud-company-zoho-is-privately-held-profitable-and-popular-with-american-small-biz/?sh=69a83a1ba6b3, accessed on 22 February 2021.

69 https://www.youtube.com/watch?v=VkH-oyNyMDA, accessed on 22 February 2021.

70 Ibid.

71 https://headstart.in/blog/the-inmobi-story/, accessed on 26 March 2021.

72 https://www.techinasia.com/inmobi-naveen-tewari-founding-story, accessed on 26 March 2021.

73 https://inc42.com/datalab/can-innovation-alone-fund-deeptech-startups/, accessed on 1 March 2021.

74 Geetha Manjunath in conversation with the authors, June 2019.

75 https://nasscom.in/knowledge-center/publications/indian-tech-start-ecosystem-%E2%80%93-march-trillion-dollar-digital-economy, accessed on 2 March 2021.

76 https://fortune.com/change-the-world/2018/reliance-jio/, accessed on 2 March 2021.

77 https://economictimes.indiatimes.com/industry/telecom/telecom-news/the-jio-effect/articleshow/65694564.cms, accessed on 2 March 2021.

78 https://sajithpai.medium.com/the-indus-valley-playbook-a66cfae8fc90, accessed on 2 March 2021.

79 https://www.fortuneindia.com/venture/uniphore-gained-in-translation/104095, accessed on 2 March 2021.

80 I.M. Pandey, 'The process of developing venture capital in India', *Technovation*, Volume 18, Issue 4, 1998, pp. 253–61, https://doi.org/10.1016/S0166-4972(98)00003-0

81 http://www.suchetadalal.com/?id=2f818746-57aa-0218-492e8b873f8c&base=sections&f, accessed on 25 February 2021.

82 itihaasa, History of Indian IT, Saurabh Srivastava, Video 'Genesis of Infinity Venture fund and Indian Angle Network', https://itihaasa.com/describe/artefact/001_001_0161?interviewee=Saurabh+Srivastava

83 itihaasa, History of Indian IT, Gopal Srinivasan, Video 'The Angel and VC ecosystem in India', https://itihaasa.com/describe/artefact/001_001_1088?interviewee=Gopal+Srinivasan

84 https://www.livemint.com/Money/4BMO0OigIfljOv3TdJsGdK/The-changing-face-of-the-VC-PE-industry.html, accessed on 25 February 2021.

85 https://yourstory.com/journal/the-decade-that-was-india-part-2, accessed on 25 February 2021.

86 https://www.bain.com/insights/india-venture-capital-report-2020/, accessed on 25 February 2021.

87 itihaasa, History of Indian IT, Sridhar Mitta, Video 'Entrepreneurship in the Late 1990s', https://itihaasa.com/describe/artefact/001_001_0325?interviewee=Dr.+Sridhar+Mitta

88 itihaasa, History of Indian IT, Sharad Sharma, Video 'Role of iSPIRT', https://itihaasa.com/describe/artefact/001_001_0290?interviewee=Sharad+Sharma

89 itihaasa, History of Indian IT, N.S. Raghavan, Video 'N.S. Raghavan Centre for Entrepreneurial Learning', https://itihaasa.com/describe/artefact/001_001_0092?interviewee=N.+S.+Raghavan

90 'Reimagining India in 2030', itihaasa Research and Digital and IIT Madras Alumni Association, 2019, https://itihaasa.com/public/pdf/ReimaginingIndiain2030.pdf, accessed on 18 February 2021.

91 itihaasa, History of Indian IT, Vivek Kulkarni, Video 'Karnataka IT and Biotechnology task force', https://itihaasa.com/describe/artefact/001_001_0497?interviewee=Vivek+Kulkarni

92 itihaasa, History of Indian IT, S. Sadagopan, Video 'Bangalore's Evolution from the 1990s as a Major Global Centre for IT and R&D', https://itihaasa.com/describe/artefact/001_001_0262?interviewee=Prof.+S.+Sadagopan

93 itihaasa, History of Indian IT, R. Chandrashekhar, Video 'IT industry in Hyderabad', https://itihaasa.com/describe/artefact/001_001_0115?interviewee=R.+Chandrashekhar

94 itihaasa, History of Indian IT, R. Chandrashekhar, Video 'Public - private Partnership in e-Governance Projects', https://itihaasa.com/describe/artefact/001_001_0118?interviewee=R.+Chandrashekhar

95 Ibid.

96 Ibid.

97 https://timesofindia.indiatimes.com/india/Supreme-Court-strikes-down-Section-66A-of-IT-Act-which-allowed-arrests-for-objectionable-content-online/articleshow/46672244.cms, accessed on 11 February 2021.

98 https://www.thehindu.com/opinion/editorial/an-inevitable-showdown-the-hindu-editorial-on-governments-notice-to-twitter/article33753442.ece, accessed on 11 February 2021.

99 https://pn.ispirt.in/aadhaar-zero-to-1-billion-in-5-5-years/, accessed on 12 February 2021.

100 https://www.visualcapitalist.com/timeline-the-march-to-a-billion-users/, accessed on 12 February 2021.

101 https://www.theverge.com/2021/1/27/22253162/iphone-users-total-number-billion-apple-tim-cook-q1-2021, accessed on 12 February 2021.

102 https://www.zdnet.com/article/daily-active-user-of-messaging-app-wechat-exceeds-1-billion/, accessed on 12 February 2021.

103 itihaasa, History of Indian IT, Nandan Nilekani, Video 'Aadhar-A large IT Led Mission Mode National Program', https://itihaasa.com/describe/artefact/001_001_0370?interviewee=Nandan+Nilekani

104 Ibid.

105 ID4D, 'Private Sector Economic Impacts from Identification Systems', World Bank Group, January 2018.

106 The Global Findex Database 2017, 'Measuring Financial Inclusion and the Fintech Revolution', World Bank Group.

107 https://www.firstpost.com/tech/news-analysis/mukesh-ambani-says-that-aadhar-helped-reliance-jio-cross-100-million-customers-3697855.html, accessed on 12 February 2021.

108 itihaasa, History of Indian IT, Nandan Nilekani, Video 'Aadhar-A large IT Led Mission Mode National Program', https://itihaasa.com/describe/artefact/001_001_0370?interviewee=Nandan+Nilekani

109 https://uidai.gov.in/aadhaar_dashboard/, accessed on 16 February 2021.

110 https://the-ken.com/story/knock-knock-whos-there-bharat-billpay/, accessed on 15 February 2021.

111 https://www.npci.org.in/what-we-do/upi/live-members, accessed on 15 February 2021.

112 https://tigerfeathers.substack.com/p/the-internet-country, accessed on 12 February 2021.

113 https://www.npci.org.in/PDF/npci/press-releases/2021/NPCI-Press-Release-Digital-Payments-well-entrenched-in-Indian-household.pdf, accessed on 15 February 2021.

114 https://gadgets.ndtv.com/internet/features/satya-nadella-and-nandan-nilekani-talk-aadhaar-india-stack-ai-and-ar-1661798, accessed on 15 February 2021.

115 'Future of Technology Services—Winning in this Decade', NASSCOM, February 2021.

CHAPTER 7: QUŌ VĀDIS: WHERE ARE WE HEADING?

1 https://interestingengineering.com/29-terrible-predictions-about-future-technology, accessed on 10 May 2021.

2 https://www.weforum.org/agenda/2016/01/the-fourth-industrial-revolution-what-it-means-and-how-to-respond/, accessed on 10 May 2021.

3 Christian Keller, Tomasz Wieladek and Iaroslav Shelepko, 'Macroeconomics of the Machines', Barclays, 2018.

4 https://www.indiascienceandtechnology.gov.in/stihighlights/sti-era-new-normal-%e2%80%93-survey-report, accessed on 17 June 2021.

5 https://timesofindia.indiatimes.com/blogs/toi-edit-page/bridging-the-5g-digital-divide-how-indigenously-developed-technology-can-reach-remote-indian-villages/, accessed on 17 June 2021.

6 https://principia-scientific.com/mrna-injections-an-operating-system-designed-to-program-humans/, accessed on 15 June 2021.

7 https://www.modernatx.com/about-us, accessed on 15 June 2021.

8 https://www.nature.com/articles/d41586-020-03476-x, accessed on 15 June 2021.

9 https://www.cs.utexas.edu/news/2019/changing-future-gene-editing, accessed on 15 June 2021.

10 https://med.stanford.edu/news/all-news/2018/11/ai-outperformed-radiologists-in-screening-x-rays-for-certain-diseases.html, accessed on 10 May 2021.

11 https://www.pnas.org/content/pnas/early/2018/03/30/1720347115.full.pdf, accessed on 15 June 2021.

12 https://www.foundingfuel.com/article/not-ai-alone-but-ai-ethics/, accessed on 10 May 2021.

13 itihaasa, History of Indian IT, Azim Premji, Video 'Where do you see Indian IT Industry in 2040?', https://itihaasa.com/describe/artefact/001_001_0045?interviewee=Azim+H.+Premji

14 https://www.livemint.com/industry/infotech/it-cos-win-record-large-deals-as-demand-for-digital-spikes-11620062735302.html, accessed on 10 May 2021.

15 https://timesofindia.indiatimes.com/business/india-business/desi-it-companies-double-mkt-share-to-28-in-10-years/articleshow/83192753.cms, accessed on 10 May 2021.

16 https://www.tcs.com/content/dam/tcs/investor-relations/financial-statements/2020-21/ar/annual-report-2020-2021.pdf, accessed on 10 May 2021.

17 https://www.infosys.com/investors/reports-filings/annual-report/annual/documents/infosys-ar-21.pdf, accessed on 10 May 2021.

18 itihaasa, History of Indian IT, N.R. Narayana Murthy, Video 'Where do you see Indian IT Industry in 2040?', https://itihaasa.com/describe/artefact/001_001_0187?interviewee=N.+R.+Narayana+Murthy

19 https://www.thehindu.com/business/Covid-19-may-have-enhanced-indias-attractiveness-as-a-gcc-destination/article33733397.ece, accessed on 10 May 2021.

20 https://timesofindia.indiatimes.com/business/india-business/theres-a-huge-part-of-india-in-every-mercedes/articleshow/57561545.cms, accessed on 10 May 2021.

21 https://timesofindia.indiatimes.com/business/india-business/bengaluru-key-to-goldmans-consumer-bank-marcus/articleshow/74092667.cms, accessed on 10 May 2021.

22 itihaasa, History of Indian IT, S. Ramani, Video 'Where do you see Indian IT Industry in 2040?', https://itihaasa.com/describe/artefact/001_001_0079?interviewee=Dr.+S.+Ramani

23 https://blog.invesco.ca/take-the-concentration-out-of-the-sp-500-with-invesco-sp-500-equal-weight-index-etf/, accessed on 14 June 2021.

24 https://www.techcircle.in/2021/04/08/meet-the-9-startups-in-india-deeptech-s-maiden-accelerator-cohort, accessed on 15 June 2021.

25 itihaasa, History of Indian IT, S. Ramadorai, Video 'Where do you see Indian IT Industry in 2040?', https://itihaasa.com/describe/artefact/001_001_0421?interviewee=S.+Ramadorai

26 itihaasa, History of Indian IT, N. Chandrasekaran, Video 'Bridgital Nation – Solving Technology's People Problem', https://itihaasa.com/describe/artefact/001_001_1149?interviewee=N.+Chandrasekaran

27 https://pib.gov.in/Pressreleaseshare.aspx?PRID=1523301, accessed on 15 June 2021.

28 itihaasa, Research and Digital, 'Landscape of Artificial Intelligence / Machine Learning Research in India', 2018.

29 https://nptel.ac.in/, accessed on 10 May 2021.

30 https://www.aicte-india.org/bureaus/swayam, accessed on 16 June 2021.

31 https://diksha.gov.in/, accessed on 16 June 2021.

32 'Leapfrogging to a Digital Healthcare System', FICCI-BCG report, September 2020.

33 https://www.financialexpress.com/industry/rbi-mulls-export-of-upi-neft-other-payment-solutions-as-many-countries-seek-to-replicate-them/1991098/, accessed on 15 June 2021.

34 https://www.business-standard.com/article/current-affairs/india-to-share-its-cowin-story-with-more-than-20-countries-showing-interest-121062101433_1.html, accessed on 15 June 2021.

35 https://www.mosip.io/news-events/the-economist-features-mosip-as-central-to-Covid-19-spurred-national-plans-to-provide-citizens-digital-identities-in-its-article, accessed on 15 June 2021.

36 https://www.forbes.com/sites/annaesakismith/2021/05/18/how-a-free-online-harvard-course-led-a-bangalore-student-to-help-walmart-develop-its-vaccine-portal/?sh=138009b9e3d2, accessed on 10 May 2021.

37 https://www.livemint.com/industry/infotech/it-eyes-20-fold-jump-in-demand-for-digital-skills-11601253032366.html, accessed on 10 May 2021.

38 https://onlinedegree.iitm.ac.in/, accessed on 10 May 2021.

39 itihaasa, History of Indian IT, Kiran Karnik, Video 'Where do you see Indian IT Industry in 2040?', https://itihaasa.com/describe/artefact/001_001_0345?interviewee=Kiran+Karnik

40 UNESCO Institute for Statistics, 'R&D Spending by Country', http://uis.unesco.org/apps/visualisations/research-and-development-spending/, accessed on 15 June 2021.

41 https://dst.gov.in/sites/default/files/STIP_Doc_1.4_Dec2020.pdf, accessed on 15 June 2021.

42 https://www.pib.gov.in/Pressreleaseshare.aspx?PRID=1554936, accessed on 15 June 2021.

43 https://www.niti.gov.in/sites/default/files/2019-01/NationalStrategy-for-AI-Discussion-Paper.pdf, accessed on 10 May 2021

44 itihaasa, Research and Digital, 'Landscape of Artificial Intelligence / Machine Learning Research in India', 2018 https://itihaasa.com/public/pdf/LandscapeofAI-MLResearch.pdf, accessed on 15 June 2021.

45 https://economictimes.indiatimes.com/small-biz/security-tech/
technology/india-needs-to-budget-for-research-funding/articleshow/
56904031.cms, accessed on 10 May 2021.

46 https://obamawhitehouse.archives.gov/the-press-office/2013/04/02/
remarks-president-brain-initiative-and-american-innovation, accessed on
16 June 2021.

47 https://www.fortuneindia.com/people/kris-gopalakrishnan-on-innovation/
105188, accessed on 17 June 2021.

48 itihaasa, Research and Digital, 'Landscape of Brain Research in India',
2018; https://itihaasa.com/public/pdf/LandscapeofBrainResearch.pdf,
accessed on 10 June 2021.

49 https://niti.gov.in/sites/default/files/2020-09/DEPA-Book_0.pdf,
accessed on 10 June 2021.

50 https://static.mygov.in/rest/s3fs-public/mygov_160975438978977151.
pdf, accessed on 15 May 2021.

51 https://www.indiascienceandtechnology.gov.in/stihighlights/sti-era-new-
normal-%e2%80%93-survey-report, accessed on 15 June 2021.

52 https://rbcdsai.iitm.ac.in/, accessed on 15 May 2021.

53 https://data.worldbank.org/indicator/NY.GDP.MKTP.
CD?locations=IN, accessed on 15 May 2021.

54 R. Buckminster Fuller, *Critical Path*, St Martin's Griffin, second edition,
1982.